IDIOT'S GUIDES.

AS EASY AS IT GETS!

Flipping Houses

by Tim W. Lenihan and Patricia Burkhart Smith

ALPHA

A member of Penguin Random House LLC

Penguin Random House

Publisher: Mike Sanders
Associate Publisher: Billy Fields
Acquisitions Editor: Jan Lynn
Development Editor: Rick Kughen
Cover Designer: Lindsay Dobbs
Book Designer: William Thomas
Compositor: Ayanna Lacey
Proofreader: Monica Stone
Indexer: Tonya Heard

First American Edition, 2017
Published in the United States by DK Publishing
6081 E. 82nd Street, Indianapolis, Indiana 46250

Copyright © 2017 Dorling Kindersley Limited
A Penguin Random House Company
17 18 19 20   10 9 8 7 6 5 4 3 2 1
001-298856-FEBRUARY2017

ISBN: 9781465459114
Library of Congress Catalog Card Number: 2016948870

Note: This publication contains the opinions and ideas of its author(s). It is intended to provide helpful and informative material on the subject matter covered. It is sold with the understanding that the author(s) and publisher are not engaged in rendering professional services in the book. If the reader requires personal assistance or advice, a competent professional should be consulted. The author(s) and publisher specifically disclaim any responsibility for any liability, loss, or risk, personal or otherwise, which is incurred as a consequence, directly or indirectly, of the use and application of any of the contents of this book.

Trademarks: All terms mentioned in this book that are known to be or are suspected of being trademarks or service marks have been appropriately capitalized. Alpha Books, DK, and Penguin Random House LLC cannot attest to the accuracy of this information. Use of a term in this book should not be regarded as affecting the validity of any trademark or service mark.

DK books are available at special discounts when purchased in bulk for sales promotions, premiums, fund-raising, or educational use. For details, contact: DK Publishing Special Markets, 345 Hudson Street, New York, New York 10014 or SpecialSales@dk.com.

Printed and bound in the United States of America

idiotsguides.com

Contents

Introduction

Since the creation of habitable spaces, human beings have always felt the need to renew and refresh their dwellings. Even if it just meant sweeping out the cave and bringing in some fresh straw to sleep upon, the desire for a brighter, fresher place to call home seems to be woven into human DNA.

At the dawn of the twenty-first century, this desire became a national obsession. The term *flipping* was coined to describe the practice of purchasing property, renovating, repairing, and modernizing it, and then putting it on the market in hopes of a quick sale and eye-popping profits. A dozen or so TV programs hit the air to show aspiring flippers how it's done.

No matter how many flipping shows a person watches, none of this viewing can actually prepare anyone to successfully take on a massive project like flipping a house. That's where *Idiot's Guides: Flipping Houses* comes in. This essential guide will lead you step by step through the process of flipping your first property. This book also gives you all the tools and information you need to launch a successful career as a flipper.

Let's get flipping!

How This Book Is Organized

This book is divided into four parts:

The odds of becoming a successful flipper are determined by the first few decisions you make. In **Part 1, Laying a Solid Foundation,** we define flipping and help you get organized. We show you how to seek out financing and build a great flipping team. Finally, we take you through a detailed planning process to get you ready to flip.

Almost nothing has more influence on a flipper's odds of success than the location of the property. **Part 2, Selecting the Right Property to Flip,** teaches you how to find great houses to flip and how to use demographic data to define your target audience of potential buyers. We discuss how best to work with Realtors and contractors, and guide you as you buy your first property.

In **Part 3, Demolition and Renovation,** we get to the nitty gritty of flipping a house, everything from pulling permits to understanding style. We take you through a quick makeover and a to-the-studs demolition and renovation, teaching you about everything from scheduling to selecting finishes and the importance of curb appeal. We also discuss what to do if you run into problems along the way.

Now you are ready to sell or "flip" your first property. Staging is an important part of effectively marketing a house. **Part 4, The Flip,** reveals the smartest use of your staging dollars, then discusses pricing and marketing strategies. We take you from your first offer through the act of sale, and finally, we show you how to analyze your results and your profits. Then it's time to start over again with a new property!

At the back of the book, we've included a glossary of terms, a list of resources to further your flipping education, and an appendix of helpful checklists.

Extras

Throughout the book, we include three kinds of sidebars to enhance the text. Here's what to look for:

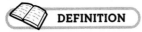

DEFINITION

The business of flipping uses several terms that may be unfamiliar to first-time flippers. These sidebars explain what these words mean.

FLIP TIP

These sidebars contain smart ideas that will save you time and money and generally make your job easier.

FLIPPER BEWARE

Heed the warnings about typical problems you may encounter during the course of your project shared in these sidebars.

Acknowledgments

I would like to thank and dedicate this book to those who have supported me and my wild dreams in both the real estate and flipping worlds for all these years. I have met many people who helped shape who I am and how far I have come, but none more so than my fellow Realtors and managers. You are all a wealth of information and an amazing resource for me. I can't thank you enough. I also want to specifically thank my assistant, Jill Rotset. You work so hard and truly understand our vision of what real estate and development really entails. I cannot thank you enough for your endless support and friendship. Last but not least, I want to thank my two boys,

Mercer and Rocco, and my wife, Celeste. You put up with the endless hours and endless phone calls, all in support of my dreams. I am forever thankful to all three of you.—Tim Lenihan

I dedicate this book to my two wonderful children, Meghan and Carter, who have continued the family tradition for a third generation with your excellent writing. I also want to thank my beloved siblings, Carol Stallings, Debi Burkhart, and Garry Burkhart, for your unwavering love and support. Thanks to my friends and fellow writers, Lou Turner, Chris Andretti, Liz Gruder and Karen Crumley, for always being on the other end of the phone. And Christopher Mayfield, what would I do without your friendship and sage advice? To my agent, Sheree Bykofsky, who knew that chance meeting in Austin so many years ago would lead to such a long and mutually beneficial friendship? Thank you for everything you do for me. A final thanks to Jim Conyers for keeping me company on Skype while I was working on the proposal for this book.—Patricia B. Smith

Laying a Solid Foundation

Before you start your flipping career, it is essential to prepare yourself for success through education and networking. Flipping is a business built on networking, and there are many organizations that can help you make the right connections to get started.

Long before you ever tour your first property, you must determine how you are going to set up your business, and the type of people you want to work with. Organization and teamwork are key. Once your team is in place, planning and securing financing for your first flip are your next priorities. Working out your entire plan on paper first can help you avoid many problems as you work to complete your first flip.

What Is House Flipping?

If you watch TV, you've probably heard the term *house flipping,* particularly if you enjoy real estate and home renovation shows. You might even have some vague idea that flipping houses could be a good way to make extra money.

Or perhaps you've watched all the shows and can't stop thinking about the idea of flipping a house yourself. You feel intrigued and want to try it, but you don't know where to begin to get into the business.

In a nation of dreamers absolutely in love with the whole idea of renovated and redesigned houses—and mostly unaware of what it actually takes to get them looking that good—it's only natural that so many people want to experience the thrill and satisfaction of successfully flipping a house for themselves.

In This Chapter

- What is flipping?
- Can anyone flip a house?
- Weighing the risks
- Profit potential

House Flipping 101

What does it mean to flip a house? It's certainly nothing like flipping a pancake; although in a way, you do turn the house upside down. *House flipping* is the process of buying a property at the lowest possible price for the purpose of repairing and renovating it and then quickly selling (or "flipping") it after the upgrade, preferably for a healthy profit.

> **DEFINITION**
>
> **House flipping** is when you purchase a house then quickly update and sell it for a profit. Flipping can also apply to other types of real estate.

It might be helpful to define what house flipping is *not*, if only to disabuse you of any fanciful notions you might be entertaining about the process:

- Flipping houses is *not* a way to get rich quick.

- It is *not* a low-stress job.

- It is *not* just office work; you'll frequently be on-site.

- It is *not* for the risk-averse.

- It is *not* easy.

This is not to say that flipping a house is something only experienced and highly qualified real estate and contracting professionals should try. Amateurs and first-timers can and do flip houses with a satisfactory rate of success. Even though I am a professional broker and Realtor, the first time I flipped a house, I didn't exactly know what I was doing.

I think anyone attracted to the idea of flipping a house should try it. However, to maximize your odds of success, you must first prepare yourself by learning everything you can about flipping. The process can be complicated unless you have an overall plan, schedule, and budget in place before you start. Once you have familiarized yourself with all that is required to flip a house, you'll be ready to take the first steps.

Why Flip Now?

House flipping was really just getting fired up as a business when the housing crisis of 2008 hit. The crash flattened the real estate market and left a lot of flippers, both experienced and inexperienced, holding the bag on properties they suddenly couldn't give away. Flipping as a business basically fell apart.

From the detritus of that collapse, a few hardy souls picked up the pieces and tried to make flipping work again. Many turned to private investors for project financing after bank loans dried up. Gradually, the market normalized and banks and credit unions once again started making cautious loans to select flippers. Slowly, the business rebuilt and expanded. Eventually, new flippers started undertaking projects once again.

Favorable Factors

Fortunately, the demand for flipped houses has greatly improved. Flipping houses is a hot trend, and thanks to the following favorable factors, the prospects for new people in the business are more promising than they have been in a while.

Mortgage interest rates are hovering at near-historic lows, meaning financing for flipping projects is more affordable and more widely available.

FLIP TIP

Always be sure to check the current prevailing trends before you jump into house flipping to ensure conditions are still favorable for success.

More than a dozen popular reality shows, such as *Property Brothers* and *Fixer Upper,* regularly tout the possible benefits of purchasing properties for renovation and resale. Millions of viewers have been entranced by the idea that they can flip a house or two, develop a new and potentially lucrative hobby, and perhaps find a more exciting and fulfilling career.

Dozens of municipalities have passed ordinances offering financial and tax incentives to flippers who work in distressed neighborhoods the city or town wants to see redeveloped.

Accurate information about the ins and outs of flipping a house is more widely available than ever before.

In many markets, housing demand exceeds supply, which creates an ideal climate for a new flipper to enter the business, assess existing inventory, and select a house with good profit potential to flip.

Many professional flippers are now actively looking for and training assistants. If you are able to go to work with one of these mentors, it can jumpstart your flipping career.

These factors combine to make entry into the field relatively uncomplicated for new flippers. But remember, trends are transient, so when I say *this* is a good time to enter the field of house flipping, I mean *now*. Not next year some time.

Reverse Migration

There are other interesting factors currently in play that also look promising for the flipping industry. Decaying inner city neighborhoods have become prime flipping grounds thanks to an emerging trend regarding where many families prefer to live. After the Korean and Vietnam Wars, many families fled to the suburbs to escape crime, traffic, pollution, and other problems associated with inner cities. The flight to the suburbs that was the story of real estate for so many decades has now evolved into a stream of people returning to the cities. Today, many environmentally conscious homebuyers reject the idea of long commutes and living in cookie-cutter suburbia. They are seeking unique upgraded homes in reinvigorated family- and career-friendly neighborhoods near amenities, such as parks, zoos, theaters, concert halls, libraries, museums, and trendy local shops that are reflective of the neighborhood. They want to relocate closer to city centers where so-called *gentrification* and *urban renewal* have ameliorated many of the problems, such as crime and pollution, that drove them away in the first place.

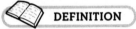 **DEFINITION**

Gentrification is the sometimes-controversial process of repairing and upgrading rundown buildings in blighted urban areas with a mix of upscale shops, office space, and residences to attract younger, better-educated, and wealthier residents to the neighborhood. It has been criticized for driving out low-income residents who frequently cannot find affordable replacement housing.

Another word for gentrification is **urban renewal.** The difference is urban renewal projects are generally subsidized by government funding, whereas most gentrification projects are undertaken with private funding. The end result is the same—slums are swept away and replaced by high-rise office buildings, pricy shops, and luxury housing.

This reverse migration trend presents an ideal opportunity for those of us in the flipping business. That sagging Victorian masterpiece with all the turrets and squeaky staircases that once you couldn't give away might become the object of an intense bidding war after you give it a modern interior upgrade, refresh the period exterior, and put it on the market. Interest will be especially fervent if the house is located in a fine old neighborhood that has suddenly become desirable again.

Keeping up with housing trends can make your life as a flipper a bit easier, as choosing new properties is simpler when many indicators point in the same direction. It saves valuable time when you don't have to invest extra hours researching suitable locations for your next flip.

I'll work the same neighborhoods over and over where buyer demand is high and inventory limited. Those two factors greatly increase my odds of a quick sale for top dollar— the sort of outcome we all want at the end of a house flipping venture.

FLIP TIP

If you are still hesitant about getting into the house flipping business now, try to find a more experienced partner who wants to free up his or her own schedule by hiring an assistant to take over some of the scheduling and project oversight on their flips. It's a win-win. You can learn as you go in a supportive environment, while your partner will have additional time to grow his or her business by finding and flipping more houses.

If you have been thinking about trying house flipping for some time but still can't make up your mind to go forward, I encourage you to read through this book, make a budget and an overall plan, and jump in.

Qualifications Needed

Unlike some careers, there is no particular training or license required to flip houses. However, there are particular types of experience that will give you a head start on the competition.

Certainly if you are either a Realtor or a contractor, you already have experience in many of the relevant specialties. Some people in the mortgage and banking arenas have also been successful in launching a house flipping business on the side, as have architects, interior designers, and draftsmen. House flipping is a natural extension of the work they already do.

That does not mean you have to be practicing one of these professions in order to pursue flipping houses. It just means that as a total newbie, you'll be entering the business with less knowledge and practical experience than someone working in one of these fields may already have.

You can come from any professional background—from janitor to to hairstylist—and still learn everything you need to know to become a successful flipper. Even if you've never had a job with any relevant experience, you shouldn't let that discourage you. Learn all you can, partner with experts, and dive in.

So what do you actually need to get going in the flipping business?

- A level head

- Some facility for planning and organization

- A creative spirit

- A great work ethic

- The desire to learn from the best

It also helps to have a fierce desire to succeed.

 FLIPPER BEWARE

Recent news stories featured unhappy consumers who each paid some self-styled guru $30,000 or more to learn about flipping houses. Many of these entrepreneurs traded on a brief TV success to push their wares onto star-struck consumers. Those same consumers are now suing to get their money back, saying they did not get any specialized knowledge or training to help them start a career in flipping houses. Stay away from people and courses that claim to be able to make you tons of money with little effort on your part. You'll be better off investing your cash on your first flipped house.

Now let's take a look at the potential advantages people in relevant professions have when it comes to flipping houses.

Brokers and Realtors

Real estate brokers and Realtors know how to locate and buy houses and negotiate the sale of both residential and commercial properties. They understand mortgages and creative financing, and all the different types of loans available to help people purchase homes. They know how to match clients to properties. They know neighborhoods inside and out, which ones are in demand, and the ones that are trending down. They know where all the schools, hospitals, churches, grocery stores, gas stations, and shopping malls are located. They are familiar with neighborhood amenities, public transportation, property taxes, neighborhood association fees, and many other important facts. They understand how to market properties so that they show to their best advantage. They have their fingers on the pulse of the home buying market, and stay abreast of the multitude of factors that can influence the market's health.

Perhaps just as important, brokers and Realtors have professional level access to the *MLS* or *Multiple Listing Service*, which allows them to instantly look up currently available or recently sold comparable houses in the same neighborhood to get a good idea of a fair price for any property.

DEFINITION

A **MLS** or **Multiple Listing Service** is a database containing information on every property for sale or rent in a given locality, including address, square footage, year built, property taxes assessed, number of rooms, and other information. There is a national public database at mls.com, and more than 900 subscription-based local databases for professional Realtors in communities around the United States.

I always recommend that new flippers find a professional Realtor they like and trust, and build a strong working relationship with them. Otherwise, locating a suitable property to flip will be a like trying to find a contact lens in a swimming pool.

The process of finding a great Realtor can be compared to finding a great spouse. Sometimes, the first one just doesn't work out. It could be a personality clash, a difference in philosophy or approach, or any number of factors. Don't stress if your first or even your second Realtor relationship doesn't gel. Keep searching until you find someone whose style and personality mesh well with your own, then work hard at building and maintaining a mutually beneficial relationship.

FLIP TIP

Not every Realtor who tries flipping sticks with it. Some Realtors flip one house, and then never do another. Others discover they prefer to focus full-time on real estate. So when you are looking for a Realtor to work with, make sure they not only have experience in flipping houses, but that they like the business and plan to stay in it.

It's important to find a Realtor with whom you work well, because he or she will be one of the most important members of your team. Your Realtor will help you to find available properties within your budget in your preferred neighborhood. They will also guide you as you place timely and strategic offers, often before the house you want hits the market or shows up in the MLS. The simple truth is you cannot get ahead of the flipping crowd if you are not partnered with a Realtor who is privy to early information about which desirable properties are about to go up for sale.

Contractors

Contractors are another important member of a flipping team. They know the labor and materials required to flip a house and can accurately assess the cost of repairs and renovations. They are familiar with local carpenters, plumbers, electricians, and other craftsmen, and know which crews are reliable and which are not. They know in which order the work must proceed. (For example, don't sheetrock your walls and then try to run wiring.)

One of the most important jobs a contractor performs is the property inspection prior to you making a purchase decision. As an inexperienced buyer, you might see a property that looks good and decide to place an offer. Your contractor can look at that same house and discover thousands of dollars in hidden damage that would blow your flipping budget and turn your winning proposition into a money pit. A good contractor can save you thousands of dollars and reduce the risk of failure by pointing out potential problems before you purchase a property to flip.

Curious about which permits your flip requires, where to get them, the cost, and how long it will take to obtain them? Contractors take care of those things. They know local building inspectors and can often work out any hiccups along the way. Their knowledge of permitting and property inspection can get your property on the market faster and with fewer headaches along the way.

Contractors know how to manage crews properly and command their respect. They keep your work site safe and free from dangerous debris. They know what to do if an unexpected emergency arises. They are licensed, bonded, and carry *workers' compensation insurance,* so if a worker gets injured on your job, his or her medical expenses will be covered. They can keep you from being held liable for a workplace injury by being able to prove that due diligence and safety protocols were in place on your job.

> **DEFINITION**
>
> **Workers' compensation insurance** provides wage replacement and medical expenses reimbursement to workers injured on the job. In exchange, laborers covered by workers' comp are required to give up the right to sue their employer for their injuries, even if they are permanently disabled as a result. Workers' comp also provides a death benefit to families of workers killed on the job.

Contractors keep you informed every step of the way during your flip. They can sometimes almost singlehandedly keep a project from going south. If hidden damage is found, your contractor can suggest creative and economical ways to fix it so that it won't devour too big a chunk of your profits. As work progresses, contractors can also let you know if the previous owners of the house made any obvious attempts to hide damage, in which case you might be able to recover some of your repair costs.

If you try to do the contractor's job by yourself, you will quickly learn you can only discover the right way to do things through expensive trial and error. Why waste that valuable time and money when it's so much easier to work with a reputable contractor? Just as with your Realtor , find a contractor you like and trust and then build a good working relationship. It will make your life and your flips so much easier.

Architects, Draftsmen, and Interior Designers

Architects, draftsmen, or interior designers might also be drawn to the house flipping business. However, we don't see them out in the field as frequently as we see Realtors or contractors.

Architects know the conceptual side of house flipping—designing buildings and hatching ideas for renovations comes easily to them—but they might not be as familiar with the more mundane tasks associated with the job. They are used to coming up with concepts and handing them off to a draftsman to record in a blueprint. While they go on-site for project management and oversight, the day-to-day requirements of building their designs often falls to a contractor who is on-site full time.

A draftsman with years of on-the-job experience can do almost everything an architect might do. However, they get paid less and have less power and authority over a project overall unless they run their own businesses.

On a day-to-day basis, draftsmen are more hands on with active projects, but most of them do not go out in the field that often. They work directly with architects to create blueprints and with structural engineers to make sure the proposed buildings are sound. In my experience, a draftsman who has started his own business is more likely to try house flipping than someone who is locked into a demanding job at an architectural or engineering firm.

That said, architects and draftsmen both have experience reading blueprints and working with contractors to see a vision that exists only on paper become a physical building. That experience is invaluable when it comes to designing a flipped house.

Another type of designer we sometimes see enter the flipping business is an interior designer. Their skill enables them to make the interior of a flipped house look spectacular, but they generally need help with some of the more technical aspects of house flipping. Houses with designer interiors do sell faster and have better appeal for more affluent buyers.

You can achieve at least a bit of that designer look in your finished flip by hiring a stager. Naturally, it's not the same as having an interior space designed inch by inch, but staging can still show your flipped house off to its best advantage. We discuss more about staging in Chapter 18.

Mortgage Brokers and Bankers

Due to their familiarity with mortgages and real property, mortgage brokers and bankers sometimes get involved in the house flipping business. Thanks to their work connections and knowledge of housing markets, they have several advantages over members of the general public when it comes to flipping houses.

Mortgage brokers and bankers know a lot of Realtors. When it's time to choose a Realtor to work with, they can cherry pick from the cream of the crop based on their prior experiences. They don't have as direct a connection to contractors as they do to Realtors, but can use their Realtor to connect with a reliable contractor.

Where mortgage brokers and bankers have the real advantage, of course, is in the financial end of things. They have intimate knowledge of the mortgage market, where rates are and where they're going, how to construct deals and secure construction financing, and a host of other financially related topics.

The Value of Sweat Equity

You might not have a lot of relevant experience to bring to the table when you start working on your first flip, but you do have something valuable—your *sweat equity*.

 **DEFINITION**

Sweat equity is a contribution you make to a project in lieu of cash investment. It consists of hard physical labor a person performs in order to earn a share of a project's payout.

If someone hires you to help them with their flipping business, they will likely have you perform the bulk of their less-demanding but nonetheless time-consuming work, such as making phone calls, ordering supplies and materials, scheduling, managing deliveries, and so on. They'll reserve for themselves the more complicated tasks, such as finding new properties and developing renovation plans.

Your contribution of sweat equity is important to a project and to the mentor with whom you are working. Your investment of your labor frees up your partners' schedules to an extent and gives them more time to focus on their families, their primary careers, or even occasionally indulge in that rarest of activities: leisure time.

Why Do These Experts Need You?

You might be asking yourself, if these experts have all this knowledge and experience in flipping houses, then why would they need you?

The answer is easy. You probably have a lot more of a very precious commodity that is in short supply for those of us working in flipping in addition to our main careers—time.

The successful Realtors and contractors I know, myself included, practically have our cellphones surgically attached to our hands. We tend to be booked almost around the clock and count ourselves lucky if we have time to say goodbye to our kids and spouses each morning, much less plan a complete flip from start to finish. By partnering with you, or someone like you, we get extra time added to our days … and for us, that is priceless.

While I cannot speak personally to the work schedules of other professionals who might also be involved in flipping houses, I feel confident many would be open to hiring an assistant to help run their businesses. If you can land one of these jobs, you'll be working and learning alongside an experienced flipping expert. This kind of mutually beneficial association is priceless. You'll be getting hands-on training that money cannot buy.

Risks and Benefits

Like any other business endeavor, house flipping has both significant potential risks and significant potential advantages. Try to minimize your risks from the get-go so that you can reach a point where you can start enjoying the benefits.

The biggest risk in flipping houses is financial. You are investing money, either your own or someone else's, in a project with an uncertain outcome. There are no guarantees you've read the market right or that your finished house will sell.

You might also run into major unexpected expenses as you are doing the renovations. These issues can blow right through your budget and decimate your entire profit margin in a matter of hours. You might find the house has hidden termite damage, foundation problems, or other major structural issues that could cost in the tens of thousands of dollars to repair properly.

When you hear of someone getting into the house flipping business and then jumping right back out again after flipping just one house, you can bet that financial problems were the cause. If you go into something hoping to make a nice profit and come out of it having lost thousands of dollars, that's not exactly an encouragement to try again.

> **FLIP TIP**
>
> There are safeguards you can put into place to minimize your risk and out-of-pocket expense. You must set guidelines for your property acquisition and rehab costs, and stay within them. It's a recipe for financial disaster if you don't build extra dollars into your budget to pay for unexpected expenses. We'll cover this topic in greater detail in Chapter 4.

We all go into a flip hoping for a nice profit, but there's more than money to be made in flipping houses. There's also the sense of accomplishment you get from completing a job on time and on budget. You will be meeting new people, some of whom will become lifelong friends. Your days will be busy and filled with activity. No more boring desk job for you! And finally, of course, there's the incredible feeling of satisfaction you get when you complete a successful flip. You'll feel especially good when your flip sells quickly and for significantly more than your investment.

By the time you have turned over two or three successful flips, you will have flipping fever, and you may well have found yourself a new career.

Income Potential

After the housing collapse in 2008, the business of flipping houses took a beating. But for the past several years, it has been growing steadily. According to RealtyTrac, a company that monitors real estate trends and transactions in the United States, in 2011, it took more than 100 days to flip a house and the average profit was about $15,100, which is not a very compelling return for the amount of time invested.

However, by 2014 (the last year for which RealtyTrac has compiled statistics), the average length of time to flip a house had fallen to just 84 days, while the average profit had risen to $58,081.

In that same time period, the number of homes flipped in the United States more than doubled, from 76,453 homes in 2011 to 156,862 homes in 2014. In most markets, demand for rehabbed homes exceeds the available inventory, meaning your odds for success are excellent.

Of course, not every penny you make is sheer profit. You still have to pay your investor, contractors, and materials suppliers. Perhaps most importantly, you have to set aside a big chunk of your profit to finance your next flip. This is especially important if you eventually want to work using only your own money, so that you get to keep all the profits. To succeed in this goal requires planning and self-discipline. Chapters 2 and 3 discuss the tools you need to get your flipping business up and running properly.

Once you have some experience under your belt and really get going in the business, it is possible to make as much with the sale of one flipped house as many people make in a year of working a regular job. Of course, until you get to that point, you will make less, sometimes far less. But as long as the market is healthy and demand remains strong for flipped houses, your business should continue to prosper and grow.

The Least You Need to Know

- You do not have to practice a particular profession or have any special training in order to flip houses.
- While flipping houses can be a great way to make money, it's not necessarily a very fast way to make money.
- There are risks associated with flipping houses, with the risk of losing money being the most significant.
- Partnering with a Realtor or a contractor is a great way to get into the house-flipping business.

CHAPTER 2

Getting Started Flipping

Now that you've made the decision to try flipping, it's time to get started. Sure, you might have watched dozens of TV shows on flipping—and they do make it look so easy—but do you really have what it takes to succeed in the house flipping business?

How do you go from sitting on the couch watching a TV show about flipping to rehabbing a house of your own? How do you even figure out if it's something you can actually do?

Try talking to some flippers in your area and asking them for their take on the business. Find out what's involved. Ask one if you can spend a few hours tagging along on her workday to see what it's like. If she doesn't want you hanging around on her job sites, then at least ask her about things that puzzle or worry you about flipping. Even the busiest flipper will usually take time to help a newbie with some basic information. If one is too busy to help you, then move on and find another one who has time to help.

You might be asking yourself, "But where do I find flippers?" That's a good question. Call a Realtor or contractor, tell him what you are trying to do and ask for referrals, as well as a couple of names. Most Realtors will want to get permission from the flipper before handing out her name and contact information, but this is a good way to meet other people who are already doing the business.

Who Makes the Best Flippers?

Like every other career, there are certain personality types that tend to be drawn to flipping and that do well in the business. Does this mean that if you don't have this exact personality you cannot be a flipper? Heck, no! We have all sorts of people in the business. However, as different as our personalities may be, most successful flippers do have at least a few things in common.

> **FLIP TIP**
>
> In a recent interview, Christina El Moussa of HGTV's *Flip or Flop* revealed that she believes the three most important qualities a flipper can have are an entrepreneurial spirit, self-motivation, and a passion for helping people.

If you have an entrepreneurial spirit, you're on your way. You more than likely don't enjoy working for others, prefer to be in charge of your own schedule, and do things according to your plan.

On the other hand, if you like to let others make the decisions, you can still be a very successful flipper. You'll just need to enlist the help of a Realtor or contractor who can be tough when it's necessary.

Flipping is a team sport, so if you are a true loner who likes to work on your own, you might want to think hard about flipping as a career choice. To be successful in the field, you must work with Realtors, contractors, laborers, inspectors, stagers, and potential buyers, among others. You don't have to be the life of the party to be successful, but you must feel comfortable interacting with a variety of people.

It might seem odd to say you must be both a team player and self-motivated. Flipping is performed by teams who all work under the direction of a single leader ... you. You drive the entire flip forward, and such an undertaking does require enormous self-motivation to keep both yourself and the flipping team moving forward, especially when the project is going sideways.

You must have a certain amount of fortitude and persistence, because a flip can take 6 to 8 months from start to finish.

If you enjoy helping people, flipping is an ideal career. You'll find yourself in the role of problem solver, helping families look for the ideal home and those who need to downsize or save their home from foreclosure.

Mapping Your Strengths

Now that you have an idea of your aptitude for the house flipping business, it's time to identify your particular strengths and weaknesses. This will help you determine what type of team you'll need to build to optimize your chances of success in the business.

For example, if you're a Realtor , you already know how to locate suitable properties but might not have any reliable contractors on speed dial to perform the labor required to do a flip. Realtors are very busy, so you might find it's a good idea to employ an on-site project manager to handle the day-to-day details of keeping the project on track.

> **FLIP TIP**
>
> I am often asked if it's necessary to become a Realtor before you enter the flipping business. If you really want to be a real estate agent, then go ahead, but it's not neces-sary to have a Realtor's license in order to succeed in the flipping business. That said, you *do* need a Realtor on your team, but that Realtor does not have to be you.

If you're an interior designer, you know you can make your interiors beautiful but might need help on the real estate and technical aspects of the flip.

As a contractor, you either have all the skills needed to rehab a house or have crews that have all the skills. However, you might not have a clue how to find a suitable house to flip before it's snatched up by someone who has better real estate connections.

Finally, if you are just an everyday person like most of us, with no particular background or experience relevant to flipping, then you'll need to build a team that has all the experience required to handle every aspect of flipping a house from start to finish.

Sit down and make a list of all the jobs required to flip a house. (We have provided a sample list in Appendix C.) Next to each job, put an *S* or a *W* to indicate whether you feel your experience and abilities relating to that task are strong or weak. The tasks that you mark as strong you can more than likely complete yourself with guidance from a more experienced flipper (at least in the beginning). The tasks you mark as weak are those for which you know you are going to need help.

For example, you might have excellent taste and be really skilled at picking out attractive colors and finishes to create a beautiful flip; you might also know you are less skilled at estimating things such as how much concrete is required to pour a 10-by-20-foot patio. That means you need to find someone for your team who can help you with estimating how much material you need to complete a particular job.

FLIPPER BEWARE

You can definitely save money if you are able to do some of the physical labor on your first flips yourself, but you should only do it if you can produce professional quality results. If you do a poor job, not only will you have wasted time, but you will also be wasting money because you'll have to buy new materials and hire an expert to come along behind you and correct your subpar work.

In addition to the list found in Appendix C, I suggest you also start a team-building list. As you review your strengths and weaknesses, mark down each category of helper you believe you will need to bolster your team in the areas where you don't have as much experience, or for jobs you would prefer someone else handle. Record all this information on your team-building list.

By the time you are done, you will have a helpful and very thorough road map to help you launch your business. As you read through this personalized list you have created just for your business, you will begin to get a very clear picture of exactly the kind of help you need to build a great team.

Filling the Voids

Next, it's time to start interviewing people in each area in which you know you will need help. Look for folks who have good reputations, pleasant personalities you think will work well with your own, and whose skills complement yours. Your goal is to find people to strengthen your team in areas in which your lack of experience affects your self-confidence.

Types of Business Entities

A flipping business works well as a sole proprietorship or an LLC and also can work as a partnership, especially a limited partnership. It's rare to see a flipping business set up as a corporation, although some larger organizations are set up that way. Look at the regulations in your city and state to make sure you select the best solution for your business.

There are five primary business entities. Entrepreneurs choose from the following options when determining how to structure their businesses. The business types are:

- Sole proprietorship
- Partnership
- LLC (Limited Liability Company)
- S corporation
- C corporation

The terms *sole proprietorship* and *partnership* refer to both the type of ownership of the business and the legal structure of the business. The terms *LLC* and *S* and *C corporations* refer only to the legal structure of the business.

Each type of business setup has its own advantages and limitations. Read through these descriptions and consult a lawyer or financial advisor if you want help in determining which setup best suits your particular situation and business goals.

Sole Proprietorships

A sole proprietorship is owned by only one person. Because a sole proprietorship is not a legal business entity, business taxes are filed on a *Schedule C* under the business owner's Social Security number, and the business owner pays personal income tax on any income the business generates. Sole proprietors are also personally responsible for any debts or legal liabilities the business incurs.

> **DEFINITION**
>
> A **Schedule C** is an IRS tax form that sole proprietors must prepare and file with their personal income taxes annually to report how much money they made or lost in their business over the preceding tax year. Sole proprietors are considered to be self-employed, and as a result, must also pay the employer's share of any Social Security, disability, and Medicare contribution in addition to the share they must pay personally on any income they have earned through the business.

While sole proprietorships are certainly the simplest form of business to set up, they have some major drawbacks. Chief among them is the risk of personal legal exposure. If you are a sole proprietor and have a client who sues your business, you are personally responsible to pay any financial judgment against the business.

A sole proprietorship is a good choice for someone who does not have a lot of money to invest in setting up a business. Generally speaking, you simply have to select a name for your business, pay a modest fee to secure a business license in that name from your county courthouse, and you're in business.

> **FLIPPER BEWARE**
>
> Because sole proprietors must pay both the employer's *and* employee's share of Social Security, Medicare, and disability contributions, combined taxes on income generated by such businesses can be surprisingly high, amounting to many thousands of dollars a year. We recommend you consult with a CPA or a bookkeeper to insure you are setting aside enough money to cover these annual taxes.

Partnerships

A partnership is a legal contract formed between two or more individuals or business entities to define ownership and responsibilities for a particular business. You may not form partnerships for corporations because they are owned by their shareholders.

Partners report their share of a company's profit or loss on their individual tax forms and remain financially and legally responsible for any lawsuits or judgments against the business.

Limited partnerships are very popular in the flipping business. Your investor may wish to form a limited partnership with you in which he or she remains a silent partner, in other words, someone who supplies working capital but wants nothing else to do with the business.

Partnerships are very easy to form and easy to run. Usually there is no state filing requirement to form a partnership.

LLCs

The chief advantage of an LLC or limited liability company is that they are independent legal entities that are entirely separate from the owner. LLCs shield your personal assets in any lawsuit or judgment situation. Adversaries cannot come against you personally because of something that happened between them and your LLC.

There is no limit to the number of owners with a LLC. Taxes are levied and paid according to the ownership structure. If you are the only owner of the LLC, you can pay your taxes as part of your personal taxes, just as if you were a sole proprietor, by preparing a Schedule C for your business profit and losses and including it with your personal tax filing. If the LLC has multiple owners or is owned by a partnership, then you should file your taxes accordingly.

While an LLC is governed by operating agreements much like a corporation, many business people prefer this arrangement over a corporation because there are no requirements to appoint a board of directors, hold an annual meeting, or record minutes with an LLC.

Most states require that you register an LLC with the secretary of state. You also must acquire a state business ID number to be used for sales tax filings and wholesale purchase purposes.

In addition, you must also acquire a federal *EIN* or *employer identification number* that you will use to identify your LLC in tax filings. Since most of your team members will be contract and not full-time employees, tax laws require that you send them 1099 forms at the end of the tax year, stating how much you paid them. Both you and your team members need this information for tax purposes, and the federal government requires that it be submitted to the IRS as well. You may only apply for an EIN if your business is physically located within the United States.

> **DEFINITION**
>
> An **EIN** or **employer identification number** is a nine-digit number assigned to each individual business by the Internal Revenue Service. It is the business equivalent of a Social Security number, and is used to track tax filings made by each individual business.

S Corporations and C Corporations

S and C corporations have completely independent legal and tax structures. Like LLCs, both S and C corporations protect your personal assets in the event of a legal action brought against the corporation. They enjoy what is known as *perpetual existence,* meaning the company will continue as a legal entity until it is officially dissolved, even if the original founders leave the business.

However, there are many downsides to forming C corporations, especially for a small business such as flipping. Their very nature makes them more suited to larger businesses. For example, C corporations are subject to a very unpopular "double taxation" as they must pay taxes on both their profits as well as any shareholder dividends. S corporations do not pay taxes on dividends. C corporations must also file their taxes quarterly, which adds additional operational expenses to your budget. S corporations and the other business entities can file annually.

The steps required to launch a S or C corporation are more time-consuming and expensive than those for other business entities. You must select a legal name for the business, check that it has not already been taken, write your articles of incorporation, and file them with your secretary of state (along with a hefty filing fee). Then you must appoint a board of directors, issue stock certificates to your initial stockholders, and apply for your EIN and any other tax identification numbers required by state or local regulations in your area. Finally, all this must happen before you conduct even one minute of business.

> **FLIP TIP**
>
> The fastest, easiest way to get an EIN or employer identification number is by applying online with the IRS. They maintain an easy-to-use electronic application at irs.gov/businesses/small-businesses-self-employed/apply-for-an-employer-identification-number-ein-online. The main advantage of filing online is that you receive your EIN immediately upon completing the application and paying the fee.

Finally, S and C corporations have many more regulations and more government oversight and reporting requirements compared to other business entities, all of which combine to make them a less popular choice for people launching a flipping business.

Setting Up Your Business

Now that you've determined what type of business entity to open, it's time to decide if you are going to flip houses as a full-time business or part-time hobby. You'll also have to consider if you truly want to go solo (not something I'd recommend for beginners) or are willing to work with partners as you learn. Finally, you'll need to determine where you want to conduct business— from your home or an office. Let's take a look at your choices.

Career or Hobby?

If you're one of the millions of Americans who have lost their jobs in the recession and haven't been able to find another, the question of whether to look at flipping as a part-time or full-time business is easy to answer. Of course, you'll want to devote almost every waking hour to getting your flipping business off the ground.

For those of you who already have a job, the answer is easy as well. If you have a family and monthly obligations, you are not going to willingly walk away from a steady paycheck to dive into the vast moat of uncertainty that flipping can engender. You'll want to do the business part-time, at least until you get established.

Fortunately, house flipping is an excellent business for part-time entrepreneurs. If you're successful with your initial endeavors, you can set a timetable for yourself to transition from part-time to full-time flipper once you consistently achieve your monthly income goals in the business.

In my experience, the first flip is a trial by fire for most beginners. Those who survive go on to flip more houses, building their experience, reputation, and income as they go. However, the annals of flipping are littered with the stories of people who barely made it through one flip and never tried another.

The only way you're going to figure out which category you will fall into is to try flipping a house and see if it's something you'd like to do long term.

Going Solo vs. Working with a Partner

The next decision you must make is whether you want to fly solo as a flipper or partner with someone, preferably someone with more experience and connections in the flipping business than you yourself have.

> **FLIP TIP**
>
> There's plenty of room to grow in the flipping business. According to RealtyTrac, in 2005 there were 259,192 people who flipped at least one house in the United States before the housing crash. In 2015, there were just 110,008 individual investors or business entities that flipped at least one home. This means competition for prime properties is still relatively low compared to precrash conditions.

I suggest you find a partner with whom to start your business even if you prefer working on your own. In the flipping business, partnerships do not mean you are shut into a small office with the same person 24/7. In fact, you might rarely see your partner if you're focused on different aspects of the flip, or if the partner is providing financing but nothing else.

As a beginner, partnering with a Realtor or contractor makes good sense for several reasons:

An experienced partner knows where the hot deals are and which neighborhoods are trending, meaning you'll turn over your completed flip much faster.

You'll learn a lot about the flipping business by working with people who already have extensive experience on the job.

You'll establish vital contacts with wholesale suppliers, building inspectors, work crews, and so on. These relationships will serve you well if you ever intend to go off on your own at some point in the future.

A more experienced partner has access to sources of financing a beginner isn't likely to know about.

To some extent, working with an experienced partner helps to protect you from your own mistakes.

If you experience a failure, having a partner can help cushion the blow and also help you see the flop in perspective so you can learn from your mistakes.

A partner can encourage you to keep going even if you have had a bad experience.

If you are absolutely determined to work on your own, be prepared for everything to take longer than you think it will. Yes, you will be able to make all the decisions without having to consult anyone else, but you will also be doing all the work.

There is a fairly steep learning curve when it comes to flipping houses. The information is not complex or difficult to learn. It's just that there is so much of it. If you are going solo, you will not have the benefit of a more experienced partner to guide you through some of the more dangerous waters of your maiden flipping voyage.

Home or Office—Where to Work?

Most flippers operate from their homes or from an existing office connected to their primary occupation. This keeps startup costs to a minimum.

It's not a good idea to shoulder the added expense of renting an office outside your home when you first start flipping. You should make every effort to minimize expenditures while you are building a solid business foundation. Even if your living quarters are cramped, you can carve out a nook where you can keep the equipment and supplies you need to run your business.

A home office has many benefits. It's virtually free. There's no commute, no snarled traffic, and no ill-tempered boss to contend with. Instead of paying for lunches out daily, you can step into the kitchen and make yourself a sandwich. You can deduct the costs associated with your home office from your income tax. Just be sure the space is dedicated to your office and is not used for anything else. IRS rules state that a space used for other purposes in nonbusiness hours does not qualify as a "home office."

A downside of having an office in your house is that it's difficult to get people to take you and your business seriously when you're running that business from home.

Another downside is that it doesn't look professional to use your home address as your business address. Depending on local zoning ordinances, you might run into trouble having an office in your home. At the very least, you need to rent a post office box so your business can have its own dedicated address. Use this business address on all your correspondence, your tax filings, and your dealings with local and state officials.

> **FLIP TIP**
>
> There are two types of mailboxes you can rent. The U.S. Post Office rents mailboxes on their premises where you can receive mail, including packages. However, you can't receive UPS or FedEx packages there, and they have limited hours making it difficult to retrieve mail after hours. Visit usps.com/manage/po-boxes.htm for more information.
>
> I recommend renting a mailbox from a mailing service. You'll get a physical street address where you can receive mail and packages, including UPS and FedEx. In most locations, you'll have 24/7 access to your mailbox but can only pick up packages during business hours. You can rent by the month or year.

A home office doesn't work for everyone. Perhaps it's simply impossible for you to work from home. Maybe you have a young child who demands your total attention, making it difficult to focus on work tasks. Perhaps your neurotic dog won't stop barking or your significant other won't stop talking. Or maybe your overly fond mom keeps dropping by with homemade cookies.

In this situation, find an office away from home so you can properly conduct your business and maintain your productivity. You'll be glad to know there are more affordable alternatives to outright renting an office that will provide you with the privacy you need without bankrupting you out of the gate.

Shared office space   Shared offices offer all the amenities of a regular office at about half the price. Shared offices are already furnished and have basic office equipment such as fax machines and phone lines already installed, so you can expect to save about $3,000 to $5,000 on office furniture and another $1,000 or more on equipment costs. Many shared offices also have a receptionist who takes messages for all the businesses in the space, so that is another cost savings for you.

Virtual office   Thanks to modern technology, your office can literally be anywhere you and your laptop are. That means you can have your office on your worksite, which is a huge time-saver, or in your car, at Starbucks, the local library, or even in a bowling alley! Virtual offices give you a physical street address, and if you choose to, you can include a remote receptionist in your package to answer your phone, take messages, and receive packages.

No matter where you locate your office, be sure to make it comfortable, attractive, and a place you want to be.

The Importance of Good Equipment

When setting up your business, it's important to choose equipment, furnishings, and supplies that will help you do your job more efficiently and comfortably. Let's look at what you need to get started.

Computers and Tablets

It is essential to have a way to digitally manage your business. You must have a computer or tablet with word processing and spreadsheet software, an email client, and internet access to keep track of the many different aspects of your house flipping business.

Most flippers I know run their businesses from a laptop rather than a desktop computer, primarily because portability is such a desirable feature when you spend significant time in the field. To that end, many flippers are now switching to tablets because they are lighter to carry around than laptops and are always connected to the internet via Wi-Fi no matter where you are.

I recommend going to a store and explaining your needs to a salesperson. Let an expert help you make the determination about which device would be a better solution for your particular needs. Buy a color printer that works with your device at the same time. You can often get a nice discount on a printer when you buy it at the same time as your computer or tablet.

Cellphone

You need a reliable cellphone to run your business effectively. There are days when I think my phone is glued to my hand because I never seem to be able to put it down.

Your best bet is a smartphone that has Wi-Fi connectivity so you can set up a virtual *hotspot* in the field if you need to. It should also be able to send and receive email and have a web browser enabled, which means you'll need a data plan as well as a voice plan. You truly don't need more features than these.

> **DEFINITION**
>
> A **hotspot** is way to gain access to the internet through your smart phone. Located in your phone settings, a hotspot sets up a wireless local area network you can use to temporarily get internet access on your computer when you are out in the field. Be careful though! Unless you have password protected your hotspot, anyone in the vicinity can hop on and potentially access sensitive information on your devices.

Camera

There are many occasions when you will need a good camera. You might want to take pictures of houses you are considering for renovation or photos of your completed flips. Unless you are a professional photographer though, your photos will strictly be for informational purposes. Many people ask why they need a camera if they have a phone with a camera, and the short answer is, you don't. But if you are going to use the photos you take for advertising flyers or any other reason, remember that the unusual aspect ratio for photos taken on a cellphone makes them look weird compared to what we are used to seeing. Cellphone photos are comparatively tall and skinny, and viewers can tell instantly that a photo is a cellphone photo. So I do recommend investing in a good quality SLR camera, such as a Nikon or a Canon, as soon as your budget will allow it.

Office Furnishings

There is no piece of office equipment more important than your desk chair. If it fits your body, provides lumbar support, and is so comfortable you can sit all day without groaning or fidgeting, you've hit a home run. If your chair is uncomfortable, your work will suffer.

Don't buy the first chair you see. Go to an office furnishings store and try out several. Select your desk first and then roll several different chairs up to the desk and sit in each one. Select the chair that feels the best to your body, not necessarily the one that visually looks the best.

The Least You Need to Know

- Assessing your strengths and weaknesses before you start will give you concrete information about the kind of people you need to hire to fill out your flipping team.

- Sole proprietorships and partnerships are the most common types of business setups used by flippers.

- Going solo is difficult for beginners. It increases the amount of time required to complete a flip and increases the odds of failure.

- No matter where you locate your office, it's important to choose comfortable furnishings to increase your productivity.

Getting Yourself Organized

Being organized while you're renovating a house will not only save you time and money, it might also save your sanity. It might even occasionally help save your flip. No, this isn't the most glamorous aspect of the flipping business. Nonetheless, keeping track of costs, paying bills as they come due, managing crews and schedules, and ordering materials in a timely fashion will keep your projects flowing smoothly and quickly help you see what is working and what is not on any given flip.

Being organized helps you stay on task with all those jobs. It keeps you informed about what is happening when and where on your flips. It shows you when you need to make midproject course corrections to stay on track. Good organizational skills also help you stick to your schedule and your budget.

I'm not just stating a personal opinion when I say this. Study after study has shown that people who maintain neat workspaces have a higher level of productivity and engagement in their work. Neat people are also better regarded by their bosses and their peers than their messier counterparts. (Although people who are *too* neat do receive their share of criticism.)

In This Chapter

- Good organization equals success
- Making your style work for you
- Managing projects efficiently
- Time and money saving tools

It may not be fair, but it's the way things are. If you want to maximize your chances of success in flipping, start with organizing your office or workspace.

Organize for Success

Right from the earliest stages of your flipping business, your desk will become your own personal equivalent of the Situation Room in the White House. It will be command central, the place where everything that happens in your business—every invoice, phone call, email, message, or sales offer—ends up.

This means you must maintain your desk and work area with some semblance of organization. When you do, that organization naturally flows from your physical space into your thinking and your workflow, making you even more efficient in your efforts. It's important to note that a leader who demonstrates the principles of organization in his or her workspace and daily actions is also a leader that commands trust and respect. That's part of the good mojo that goes along with being organized.

Going Digital

We are living in a digital age in which most communications, many purchases, and even property transactions happen online. That means you won't have as much paper to deal with as we did in the past. That should help you minimize paper clutter.

Of course, some things will still come to you in paper form, and it's that potential clutter you need to manage. File bills and correspondence as they come in and notes as you make them. Follow the time-honored principle of handling each piece of paper only once. When you first put your hands on it, deal with it then and there, or have an assistant take care of it. Don't allow unfiled papers to accumulate on your desktop. That is the fastest way to create a big mess in your office.

> **FLIP TIP**
>
> The best way to keep track of notes is not on paper, but on your phone or tablet. Unlike paper notes that exist in just one place and can easily be lost or misplaced, a digital note can be remotely accessed from your electronic device wherever you can receive a phone or Wi-Fi signal.

Move whatever you can into a digital format, including contracts, invoices, building plans, notes, sketches, reminders, your calendar, and so on. Digital documents are available to you wherever you are; they're also particularly easy to access and edit if you use a tablet or smartphone. Later in this chapter, I'll discuss how new mobile apps and cloud-based subscription software are streamlining and revolutionizing the flipping business, saving flippers time and money in the process.

Just Clean It Up!

Some of you are resisting this advice even as you read it. I can almost hear the protests now. "My desk may be messy, but I can tell you exactly where everything is!" That might be so, but I'll bet you cannot find what you need when you need it as quickly as your more organized friends.

Buy whatever desk accessories you like, but at the minimum, get some sort of organizer to keep track of current working files. A drawer organizer will handle small items, such as pens and pencils, sticky notes, and the like. Have a place for everything you need and use, and put items back in their designated spots when you are not using them. If you're still getting ready to trot out photos of Einstein's messy desk to defend your position, put them away. Einstein got a pass (he did invent the theory of relativity, after all...), but you should try to do something similarly amazing. Take several deep breaths and tackle the basic organization of your entire workspace, including your desk. Follow whatever system seems best for you, and get it done. I guarantee you will feel calmer, happier, and ready to take on the world after you're done.

 FLIP TIP

> While messiness hurts you in many ways in the flipping business, being disorganized is not 100 percent bad. In a 2013 study comparing organized to disorganized people, researchers at the University of Minnesota found that people who have cluttered workspaces were better at creative problem-solving than people with neat desks. They concluded that people who are organized tend to perform and make decisions to conform with what they believe was expected of them. But messy people who feel no such constraints on their performance were more likely to think of completely novel but still viable solutions.

For those of you who already have a well-organized workspace, congratulations. You just saved some time you can devote to developing other aspects of your flipping business.

Effective Project Management

When you have your own flipping business, you wear several different hats. You put your teams together and find projects for them to work on. You arrange financing for the project and come up with a good plan and a timetable to renovate your flip. You hire crews and select and order materials. You are the leader of your team, and unless you specifically hire some to oversee your flips, you are essentially the *project manager (PM)*. Team members will look to you for guidance as work progresses on your projects.

DEFINITION

A **project manager** or **PM** is a person who is responsible for overseeing the planning, execution, and management of every aspect of a project from beginning to end.

More than anyone, a project manager is ultimately responsible for the success or failure of any specific project. It's a big job with lots of responsibilities, and many house flippers find that hiring a PM helps them stay profitable and grow their businesses.

Not only are you ultimately responsible for bringing in each flip on time and on budget, but you are also the team manager. You run the schedule and make sure materials are delivered on time and in the proper order. You must have work crews onsite at the right times. It won't do you any good to have a truckload of flooring sitting in your house if you forgot to schedule the installation crew. Every job in flipping requires precise coordination. A lack of coordination usually means cost overruns and a failure to meet your scheduling goals.

As project manager, you must be adept at mediating and negotiating, smoothing over differences between team members, and addressing and offering solutions for any problems that crop up along the way. And believe me, you'll have to deal with all sorts of unexpected problems ranging from personnel disputes to late deliveries, permitting issues, mistakes, weather delays, and defective materials. The list goes on and on, and your crews will always look to you for answers as issues arise.

You must also manage the risks associated with your project—the potential physical risks to the workers and the financials risks you and your business partners are shouldering. You also might have to contend with the risks of vandalism and theft of materials from your worksite.

FLIPPER BEWARE

One thing that does not go over very well with contractors and work crews is a bad temper. If you blow up at people who are working on your flips, you may soon find yourself with a crew of one. Contractors and craftsmen who do jobs like plumbing, electricity, and carpentry are too much in demand for them to put up with being treated disrespectfully. If you have a quick temper, don't bring it to your job sites.

Perhaps the most important skill you need to manage your projects is the skill of effective communication. When you can express your expectations for a project clearly, whether verbally or in writing, it makes it much easier for team members to fulfill those expectations correctly right out of the gate. On the other hand, if you don't express yourself clearly or give confusing instructions to your crews, it's likely that your results are not going to be what you wanted.

Clear communication is essential in the flipping business. It's always a good idea to have things in writing so that if a disagreement or misunderstanding arises, your original intentions can be verified by referring to a work order or the original contract. This is truly important when it comes to deciding who covers the cost of mistakes. If the work that was done clearly does not conform to what you have in your written orders, then the contractor, subcontractor, or supplier should cover the error. If the mistake is on your end, then you'll have to pay the costs of fixing any mistakes.

Multitasking

You probably already realize just from reading the first few chapters that you are going to be performing and overseeing multiple jobs as a house flipper. The ability to multitask is critical for anyone who wants to flip houses. This is a job with many moving parts which must all be properly coordinated to ensure a great outcome.

If you feel overwhelmed at the mere idea of handling all those tasks and the associated stress, consider hiring a project manager. Yes, that means more money out of your pocket, at least in the beginning. But a good project manager can free you up to focus on finding more flips, selecting finishes, or pricing comps. As you've already discovered your areas of strength and relative weakness in Chapter 2, you can now assign your project manager tasks in line with that information. Keep the jobs you like under your management, and assign the jobs that are less appealing to you to your project manager.

One of the tasks that is most difficult for many beginners to manage is the creation of a *takeoff* list, which is a list of materials required to do your flip. It's a technical job that requires accuracy, familiarity with building materials, and precise estimating skills. Since a big chunk of your costs are tied up in your materials, it's essential that you stay on top of the items needed to transform your flip into a dream house. A lot of money can go down the drain if you order too much material, and you'll lose time as well as money if you don't order enough.

DEFINITION

A **takeoff** is a list of materials required to complete any building project, including a flip, along with the estimated cost of those materials.

Usually, a general contractor or project manager is adept at creating takeoff lists, but watch them closely to make sure everything that is being ordered is in fact needed.

As you grow your business, you'll be able to assign more responsibilities to other team members. Just remember, as the team leader you are still ultimately responsible for everything that happens on your project, whether you have a project manager or general contractor on the job or not.

Hiring Assistants

If you have the budget to hire an assistant from the beginning of your flipping business, you'll be well ahead of the game. Many aspiring flippers are husband and wife teams or teams of close friends. When that is the case, it's easy to split the workload among the participants.

Where you might run into difficulty is if you are a lone wolf flipper, coming into the business all by yourself with no support from friends, family, or existing business associates—and no prior relevant experience. It's easy to get overwhelmed by the sheer volume of work that must be done to complete a flip. There are so many different jobs to do, requiring so many different skill sets. In Chapter 6, we'll give you some great ideas for breaking down big jobs into more manageable tasks. And in Chapter 5, we'll show you how to put together a great team to help divide the labor and ease the burden from your shoulders alone.

Organizational Tools

As we've mentioned, flipping is a job that involves many elements. Organization is key to staying on top of all the different jobs you have to do, figuring out the when they must be done, and the order in which they must be completed. Trying to keep all those facts, dates, and figures in your head, or even down in one notebook, can seem an almost Herculean task.

Fortunately, the digital age has brought literally hundreds of new tools to market to help flippers manage their projects. Some are apps you can run on your smartphone or tablet, while others are feature-rich cloud-based software that come along with a monthly subscription fee. However, don't let cost alone deter you from trying these tools. Many are so handy they can earn back your investment in a day or two.

Most offer 7- to 14-day trial periods so you can test drive them in the real world and see if they offer significant value for your business. Try out several to see which apps you like and will use. There's no sense investing in a tool if it's just going to sit unused on your phone or tablet.

Estimating

Estimating is one of the most important jobs you will have as a flipper. When you compile your takeoff or list of materials required to complete your flip along with their costs, it's truly helpful to have digital assistance as you are doing it. While creating takeoffs is normally something your contractor or project manager would handle, it's important for you to know how to do it, if for no other reason than to insure the proper amount of material is being ordered in a timely way. It also helps you ascertain that the material you ordered is in fact the material that was delivered.

Like many of the tasks we are discussing in this section, estimating is often best handled by using one of the new digital apps designed especially for the purpose. Like the other apps I'll discuss later, there are estimating apps that range in cost from free to expensive. However, even expensive apps can prove well worth the investment if they can save you significant time and money on your projects.

The number one estimating app for contractors is Contractor Estimating and Invoicing Tool by Joist Inc., and it's free. It quickly creates professional estimates and, as a bonus, invoices. BuildCalc is also very popular. Users love it because the company frequently updates the interface to ensure it works properly on the latest devices. It creates detailed takeoff lists and makes it easy to share estimates between team members, which is a lot of functionality for just $24.99.

Apple fans also like Construction Cost Estimator. At less than $20, it's a bargain compared to some other programs which I have not included here, but it can only create on-the-spot estimates and is not capable of most of the more advanced functions BuildCalc provides. No matter which estimating tool you choose, having a digital app handle big jobs like estimating can be a huge time and money saver.

Project Timelines

You should never start a flipping project until (and unless) you have a complete and detailed project timeline in place. The project timeline sets expectations for the entire team and lets crewmembers know when you need certain tasks completed. A schedule helps your contractor to accurately schedule work crews and delivery of materials.

Keep in mind that bad weather and slow shipments can negatively impact your schedule, so always factor in an extra couple of weeks to account for any contingencies that may crop up during the flip.

FLIP TIP

There are several good timeline management apps and cloud based software programs that let you easily create schedules and keep track of every aspect of your project from demolition to open house. LiquidPlanner is cloud based and highly rated, but also expensive, starting at $29 per month per user for just the basic app. Smartsheet is also cloud based and has mixed reviews, but is more affordable at just $10 per month per user for the basic plan. Microsoft offers Project Timeline, which is free with some very affordable add-ons to expand its capabilities. However, it only works on PCs and Android devices. There are dozens of apps available if none of these suit your needs. Just search for Project Timeline apps to review what is available.

Of course, you can manage your timeline manually on a spreadsheet if you wish, but it would be much faster and easier to use one of the various specialized timeline management apps to get the job done.

Budgets

In many ways, your budget is probably the most important document relating to your flip. It's the center tent pole that supports everything else. Without a proper budget in place, you really have no way of knowing if your flip has the potential to turn a profit or not.

Many people like to use a spreadsheet program like Excel to manage their budget. There are actually a number of free construction budgets templates available to use with Excel. A Google search will quickly lead you to them. Using a template is a real timesaver because all the required fields and formulas are already built in.

For those of you who prefer Quickbooks for budgeting tasks, template and plugins are available to help customize the software for construction budget management. BuildStar offers one such program, Construction Budget Management software, that ties right into QuickBooks to help you oversee and manage construction costs on each flip. For more information on creating flipping project budgets, see Chapter 4.

Materials Management

The estimating, ordering, and managing of all items required to complete your flip is called *materials management.* It covers everything from concrete for a patio to sheetrock, insulation, cabinets, plumbing and light fixtures, paint, landscaping—anything you purchase to help convert your flip into a lovely home ready to sell. Proper materials management enables you to stay within your budget and your timetable. If you don't stay on top of it, you may see your budget swing wildly out of control.

As with timeline management and budgeting, there are many good apps and software programs that will help you keep track of the materials required to do your flipping projects. Being able to handle all this information digitally is a huge plus. It reduces paper clutter and enables you to manage your business remotely or onsite as your schedule demands.

Because materials management and construction apps are fairly complex and can do many things, they are also rather expensive. The most popular Buildertrend, costs $99 per month per user but has many useful features. You can keep track of all your materials in the app, as well as your timetable. It also can handle *change orders* and even lets users mark up previously uploaded digital construction plans to instruct subcontractors.

> **DEFINITION**
>
> A **change order** is a legal amendment added to a contract whenever jobs are added or removed from your flipping project or you make any change to the work in terms of budget, schedule, scope, or materials used.

You may have some specific need and not know if there are any apps available to handle it. Do a bit of Google research and you're likely to find something that will work for you. Also ask other flippers to recommend any digital tools that they find particularly useful.

Finally, remember to back up your phone or device nightly so you will still have a copy of your critical files even if you suffer from equipment problems and lose the files on your phone or tablet.

The Least You Need to Know

- Good organization is critical in the flipping business.
- Disorganization can cost money and cause many problems.
- Excellent project management is key to flipping success.
- Digital tools can make house flipping easier to manage.

CHAPTER 4

Securing Financing

You might think it's a little premature to have a chapter about financing flips so close to the front of the book. In fact, you might not even have gone out looking for suitable properties yet. But unless you are independently wealthy, you *will* require financing for your flipping projects, and it's one of the jobs you must take care of early in the game.

It's important to pull your financing together before you need it so you can act quickly when you *do* find a great deal. If you come across an ideal property before you have your financing in place, you risk losing that house to another buyer while you are trying to secure a loan. You need to be in a position to take quick action when that perfect flip does become available. We're not saying you must go take out an actual loan today. Just get prequalified so you can be ready to move when the time comes.

If you're going to use traditional financing, such as a bank mortgage, getting prequalified tells you the maximum loan you qualify for, which is important knowledge. Why waste time looking at $300,000 properties when you can only get financed for $200,000?

In This Chapter

- Flipping risks
- Estimating costs and profit potential
- Using budgets to make decisions
- Loans available to flippers
- Creative financing options

Many of the initial decisions you'll make as a flipper involve money and financing. Out of your maximum property budget, how much can you personally finance? How big a loan will you need? How much will you (or a partner or a private investor) have to come up with in cash to close a deal? How much are you personally willing (and able) to lose? The answers to these questions will shape the hunt for your first property.

The good news about the flipping business is that there are several creative ways to get loans in addition to the old standbys available through banks and credit unions. So get your ducats in a row, and start working on putting your financing in place. Let's take a look at the possibilities.

Assessing Risks

Before we discuss the types of loans available to flippers, we want to talk about managing risks in your business. One of the most important questions you'll have to answer when seeking financing for a property is "How risky is this flip?" Your potential lenders and investors need to know the answer to that question as well.

In an ideal world, a flip runs smoothly, with no glitches, hitches, or mistakes to spoil your dreams of success. In the real world, things might not go quite so smoothly.

The First Rule of Flipping

Unlike the "sure thing" you see on television, where every flipped house sells quickly and for an eye-popping profit, flipping in the real world is a business where things can and do go wrong. There's a risk your rehab will cost significantly more than your estimate because you find expensive hidden damage that must be repaired before you can sell the house. You could watch your potential profit melt away in a matter of minutes with one bad inspection report.

There's also the risk the house won't sell quickly or at all. Maybe you misread the demand for the neighborhood, or perhaps people don't like your sales price or the finishes you've chosen.

Realize that every day that ticks by without selling a completed flip costs you more money. You need to factor these potential "after the flip" *carrying costs* into your budget as you plan.

> **DEFINITION**
>
> Known as a *holding* cost in some areas, a **carrying cost** consists of any money you must spend to hold a house in inventory until it sells and goes to an act of sale. This includes things such as loan interest, utility payments, hazard insurance, yard maintenance, rental of staging furniture, and other related expenses.

Because of the potential risks involved, we always advise new flippers never to invest more money in any given project than they can afford to lose. This is "The First Rule of Flipping." We call it the pain point, or put more directly, the most money you are willing and able to lose on a flip.

Figuring out this number also gives you an idea about your tolerance for risk. While flipping houses is a very enjoyable business, it's not something we recommend for the fainthearted. If the thought of losing several thousand dollars on one project makes you sick, you might want to pause and think about what you are actually prepared to risk to gain the opportunity to earn a significant payday.

Some of you may be thinking, "But wait a minute. I don't have a spare penny, so how can I invest any money in my flip, much less afford to lose money?"

That's a great question. Many new flippers start out in that same position. Later in this chapter, we'll introduce you to loans where you can borrow 100 percent of the price of a property even if your credit is not stellar, so yes, you can still get into the flipping business even if you don't have a pot of cash buried in your backyard.

The chance to earn handsome returns on an investment of their *sweat equity* is what attracts many people to the flipping business in the first place. Your labor and ideas, perhaps even expertise, are what you invest instead of cash.

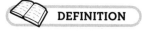 **DEFINITION**

> **Sweat equity** is labor, ideas, and expertise you invest in a project in lieu of cash. In exchange for your sweat equity, you receive an ownership position in the project and a share of any profits realized.

Just be sure you and your business partners agree on the cash value of the labor and expertise you plan to contribute to a project. The terms of your agreement should be laid out in a written contract prior to starting any project.

 FLIPPER BEWARE

> If, like many new flippers, you are investing sweat equity in a project, make sure you get the estimated value of your contribution in a written contract. When it's time to divide the proceeds of a sale, and you believe your sweat equity investment is worth 50 percent of the profits earned, but your private investor says it's only worth 25 percent, you'll have no recourse unless those terms were laid out in writing in a contract signed by both parties. We have included a basic sweat equity contract in Appendix C, but check with a local attorney to ensure its provisions comply with the laws of your state and completely protect your interests in your jurisdiction.

Risk Mitigation

Of course, you don't have to just blindly accept risks as they come. There are many ways to mitigate the potential risks associated with flipping houses and reduce your chance of failing before you sign your first deal. Here are a few:

- Pick the right neighborhood.

- Buy low and sell high.

- Control costs and stick to your project budget.

- Price your property competitively.

- Choose finishes and colors that are on trend for the time, the neighborhood, and the style of the house.

Many of these techniques are best deployed in the early stages of a flipping project. For example, you can significantly increase the odds of your flips selling quickly by only buying houses in trending neighborhoods with high demand and relatively low inventory. If you have a choice between buying a beat-up house in a hot neighborhood, where there are only one or two other houses for sale, or a great-looking house in a neighborhood people are leaving, where houses sit on the market for months without a nibble, always buy the lesser house in the hotter neighborhood. Assuming you do a great job on the rehab, a prime property in a location where there are not enough houses to meet the demand could end up in an auction situation. That means you'll make even more money than you had planned.

Another way you can reduce risk is by maintaining hazard insurance on your property. Just because a house is in the process of being rehabbed doesn't mean it isn't subject to the whims of Mother Nature, an accidental fire, or an opportunistic thief. Work with your insurance agent to determine how much coverage you need and maintain it until you sell the property.

Estimating Costs

We discussed the tools to estimate costs in Chapter 3, but there we were discussing estimates for the cost of materials required to completely rehab a flip. Here we are talking about the costs of acquiring the financing that makes your flips possible.

Of course, in order to know how much money you'll need to borrow, you need to work out the following information:

- You first must determine the cost of your target property acquisition.

- Then add the acquisition cost to the cost of the labor and materials required to get your flip ready for market, plus an estimate of your carrying costs. These three items will give you the basic investment required to do the flip.

- Next, run comps on the property to get an idea of your potential sales price.

- Once you've set your sales price, deduct your total investment along with real estate commissions, insurance, loan, and closing costs from the sales price to calculate your potential profit.

Be aware that not every flip sells for its asking price. That means you must be sure to leave yourself plenty of room to cover your costs and still make a profit even if you do have to accept a lower offer to get the house sold.

> **FLIP TIP**
>
> To quickly figure your potential profit on a flip, subtract your property acquisition cost, rehab costs, real estate commissions, insurance, loan, and closing costs from your proposed selling price.

These numbers are important, because lenders want to know they are investing in a viable project. After all, they not only want to make sure they get paid back, but they also want to earn some money on the deal. Understandably, they prefer to invest in projects that have the best chance of returning a healthy profit. Numbers are especially important for private investors. Estimated profit potential helps them select which projects they want to finance.

Other Influencing Factors

There are other factors, of course, that can influence your costs in either a positive or negative way. Average days on market (DOM), perceived demand for the neighborhood, and of course, average return on investment for flips in that neighborhood are all things that can impact how much money you end up earning on any given flip.

For example, if the average days on market for a house in your target neighborhood is more than 90, most investors will shy away because they don't want their capital tied up for that long. In that case, consider finding a property in a trending neighborhood with a lower *DOM*.

> **DEFINITION**
>
> **DOM** is an acronym that means *Days on Market*. Average DOM in your locale is an important indicator of potential for a successful flip. The lower the average DOM, the faster your flip is likely to sell. New flippers should stay away from neighborhoods with high average DOM, because houses there will keep your working capital tied up for too long, which hurts your flexibility.

Perceived demand for a neighborhood can be a big help with lenders. They know the market almost as well as Realtors, and if you bring them a proposal for a neighborhood they know has high demand, they are more likely to finance your deal. However, if you are trying to flip a house in a low demand neighborhood with many available properties, financiers might say no. They don't want to run the risk of a bad loan, which is a possible scenario with a new and inexperienced flipper when the average DOM is high. You can get buried in carrying costs and burn through a large chunk of your profits if you are not able to sell a completed flip quickly.

The same goes if the average return on investment for your proposed flip is too low, just $15,000 or $20,000. That's generally not enough of a return for someone who is bankrolling a potentially high-risk investment.

Conversely, if you buy a house in an old neighborhood that has suddenly become hot again, and comps are showing the average return on investment for flips there is about $50,000 to $70,000, you'll have a much better chance of bringing a lender on board. That's because the lender knows that property will sell quickly and bring a nice return on investment (ROI).

Given the choice between a flip that has the potential to sell quickly and produce a healthy profit and one that is likely to sit on the market and bring a low return, why wouldn't you choose to work on the flip that will bring you much better results faster?

Gathering Your Ducks

As you begin to collect all this information, keep it organized and stored in one place. You need it to create a project budget, and you need the project budget to present your deal to potential lenders.

Some people prefer to work with QuickBooks, Excel, or some other budgeting or spreadsheet software to manage their numbers. You might even like to write reports out by hand in ledger books. Your personal style is not nearly as important as the accuracy of your numbers and the knowledge and enthusiasm with which you present your report to a lender. If he or she can see that you know your stuff, and your proposal is supported by the data you submit, you are more likely to get a green light than if you are disorganized and appear uncertain when you make your presentation.

Creating a Project Budget

Before you seek financing for any project, you must know exactly how much money is needed to complete your flipping project. By this time, you should already have gathered all the necessary facts and figures required to complete an accurate project budget. You must include the acquisition cost of the property, real estate commissions, and loan costs on both the acquisition and ultimately, the sale of the property, plus the cost of all the labor and materials required to get your flip ready for market. Don't forget to include staging, marketing, and carrying costs. All those pretty color flyers you hand out to potential buyers don't come for free. Weigh every expenditure against its potential to increase the price you can get for the property.

Once you have all these figures compiled, add 10 to 15 percent more for unforeseen contingencies. You may never use it, but if a problem crops up that will cost you several thousand dollars to fix, you'll be glad you have that money in your budget. Use these figures to create your project budget, which will help you determine how much money you need to do the flip.

FLIPPER BEWARE

Make sure the budget you present to your potential lender is as accurate as possible. Lenders rely on you to give them reliable information. If you mess up your budget and cannot complete a flip as a result, don't expect your lender to be too eager to conduct business with you again.

For example, it would make no sense to borrow $100,000 when you really need $125,000 to finish your flip. However, if you're just "guesstimating," trying to work without a complete and accurate budget, then you could end up borrowing less than you need. You can't bring a house to market that doesn't have plumbing fixtures or an HVAC system, but if you run out of money before you finish your flip, you could find yourself in a similar difficult situation of having to market a house that is, by definition, uninhabitable. Most investors will not be too happy if you keep going back to them and hitting them up for more money after the initial loan because your budget numbers were wrong. That is not a scenario that builds trust or long-term working relationships.

If you run out of money before you complete your rehab, and cannot get additional loans to finish it up, you might end up having to post your property as an *as-is listing* to get back at least some of your investment and get your investor repaid. But kiss any idea of decent profits goodbye if you find yourself in this situation. People who buy incomplete or distressed properties that still need work done usually insist on getting a bargain sales price. And you can pretty much count on kissing your investor goodbye as well. Most investors don't feel comfortable giving money to flippers who have proven themselves unreliable and who cannot complete their flips on time, and within the original budget.

DEFINITION

An **as-is listing** is a property sold in its existing condition, without any warranties or guarantees. When you buy an as-is listing, you accept the property exactly as it is, including any damage and physical defects. You give up your legal right to make any claims against the seller. It must be stated within the sales contract that the house is being sold as-is.

Of course, there will be occasions when, halfway into a flip, an inspector finds hidden damage that must be repaired. While this won't necessarily make an investor happy, it's a completely different situation than you just screwing up the budget. Generally, an investor will give you additional funds to repair newly discovered damage in order to protect their original investment. He might not be happy about it, and he might feel obliged to run you over the coals a bit. However, unless you and your contractor were just grossly negligent in your initial inspection of the house, an experienced investor will understand that sometimes unexpected expenses do crop up mid-flip.

A budget is essential in this process. With a budget, you know exactly how much everything you need is going to cost. You will also know your labor costs, real estate costs, and the cost of borrowing the money needed to complete the project. New flippers sometimes fail to take into account the cost of borrowing money adds to the overall expenses associated with the project. But without that loan money, many of you would not be able to enter the flipping business. So don't think of it as a necessary evil, but rather as a necessary cost of doing business.

Project Financing

Once you have found a property and completed your budget, it's time to think about how you are going to finance your flip. One of the most important things you must do is get yourself out in the business community and establish yourself in the minds of potential investors as an active flipper. Have professional-looking business cards designed and printed up. Join the local chamber of commerce and hand out your card to everyone you meet. Let them know you are looking for investors. Conduct yourself professionally, and within a reasonable period of time, potential investors might start contacting you to see if you have a project they can put some money into.

Of course, this approach takes time, and in the meanwhile, you might already have a flip you need to finance. In this section, we'll review the various ways to get the money you need to turn your rundown house into someone's dream home.

As entrepreneurs in the flipping business, we fortunately have access to a number of different ways to get money. We are not limited to just banks, mortgage companies, credit unions, or savings and loans associations (S&Ls). Let's take a look at what's out there.

Using Your Own Money

The fastest and easiest way to finance a flip is with your own money, but let's face it … that's not a viable option for most beginning flippers. But for those of you fortunate enough to be able to do this, a few cautions.

Just because the money is yours and you don't have to answer to anyone about how you spend it is no reason not to exercise all the due diligence we suggest throughout the course of this book. You still need to …

- Research hot neighborhoods.

- Locate and buy a good potential flip.

- Perform a thorough inspection with a licensed contractor to make sure you know what you are getting into.

- Draw up a plan for the rehab.

- Create a project budget.

- Put together a reliable team to do the rehab work.

- Find a top producing Realtor to sell your finished flip.

Having your own money does not insulate you from mistakes. If you try to take short cuts on any of the required steps, it will hurt you just as surely as it would hurt someone working with a private investor.

If you're worried you might be tempted to cut corners just because you are king of your own world, hire a project manager to oversee the flip to insure everything is done professionally.

Banks and Mortgage Companies

We are in an era of relatively low mortgage rates, so this is a good time to enter the flipping business. Loans granted by lending institutions are the most affordable way to finance a flip.

While many new flippers approach banks, mortgage companies, credit unions, or S&Ls to seek financing for a flip, it's not as popular a way to underwrite a flipping project as you might think.

First of all, it's slow. Lending institutions generally require 30 days or more to approve and process a loan. The process is fraught with dozens of "gotchas" that can bog down approval or access to funds, and in some cases, scuttle a loan entirely.

Then there's the fact that these companies make potential borrowers jump through hoops of fire in order to get a loan. We're not saying you have to pledge your first-born son, but it sometimes can feel almost that bad.

There are stacks of papers you must read, digest, sign, and get notarized. There are many forms that must be filled out. W-2s, 1099s, income tax forms, and proof of income must be provided and so on. They look into your bank accounts, credit history, and check to see if you have a criminal record. And if you've got a bad credit score or have ever had any sort of financial downfall such as a bankruptcy or foreclosure, you can just about forget getting approved for a loan from one of these institutions.

Since these types of loans are heavily regulated by both state and federal laws, you also must meet certain down payment and income requirements, and have enough cash on hand—usually 20 percent of the purchase price—to put down before you can be approved. And that cash must be *yours*. It cannot have been borrowed from a relative or another financial institution.

All that agony might be fine for people who are investing in their dream home or the home where they plan to raise their families … any place they plan to put down roots and stay awhile. Eventually, the torture of the mortgage process fades and the pleasure of living in a house they love supersedes any remembered pain.

> **FLIP TIP**
>
> If you are a new flipper and haven't yet made many connections in the business, you might have no choice but to apply to a lending institution to finance your first flip. The requirements will be a lot more stringent and loan approval a lot slower if you go through a bank or mortgage company rather than a private investor. Make allowances in your planning for these contingencies, because dealing with lending institutions can really slow down the pace of a flip.

Can you imagine going through this loan process four or more times a year, every single time you want to flip a new house? Yes, it does get easier as you go along, but like getting a root canal, it's not something you look forward to.

That said, at least some of you, particularly those of you in smaller towns where there might not be a lot of private financing options available, will have to rely on lending institutions to finance your flipping business.

I suggest chatting with at least three different loan officers prior to making a decision about whom you want to work with. You are creating a long-term business that will bring the lending institution repeat business for years to come, so you want to find someone you trust and like, someone you believe you'll be able to rely upon.

Don't forget to negotiate for the best interest rate. Shop around for the loan if you need to. Interest rates do vary from one lending institution to the next, sometimes from one day to the next. Read the loan papers thoroughly, including all the fine print. It's important for you to know and understand exactly what you are agreeing to before you sign a loan contract. If you feel uncomfortable with the jargon, pay an attorney to review the loan papers before you sign them.

When dealing with lending institutions, you should be working toward becoming established enough and having enough creditworthiness to be granted a large line of credit. That way, whenever you want to buy a house, you just buy it with your line of credit, without having to endure the mortgage process. The same is true of all the costs associated with flipping a house. They can be covered with the credit line as well.

FLIP TIP

Getting a line of credit is an ideal way for a flipper to finance his projects. The rub is, you must have a good relationship with your lending institution and have completed several transactions successfully before you will be offered this method of financing. Just make sure to tell your lending officer that you are interested in a large line of credit to run your flipping business and working your way toward getting one. They might be able to help you qualify a little sooner if they know you are interested.

Once you have established your own credit line, you won't have to rely on outside money to run your business. The only difficulty is that you must have a long and credible history with a bank or other lending institution in order to qualify for a line of credit. But we must mention it here, because it's something every flipper should be building toward as they grow their businesses. Having a large line of credit really does make the entire process of flipping a house much easier.

While a loan officer from a lending institution doesn't have nearly the flexibility or authority that a private lender has, find a way to make it work for you if banks and mortgage brokers are all you have to work with in your particular location. The important thing is to secure the financing that will enable you to launch your flipping business.

Finding and Working with Private Investors

Based on personal experience, we would have to say working with private investors is a preferred way to secure financing. A private investor offers many advantages to flippers. You can secure a loan quickly, particularly if the investor likes your deal. You don't have to jump through a lot of hoops. You just have to bring a good deal to the table, and convince the investor you're the person to bring it across the finish line.

Another advantage is that money borrowed from a private lender, while more expensive than money borrowed from a lending institution, is much more affordable than money available from other sources, such as *hard money loans*. And often it is possible to get the entire cost of your project funded.

DEFINITION

A **hard money loan** (HML) is based on the value of the real property you are buying, not on your perceived creditworthiness. Sometimes called "the loan of last resort," these loans provide funds in 1 to 2 weeks instead of the 30-plus days a mortgage requires. They're expensive, costing three to four times as much as a mortgage loan, plus they have high origination fees.

You might be asking, "Why would someone I don't know be willing to give their money to me?" Think about it. Investing in the stock market brings uncertain returns at best. Bonds, even government bonds, pay miniscule returns these days. By investing in a flipped house, private lenders not only earn a handsome and consistent return on their investment (8 to 12 percent), but the loan is also guaranteed by the real property she is lending against. In other words, if you take her money and run off to Acapulco, she gets the house. So she is pretty much insulated against big losses when lending to house flippers.

When you work with a private lender you must give her three things:

- A promissory note that lays out the terms you have agreed to for the deal. This serves as your contract.

- A deed of trust. This document secures the private lender's loan to the property you're flipping. It allows the lender to foreclose on you and seize the property if you don't keep up your end of the bargain.

- Hazard insurance naming the investor as an additional beneficiary so that if anything happens to the house during the flip, their investment is protected and they'll get their money back.

Private investors usually like to keep their *loan-to-value* (*LTV*) *ratio* below a certain amount. The amount can vary from investor to investor but is generally in the neighborhood of 70 to 75 percent, which is lower than the risk a lending institution might be willing to take.

DEFINITION

A **loan-to-value (LTV) ratio** is a risk assessment lenders use to determine risk on any particular loan. Most lenders prefer loans with an LTV no higher than 80 percent. If a property has a high LTV, it can be more difficult to get financing for it. The more equity a buyer has in a property, the lower their LTV will be.

Sometimes the most difficult part of working with private investors is finding them in the first place. If you are active in the local business community, you are likely to meet many private investors. However, those investors won't know you are seeking money to finance your flips unless you tell them. You can also network with Realtors and tell them you are looking for private investors. Generally speaking, an active professional Realtor will know several private investors and they may be willing to share their contact info with you.

Perhaps the best way to find a private investor is to check and see if there is a chapter of the Real Estate Investors Association (REIA) in your town. If there is, get in touch with them and ask to attend a meeting. During the meet and greet preceding the meeting, introduce yourself to several people, tell them what you are doing, and give them your business card. You might just find the perfect investor!

The All-Cash Deal

There's a reason that celebrity flippers usually pay all cash for their houses. When you are an all-cash buyer, sellers treat you preferentially and take you more seriously. It makes sense. So many things can derail a mortgage approval. However, if a cash offer is on the table, all other factors being equal, it will automatically trump any financed offers.

That said, just because celebrity flippers usually pay all cash for a house doesn't mean you have to do the same. Realistically, most aspiring flippers will not be able to start their businesses this way. These celebrity pro flippers have been doing it a while and have built relationships with several reliable investors, as well as cash reserves to maintain their flexibility and ability to move quickly on great deals. You can certainly aspire to move to all cash deals in the future, but don't feel bad if you can't work them to start with.

> **FLIP TIP**
>
> According to *World Property Journal,* all-cash transactions accounted for 36.4 percent of all home sales in the United States in November 2015, the latest month for which complete data is available. Prior to the 2008 housing crisis, cash sales accounted for just 25 percent of all home sales. Experts say the growing popularity of flipping as well as an influx of international buyers into the U.S. housing market account for the increase. International buyers must pay cash because U.S. banking laws do not allow foreign nationals to apply for mortgages to finance property purchases.

It's interesting to note that the percentage of all-cash sales vary according to the type of sale. *Real estate owned (REO)* properties have the highest percentage of cash sales. *Short sales* have the next highest percentage of cash sales, followed by resales of existing property, with new construction having the lowest percentage of cash sales of any of the categories.

> **DEFINITION**
>
> **Real estate owned (REO)** property is owned by a bank or other lender, such as a credit union. They become owners of the property after the original purchaser defaults on the loan and the property is foreclosed and repossessed by the lender. Lenders generally try to sell foreclosed properties at auction, but if no one bids, ownership reverts back to the lender, becoming an REO property.
>
> **Short sale property** is sold at a price where the net proceeds of the sale will not cover the debt remaining on liens against the property. A short sale can only go through if all lienholders agree to accept less than is owed to them. Short sales are viewed as a more responsible alternative to foreclosure for homeowners struggling to meet mortgage payments.

Other Creative Financing Options

So far, we've discussed more typical arrangements an individual might make to finance a flip. But there are several other ways to get the financing you need to launch your flipping career.

Bridge Loans

Bridge loans are short-term loans flippers use to float a project until they can sell a flip or secure a more permanent loan. They go by a lot of names: *swing loans, gap financing,* or *interim financing,* but all of these names refer to the same type of short-term loan. They usually have terms of a year or less, although they can run for as much as three years.

Bridge loans have higher interest rates than most other loans, but provide quick cash flow. They are secured by collateral, such as a piece of real property.

Bridge loans can be useful for people who flip houses. They provide flexibility for cash-strapped businesses. For example, if you want to get started on your next flip but you're waiting for the sale to close on your last rehab to free up capital, a bridge loan can provide the funds you need to purchase and renovate a second property. Yes, you'll pay more in loan costs, but it's better to pay higher interest rates for a short time so you can secure and profit from a second flip than to risk losing a house you want while waiting for your funds to clear.

Not all financial institutions offer bridge loans, so check with the banks and mortgage brokers in your area to see which ones provide this type of financing.

Hard Money Loans

A hard money loan (HML) allows you to borrow 100 percent of the cost of a property and rehab even if you have bad credit. These loans are made by private individuals who are interested in the very high rates of return on HML loans and not much else.

Hard money lenders typically charge between 14 to 20 percent interest on their loans plus 6 to 8 points. That can add up very quickly.

Frequently, the individual providing a hard money loan will require you to guarantee the loan with real assets. Because of their high costs, HMLs are *not* recommended for long-term investments but can be a good solution to finance flips you know you can turn around quickly. Many flippers use a hard money loan to secure a property and do some initial upgrades. They then turn around and get a bridge loan at a more competitive rate to carry the property until it can be sold.

Partnerships

Most partnerships established by new flippers work this way: one partner invests all the money and the other partner puts in all the work. Then, they spilt the profits 50/50. Typically, you will be the person putting in the sweat equity.

Where do you find these partners? The same places you find private investors. The difference with a private investor is you are only paying him 8 to 12 percent interest on the money he loans you. With a partnership, you are giving up more.

So what are the advantages? The primary advantage is that while you are splitting the profits, you are also splitting the risks. If a deal goes south, having a partner can help you weather a storm until you can get things back on track.

Most partnerships of this type work on a deal-by-deal basis. We actually recommend partnerships to new flippers because it can be a great way for them to get into the business, earn some money, build credibility, and gain experience in a relatively protected environment. This can lead to them being able to confidently launch on their own after a few more flips.

Friends and Family

Borrowing money from friends and family really falls under the category of private investors, but unlike a private investor, your parents will probably not charge you 12 percent interest. They might be quite happy with a return of 4 or 5 percent interest to help you start your flipping business. That is still a far better return than they can find almost anywhere else.

The same goes for friends. If you have a friend who has money to invest, see if they are interested in financing all or part of one of your flips. The worst that can happen is they say no, but they might say yes and could even become a full permanent partner in your business if things go well.

Mix and Match

You can also mix and match several different types of financing to gather all the money you need to do a flip. For example, you might use a hard money loan for 20 percent of the total, a bridge loan for 50 percent, and a loan from a family member for 30 percent. Don't be afraid to explore these creative types of financing to help you put deals together.

The Least You Need to Know

- Flipping is a great way to make money, but it is not risk-free.
- Most flippers prefer to work with private investors because of the speed and flexibility they offer.
- You can get loans that cover 100 percent of the cost of purchasing and renovating a flip, but they can be expensive.
- Work toward being granted a large line of credit. It will help you finance your flips relatively cheaply and make your life easier all around.
- You can mix several types of financing to get all the funds you require to complete a flip.

CHAPTER 5

Building Your Flipping Team

How and when do you dip that first toe into the flipping pool, and whom do you need to invite into the waters with you? Those are questions every new flipper must answer.

You can choose to do everything yourself. Most people start working on their own. But very few successful flippers remain solo operators for long.

You'll launch faster and with a higher trajectory if you build a professional team first. Then, you can leverage your team's flipping knowledge, experience, and expertise to help make your first project, and all projects that follow, successful. As you put your team together, you should be thinking about the best use of your time, and find people to do the jobs that require expertise you don't have or jobs you don't actually want to do.

How do you go about making these essential connections before you launch your business? Let's explore that now.

In This Chapter

- What kind of help do you need?
- Working with building inspectors
- Assigning responsibilities
- Hiring as you go
- Do you need a personal assistant?

Building Successful Partnerships to Increase Profits

The most successful flippers have entire teams working with them to keep their businesses moving forward. Why? Because there are more jobs to oversee and details to manage on a flipping project than one human being can possibly handle alone.

A few of you might think you'll make more money if you work alone, but that's false economy. You might save a few dollars now but lose money later when other expenses crop up because you are trying to do too much by yourself. We recommended earlier in this book that you only tackle jobs for which you have experience and expertise. We stand by that advice.

Not every flipping team looks exactly like all the others, nor do they necessarily have the same kind of team members. But generally speaking, most teams consist of:

- You, the team leader. You make the decisions, hire crews, choose the remodel design, buy materials, select finishes, oversee the project (unless you hire a project manager), write checks, and serve as the general factotum on the job.

- An investor to lend you the money required to buy a property and make any necessary repairs or upgrades.

- A professional Realtor who is experienced in locating properties for flippers.

- A general contractor who can oversee the demolition and renovation of your property.

- A *stager* to decorate your finished house to maximize your chance for a fast sale.

> **DEFINITION**
>
> A **stager** is a person skilled in the art of using furniture, accessories, lighting, scent, and plants to create an inviting space that appeals to the largest possible number of buyers prior to putting a house on the market.

As you grow your business, you might continue to add team members, such as a personal assistant, who keeps you on track and handles most of your clerical work, such as answering emails and phone calls and scheduling appointments. Many flippers also hire project managers once they get busier and have more cash flow. A project manager allows you to run two or more flips at once, with a project manager overseeing one flip while you oversee the other. This strategy allows flippers to keep expanding their businesses and increasing the number of flips they can handle each year.

There is no rule that says you must keep hiring more people and growing your business. You might be happier running 2 to 3 flips a year with a small team. That can still give you a nice annual income. A smaller number of projects gives you more leisure time and a less hectic pace, if that's what you prefer.

Your Investors

We talked about the different kinds of investors you might work with in Chapter 4. Do some research to get names of potential investors then set up meetings and talk with each one. Tell them your plans and goals, and find out what they are looking for in an investment project like a house flip. Ask how much of a return they want and how fast they can turn around a loan. By the time you speak with several investors, you'll know which one you want to work with. It will be the one whose goals align with your own and whose personality best meshes with yours, and the one you feel the most comfortable and relaxed working with.

 FLIPPER BEWARE

Whatever you do, make sure you keep your reputation clean. Even a whisper of scandal attached to your name could turn you into someone people don't want to work with. In the flipping business, earning a reputation as someone who is less than trustworthy is one of the worst things that could happen to you.

Once you settle on an investor, focus on cultivating an ongoing relationship. When the investor sees you are dedicated to your work, reliable, and hardworking, and you pay your bills on time, they will want to keep working with you. Flipping is an attractive and potentially lucrative proposition for an investor. When they find someone who not only takes very good care of their money but also returns them a handsome profit on each outing, they'll want to continue doing business together. If you consistently make money for your investor, you will soon have other investors seeking you out and wanting to give you money as well.

While it's tempting, never take on more projects at one time than you can truly handle and turn out to a consistent high standard of excellence and quality. All it takes is one big screw-up from you for the money tree to wither and possibly die. If you fail to bring a flip in on time, consistently blow your budgets, or manage to lose money on your deals, you might soon find yourself without a source of funding. Investors tend to be friends with other investors and they do talk to each other, so your mistakes will not stay private for very long.

Your Realtor

In many ways, an experienced professional Realtor may well turn out to be the most valuable person on your team. Your Realtor will serve as the vital link between you and properties that might be suitable for your flipping business. He or she *should* have access to insider data that puts them ahead of the curve when it comes to being in the know about available houses before anyone else might find out about them. Not all Realtors do, so make sure the one you choose is established enough in the profession to have already built the connections that provide this kind of advance information. In flipping, knowing about an upcoming listing even an hour ahead of the crowd may put you in the winner's circle.

> **FLIP TIP**
>
> Realtors can take extra classes to earn specific credentials. Find one who is a Certified Residential Specialist (CRS). They have completed training that makes them especially well-qualified to handle all transactions related to residential real estate.

Half the battle of being a successful flipper is finding affordable houses to flip in high demand neighborhoods. No one knows how to do this better than a Realtor.

Just as with investors, look for a Realtor who makes you feel comfortable and inspires your confidence. Ask around to see if you can get some names of Realtors active in the flipping business. Not all agents are, so this is important information. You wouldn't want to try and partner with an agent who has never worked with a flipper before and isn't familiar with the business. You want to work someone who is on top of everything happening in your area that could positively or negatively impact your flipping business.

While you definitely want a Realtor who has experience, particularly in handling sales of houses that will be flipped, don't always go with the top-selling agent at a brokerage. Top sellers are far more focused on maintaining their status as a top seller than they would be on your new flipping business. Look for a Realtor who is willing to spend a little time with you learning your preferences and what you are looking for.

You and your Realtor will spend a fair amount of time together at first, but once you get established in the business and your relationship has solidified, you'll be able to work in a kind of shorthand way. After a while, your Realtor will know instinctively which properties will appeal to you and work with your budget and will only contact you when houses that fit your parameters come on the market. He or she won't waste your time sending you to look at houses in down-trending neighborhoods, where the average days on market is so long it could kill any hope of a fast sale or a reasonable profit on your flip.

Some Realtors work with many flippers. You might not like the idea of "your" Realtor working for your competitors, but if you think about it, it makes sense, especially when you look at it from a Realtor's point of view. His job is to list and sell houses. He only earns money when he moves inventory. He often has more properties to sell than you can handle alone, so it's logical to have other flippers ready to step forward and buy properties you don't want. If you were a Realtor's only client, his annual sales total would look pretty sad compared to his fellow agents, unless you are flipping entire blocks at once.

It's also true that some flippers work with many Realtors. The various agents might focus on completely different neighborhoods, work in different towns, or just bring in different types of property.

FLIP TIP

Looking for another way to pick a Realtor who's a winner? Look for someone who has been awarded the Realtor of the Year award. The award is voted upon by the Realtor's peers, so if you can find someone who has won it, then you'll know you have a Realtor who is highly regarded by his or her peers for real estate expertise, ethics, and business conduct. The awards are sponsored by a local branch of the National Association of Realtors.

Whether you work with one Realtor or several is up to you. You'll discover the protocols and practices that work best for you through trial and error as you gain experience in the business. No matter how you end up putting your team together, having that one über Realtor who is always no more than a phone call or text message away can truly be one of the most important aspects of your success as a flipper.

As a final FYI, even though you might be a broker/Realtor in addition to being a flipper, you shouldn't rely 100 percent your own resources to find properties. We do coordinate with other Realtors who stay on the lookout and alert us when likely properties in neighborhoods we focus on are about to come on the market.

Contractors

A good contractor is another vital team member who will help propel your flipping team forward. He or she can take the house in your head and make it appear before your eyes. They oversee all the work that is being done on your house and ensure that it's being performed correctly. They hire any subcontractors needed on the job, like electricians, roofers, plumbers, and so on and receive shipments of materials for use on the project.

Because the contractor is the one team member you'll be working with most closely, almost on a daily basis, it's especially important for you to select someone whose personality and work style mixes well with your own.

By now, you are familiar with the routine of networking to get contractor's names. You can also drive the neighborhoods that interest you, and if you see a crew working on a house, stop and spend a few minutes chatting with the contractor. However, *don't* conduct your job interview while the contractor is busy working on another person's job. That's not considerate. Keep your conversation brief. Tell him what you're looking for, give him your business card and get his, and tell him you'll call later to set up a mutually convenient time to chat about your job.

FLIPPER BEWARE

Licensing requirements for contractors vary from state to state. Some states only require a contractor to be registered, not licensed. Licensing requires a contractor to pass exams and prove that he's competent in the field of work for which he is trying to become licensed. Registration doesn't provide the same protections to potential employers, because it simply is a written record that someone is performing contracting work. It in no way guarantees competency to do the job or any sort of relevant expertise.

Ask the contractor about his experience, how long he's been doing flips, and how much of the work he likes to handle. This is important because contractors have different working styles. Some contractors want to be 100 percent in charge of the work site and barely tolerate the flipper showing up. Personally, this style doesn't work for me. We don't want to sleep on a cot in our flips, nor do we want to feel constrained from being able to drop by and check on things whenever we want just because the contractor thinks we are intruding on his territory.

On the opposite end of the spectrum is the contractor who doesn't want to take responsibility for anything. He wants you on the site all the time and won't even make the smallest decision without calling you in. What you should be looking for is a contractor whose style is somewhere in between these two extremes. You want someone who assumes most of the responsibility for keeping the job running on time but defers all important decisions to you. He keeps you informed and in the loop regarding what is happening with the flip, with inspections and with any potential problems, so that you are always informed of everything that's happening and can offer timely and informed responses to problems based on the contractor's ongoing feedback.

We cannot overemphasize the importance of hiring a competent, reliable, and ethical contractor. Ask for the names of previous clients and interview them. A contractor who is proud of his work will not hesitate to give you his references. Don't always select the guy with the lowest bid.

He may lowball you to get the job and then come back and hit you with a bunch of unexpected charges on the back end.

Hire a licensed contractor if you can. It might cost you more, but you should factor that into your budget. It's really that important. If you don't have a capable contractor, then you are not going to end up with a quality flip. And if you don't end up with a quality flip, you might have trouble passing your final inspections and selling it. Invest a little more now in a great contractor to ensure you will be getting a quality finished product. Doing so will save you money and headaches down the road.

Project Manager

A project manager can free you up to work on putting together the next flip while the current flip is progressing toward completion. You won't have any gaps or downtime in your flipping schedule. This is important because contractors and subcontractors only get paid when they're working, which means they don't like to have too many idle days.

That said, a project manager isn't someone you often see on a brand-new flipper's team. We include the job description here in case you have an unusual situation, such as a husband-wife team in which one of the spouses is going to serve as the project manager while the other spouse oversees other aspects of the business. Or, of course, it's possible that you want to hire an outside project manager right from the beginning (someone to whom you are not related). Sometimes a new flipper will hire a project manager in lieu of a general contractor, because it's more affordable. Just be sure you hire someone who really knows what he's doing.

For example, you might have a master carpenter who is very experienced, who is willing to serve as your project manager, and who will oversee the entire job for you for either a flat fee or a percentage of your profit. The good news about this type of arrangement is that if you find the right project manager—someone who is experienced in construction and respected by the subcontractors—you might not need a general contractor, and that will save you a lot of money.

> **FLIP TIP**
>
> We've found a really good way to get a project manager on board is to offer a flat fee plus performance bonuses along the way for meeting scheduling and budgetary goals. This gives your product manager a little bit of ownership in your flip and a big incentive to get things done on time and within the budget. You can usually make up at least part of the bonuses with the lower carrying costs you'll have by being able to bring your house to market a few days earlier.

As you go along, you might even find it advantageous to form a partnership with your project manager, particularly if he or she is very good at her job. We suggest this because as we have mentioned before, people do develop reputations in this business. If your project manager is first rate, some other flipper might come along and try to lure her away from you. But if she owns a piece of the business, she is much less likely to want to leave for another position.

Stagers

Stagers are the people who essentially put the icing on your cake. They transform the blank canvas that is your completed flip into a home worthy to be featured in the pages of a magazine. They spark the imaginations of potential buyers with visions of living in your house with that exact furniture and those accessories and can really help you get the offers rolling in on a recently completed flip.

You, as the flipper, can discuss your property with the stager and convey the feeling, design period, and color palette you are looking for. Or, you can leave those choices to the stager's own excellent taste. You then pay a fee to the stager for decorating your house and any additional rental fees based on the length of time you keep the furniture in your house. When your houses sell quickly—as they tend to do when they are professionally staged—the cost of a stager is nominal and the service more than pays for itself.

If you really don't want to pay a stager, try renting the furniture yourself from a furniture rental company. The problem is, you will not be able to rent the expert eye and stager's design and color sense if you go this route. That means your results are not likely to be as impressive.

The cost of staging varies from locale to locale and is higher in places such as California and New York. Generally speaking, the cost to stage a 1,500-square-foot home will run in the neighborhood of $1,500 to $2,000. There's usually a time clause in staging contracts and if your house sits on the market for too long, you might have to pay additional rent on the furniture and accessories used in your staging.

Building Inspectors: Friends or Foes?

There's no doubt that a bad inspection can almost singlehandedly sink a flipping project. But the best way to insulate yourself against that is not to regard your local inspectors as potential enemies but rather, as your friends.

Inspectors are your friends because their job is to make sure the work being done on your house meets all the current building codes and legal standards for quality, safety, materials, and correct installation prevailing in your city or town. They're your friends because houses with clean inspection reports sell faster and cost you less to sell since you will not be on the hook for thousands of dollars in required repairs to make the sale go through.

Building inspectors are typically certified as either residential or commercial building inspectors, or as plumbing, electrical, or mechanical inspectors. That's why you will see more than one inspector on your projects.

What They Do

Building inspectors thoroughly examine buildings to make sure they are up to code and safe to use. They flag violations and give building owners a reasonable amount of time to make repairs and bring the building up to code. If a building has too many problems and cannot be made safe to inhabit, a building inspector has the authority to condemn the building, which means it can no longer be used and must be torn down. A property owner who repeatedly ignores violations or who has too many violations can face legal consequences including fines or condemnation of property.

Inspectors generally visit early in the renovations to check structural elements in the framing, the foundation, and so on. They visit again when the renovations are done for a final inspection and to issue a certificate of occupancy stating the house is safe to occupy.

There are several kinds of inspectors. Electrical inspectors are responsible for making sure every element of the electrical system in your home is safe and ready to use. They will crawl under a house, go up into the attic, follow every wire to the electrical box, and test every switch, outlet, and light fixture in the home to make sure they work properly. They do their work after all the repairs and wiring to the electrical system are completed, and must be called in before the sheet-rock is installed so they can visually inspect the entire electrical system, including all the wiring.

Plumbing inspectors are also called in before the walls are enclosed so they can visually inspect and ensure proper operation of all pipes, drains, and plumbing fixtures. They should test every faucet, spigot, and showerhead for adequate water flow. Also, they should make sure the toilets flush quickly and completely and that sinks and tubs also drain quickly.

Mechanical or HVAC inspectors inspect a home's heating and air conditioning systems. They will look inside the system, inspect the coils, fans, blower system, and duct work, and also check for mold, and whether or not any animals have made themselves at home inside your system. Yes, that happens! They will also test the thermostat to make sure it works and gives an accurate reading. They will check the outside condenser on your A/C system to make sure it is free from rust and debris. Finally, they will turn the system on and check each vent to ensure there is adequate flow to distribute the air you are paying to heat or cool.

Building Inspectors vs. Home Inspectors

We want to make clear here that when you deal with an inspector as a flipper, that's a completely different inspector than a potential buyer would hire to make sure a house she is considering did not have any hidden problems. The inspectors you will be working with are employed by government agencies in cities, towns, and counties. A little more than half of the 100,000 building inspectors in America are employed by municipalities to enforce codes.

Home inspectors work for themselves and inspect houses with pending sales contracts to make sure there are no defects or hidden damage that could affect the safety or habitability of the structure. As a flipper, you will only see this inspector after you have an accepted offer on your house.

 FLIPPER BEWARE

If you aggravate an inspector, he can make your life difficult. He can add requirements for your property to pass inspection by demanding a higher grade of materials or require you to replace something you believe could be repaired. He can nitpick everything on your house from the foundation to the roof and delay your entire project by refusing to okay your inspection for any reason he wants, and he is well within his authority in doing so. His only goal is to make sure your property is up to code and safe for habitation. Your only goals should be to make sure your property meets the required standards so it will easily pass inspection and to maintain a cordial working relationship with your inspectors.

All the inspectors we know are nice people—professionals who are interested only in doing a good job. However, they prefer property owners who are courteous and who respect their authority. Remember, you might think the inspector is working to protect the interests of the home's future owner, but he is actually working to protect your interests as well. He doesn't want you to put a house up for sale that poses hazards to its new owners. For example, if he does a sloppy job and let's a marginal electrical box slide when it really needs to be replaced, then the new owners could have a short and an electrical fire and come back against you for damages once it's discovered the fire originated in a defective electrical box.

Figuring Out Who Does What

Another important aspect of flipping is determining the division of labor. You don't want contractors tripping over each other on your work site, nor do you want two sets of cabinets showing up because you never made it absolutely clear who was responsible for ordering them. If you are the team leader, you must decide who is responsible for each job on your list and make sure that every single job has been assigned to someone. You don't want crew members standing around because you forgot to ask your assistant to order countertops.

Part of your task may be to cede authority to others to assign jobs. For example, if you have a project manager, assigning jobs may come under his or her purview. Your general contractor will handle any work assignments that fall under his authority. Those are things you can comfortably take off your own plate, secure in the knowledge they will be handled properly.

We'll further discuss assigning tasks and division of labor and how to keep up with it all in Chapter 6. In addition, we provide a handy jobs checklist in Appendix B that you can use to ensure you have everything covered.

Hiring a Personal Assistant

There could come a time in your life as a house flipper when you realize you just cannot do it all. That's the moment when you should consider hiring a personal assistant. A personal assistant will help keep you on track and handle all the small details that could bog you down from day to day. If you have a family member who has been anxious to join you in the business, hiring them as a personal assistant could be a good way to introduce them to flipping.

Start with only a part-time position, hiring someone for 10 to 15 hours a week to answer the phone, take and relay messages, do your books, pay bills, respond to emails, and coordinate things such as inspections and deliveries. As your business becomes more successful, this might easily turn into a full-time job. In fact, some of the busiest flippers have an entire office full of assistants to help them run their flipping empires.

If you are feeling overwhelmed, forgetting to eat, and not getting enough sleep, hire a personal assistant to give you some relief, even if it's only for a few hours a day.

The Least You Need to Know

- A flipping team will help you launch your business faster and with a greater chance of success.
- It's essential to find an investor, Realtor, and contractor you feel comfortable working with.
- Building inspectors are actually your friends, although they may sometimes feel likes your foes.
- As your business continues to grow, you may find it helpful to hire a personal assistant.

CHAPTER 6

Planning Your First Flip

We are starting to get into the heart of the flipping process now, and it begins with planning. Yes, you need a thorough, comprehensive plan to make a flip come together properly.

This chapter may contain some surprises for those of you used to TV flipping shows. It takes a lot more to flip a house than just slapping on a fresh coat of paint and sticking a vase of flowers on a counter somewhere. Planning is a truly essential ingredient in the recipe for a successful flip. Let's get started!

In This Chapter

- Emulate successful flippers
- Manage expectations
- Plan, budget, and schedule
- Use checklists to manage your flip
- Contingency planning

Follow the Leaders

Businesses can be invigorated and changed for the better by the influx of newcomers. But flipping is a business that doesn't need to be reinvented all the time. When the economy is stable and demand consistent, flipping works well. Instead of twisting yourself into a pretzel trying to think up new ways to flip a house, a beginner will do far better to follow the leaders.

By that, we mean do what established flippers who are working in your target neighborhoods are doing. If they're focusing their efforts on houses on the east side of the freeway, you can bet they have strong demographic data and sales results supporting that decision. So why would you want to buy a house on the west side of the freeway where no one else is flipping? Yet many new flippers make illogical choices when purchasing their first home and then wonder why they can't sell it. No amount of fancy renovation or clever staging can make buyers want a house in a neighborhood where people are moving out instead of in.

We're not saying you can't ever do your own thing. As you gain experience and expertise in the business, you could be the one to turn the first successful flip in a neighborhood. But when you're just starting, why take unnecessary risks? If the local flipping pros are focusing their efforts on two or three distinct neighborhoods, concentrate your own efforts there as well.

Getting Along

Be courteous and respectful toward your more established competitors. You'll be seeing each other at courthouse auctions, chamber of commerce meetings, and around the most active flipping neighborhoods. So smile and shake hands! The last thing you want is an ongoing feud with a fellow flipper.

> **FLIP TIP**
>
> Establish and maintain friendly and professional working relationships with other flippers in your locale. Even if a flipper had the money to snap up every property as it came on the market, he more than likely wouldn't have enough time or team members to flip them all. As a result of these constraints, flippers often share information about properties they are not going to buy with their friends in the business. Make sure you keep yourself in good standing amongst the local flippers so you get the scoop about upcoming available properties!

That doesn't mean you can't be competitive with other flippers or place offers on the same houses. Just keep it friendly. You never know when someone will reach out to help you or ask you for help. If you have a good reputation, an established flipper might contact you with info about a house she can't buy because she is tied up elsewhere or ask you to partner with them on a deal.

However, if you are rude, arrogant, or unfriendly toward your competitors, you will get a bad reputation, and other flippers will avoid you. If that happens, don't expect any inside information to come your way without you having to dig for it.

Setting Realistic Expectations

Almost every newcomer in the flipping business expects a big payday on the first house he flips. While that can happen, particularly if you make a good plan and stick to it, you are more likely to make larger profits once you have more experience. Don't be disappointed if your early flips show relatively small profits. The important thing is to stay in profit; you can and go after more expensive houses as your working capital grows.

> **FLIP TIP**
>
> When deciding where to purchase your first flip, keep in mind that houses in high demand neighborhoods sell faster. It's not unusual to get several offers the first week a desirable house is on the market. You might end up with a bidding war! Even if you get a screaming deal on a house in a neighborhood where there's not much demand, walk away. The most gorgeous flip in a down-trending neighborhood might not sell for a while. You must pay carrying costs for every day it sits on the market, and it ties up your working capital so choose your neighborhood carefully, with the fastest possible sale in mind.

As you move from flip to flip, you will learn what improvements work best in what neighborhoods. Over time, your experience will start to add up and show in larger profits on each flip. You'll make fewer mistakes and the work will become more enjoyable as you become more knowledgeable about what you're doing.

Staying on Track

Hidden damage is the biggest schedule and budget buster in flipping. You can be dreaming of selling your flip when your contractor tells you he found a cracked foundation when he took up the flooring. Or you discovered rusted pipes when you removed the bathroom walls, and now you need a complete *repipe*. These are huge expenses, but the repairs must be made or you will not be able to sell your property.

> **DEFINITION**
>
> A **repipe** is the total replacement of every plumbing pipe, including underground pipes, in your house. Repipes are often required on older homes in which pipes have rusted through, or are leaching lead into the water. A typical repipe can cost from $3,000 to $20,000 or more, depending on the materials used, the number of bathrooms, and the number of fixtures and appliances that are attached to the lines.

When something happens that knocks you off schedule or out of budget, work hard to get yourself and the project back on track. Think positively. No, you didn't plan to spend $10,000 to replace the roof when you started the flip, and you certainly didn't budget for it. But now that you *have* to do it, think of it as a positive. A new roof is a great selling point for any older home. It assures sellers they won't have to deal with roofing issues for many years to come. It tip a decision in favor of placing an offer on your house instead of another.

Accurate Scheduling

Managing a flip is a little like working a giant jigsaw puzzle with hundreds of pieces. You have to fit all tasks into the schedule as you rehab your flip.

Jobs must be done in a specific order when you are renovating a house. Otherwise, you will run into major problems and cost yourself a lot of unnecessary hassle and expense. See Appendix B for a template that will help you lay out a good basic schedule for your flip.

The Inspection

Prior to buying any property, have your contractor make a thorough inspection to check for damage, hidden or otherwise, and give you an estimate of what it will take to complete any necessary repairs. This inspection tells you if the house is essentially sound and if it has sufficient profit potential to make it worth buying.

After you have purchased the property, conduct a second inspection so you can visualize your renovation. This is where you plan your demolition and decide what must be done to make the property look like the house you've pictured in your head. All your initial construction decisions and cost estimates are made during this inspection. You will decide whether to keep or replace plumbing and lighting fixtures, cabinets, and flooring. The kitchen and bathrooms are where you will spend the most time and money, because those upgrades really help sell houses.

Once you have finished this second inspection, you will have the information you need to accurately plan both your timetable and your budget for the flip.

Laying Out Your Order of Work

Now it's time to actually lay out a work schedule for your project, starting with what happens on Day 1, Day 2, and so forth.

You have an estimate from your contractor of the total number of days your flip will require to complete. Write down the estimated number of days to complete each job. This will help you stay on track as you go along. It will also remind you to hold your contractors accountable to complete work within the promised schedule. Add 10 percent more time to allow for unexpected contingencies, such as bad weather, illness, and so on. For example, if your data suggests that you will need 6 weeks or 42 days for your flip, add 4 to 5 extra days to that total to allow for time to deal with any unexpected developments that could delay the project.

 FLIPPER BEWARE

> Now that work is beginning on your first flipping project, make sure that safe working conditions are maintained to minimize the risk of accidents on your work site. For example, make sure crewmembers wear goggles and masks during demolition to avoid eye injuries or breathing in irritants. Goggles should also always be worn whenever power tools are in use. Masks should be worn while painting. Following a few simple, commonsense rules will keep your crew safe and help you avoid time lost to accidents.

As you write out your schedule, keep in mind that jobs must be done in a particular order. You can't work on the cabinets one day then the plumbing, and next install flooring, and finally circle back around and install sheetrock and paint the place. It just doesn't work that way. You'd get paint all over your nice new floors if you went about your flip in this fashion.

Here's a suggested order of work to help you know what gets done and when:

Design   An experienced contractor can create a redesign on the back of a fast food napkin, but until you become familiar with your contractor and his work, it's better to hire an architect or draftsman to draw up the plans for your renovation.

Demolition   Demolition gets a house ready for renovation. Trash and damaged material are removed—and all the debris from the demolition itself, including sheetrock, old carpet and flooring, cabinets, insulation, and so on. The goal is to leave your contractor a clean slate upon which to work his magic. Remember to rent a dumpster so your crews have a place to put trash.

Roof and foundation   Next focus on any necessary repairs to the roof and foundation of your house.

Windows and siding   Replace windows and/or siding next. The idea is to close your house in and make it absolutely weatherproof before you start on any interior renovations.

Structural carpentry   If you are going to move or build any walls, install beams, or add new doors, you'll need a structural carpenter. If you are adding new windows or enlarging exterior door or window openings, you will need your structural carpenter to frame those out before they are installed, and steps 4 and 5 will be reversed.

> **FLIPPER BEWARE**
>
> *Never* allow a crew to remove a wall unless you are 100 percent sure it is not weight-bearing. If you remove a weight-bearing wall without first installing a beam to carry the weight the wall was supporting, the entire house can come crashing down on you in a matter of minutes. Seriously.

Plumbing, electrical wiring, and ductwork   Anything that is inside the walls or ceiling needs to be repaired or installed at this time before the new insulation and sheetrock get installed.

Inspections   Before you close the walls, have your plumbing and electrical work inspected to insure it's up to code. Before you get to this point, check with your city inspectors to get an idea of how far ahead you must make your inspection appointments. It's no fun losing workdays sitting around waiting on inspections because you forgot to schedule them in time.

Insulation   Next, new insulation gets installed into the exterior walls and the attic.

Sheetrock   Sheetrock goes up next. Crews need a day to install and tape the sheetrock and apply the first coat of joint compound over the seams and nail holes. They'll come back the next day to add a second and third coat of joint compound. After the joint compound is completely dry, they will return and sand down the seams to prepare the walls for painting.

Painting   Walls and ceilings get painted next. You can paint the exterior now, or wait and paint it later in the flip.

Cabinets   If you are putting new cabinets in your kitchen and bathrooms, now is the time to install them.

Plumbing fixtures   Sinks, toilets, tubs, and showers go in next in the bathrooms and the kitchen.

Tile and countertops   If you are using decorative tile in your rehab, it gets installed now, along with any new countertops.

Flooring   New flooring, whether hardwood, laminate, tile, or carpet, gets laid down now.

Trim carpentry   Baseboards and moldings (painted or stained before installation) get installed next.

Exterior painting and gutters   You're almost done. Have your crews do any exterior painting that might be required and install new gutters.

Landscaping   Plant attractive flowers and small shrubs to enhance curb appeal.

Staging   Hire stagers to show potential buyers what your house looks like with furniture.

List and market your house   If you've done your job right, your first sale will soon happen!

A Warning About TV Flipping Programs

In my experience, the primary way people get interested in flipping houses is by watching one of the dozen or so house flipping reality shows currently on television. There's no doubt they are entertaining and filled with many great ideas. While watching these shows is as good a way as any to get acquainted with flipping, we want to address some misconceptions TV creates.

One of the things that bugs me most about TV flipping programs is that they show so many important decisions being made on the fly and out of order. No, you don't have to select and buy new flooring the moment you start your flip, but you shouldn't wait until the day before the contractors need flooring to order it, either. Not if you want to stay on schedule.

My biggest concern is the frantic timetables these shows present as reality. Exacting work that normally requires weeks or months to complete gets compacted into an hour or less of airtime. This rapid pace convinces some viewers that house flipping is a much faster and easier business than it actually is. It often appears that a complete demolition and rehab is being completed in one short week, and that's misleading.

 FLIPPER BEWARE

No matter what you might see on television, it's simply not possible to flip a house in a week or even 2 weeks. The closest you could come would be to buy a house that was already in very good condition and then just repaint it and maybe lay down some new carpet. That could be done in a week to 10 days. But a full rehab generally requires 2 to 6 months or more to complete, depending upon the amount and complexity of the work being done.

To make things even more confusing, producers often speed up video to make repairs that might have required days or even weeks to accomplish appear to be happening in a matter of minutes. While this can be a very effective production technique, if you are not fully aware that's what they are doing, it might lead you to have unrealistic ideas about what can be accomplished on your flip in your allotted schedule.

These glossy portrayals fall under the heading of TV magic, and while we cannot blame the shows' producers for wanting to present unbelievable transformations to their viewers, we do fault them for not emphasizing the actual amount of time required to work such feats of legerdemain. These programs can plant some very unrealistic ideas in the minds of aspiring house flippers, whose only acquaintance with the house flipping business might be through watching reality flipping shows.

Yes, flippers are always under the gun timewise, but we still need to eat and sleep like other mortals. We've seen shows that required crews to work through the night to make an artificially imposed deadline. If you asked a real-world crew to work overnight, they would laugh and walk off the job. They have families they want to get home to and leisure time activities they want to enjoy. Most good crews will do their best to produce quality work and meet your deadlines, but you have to be reasonable with your expectations.

That's why writing out an accurate work schedule before the renovation ever starts on your flip is so important. A written schedule ensures that everyone knows your expectations. They know what must be done and when, and if there is ever any confusion, everyone can refer back to the written schedule for confirmation.

Checklists for Success

We're big fans of checklists, especially for beginning flippers. Checklists keep you on task and on target and remind you of important deadlines and goals that must be met. Checklists fuel productivity and keep you from forgetting critical details. They ensure that your contractor and crew are in alignment with your vision for the project, and know your expectations and schedule, because it's all down in writing.

FLIP TIP

All of these checklists can be easily maintained on a smartphone or tablet so you can carry them with you in the field. Of course, if you are a clipboard and pen kind of person, you can maintain your lists that way instead. But considering the digital age we live in, just be prepared for a few strange looks when you show up with your clipboard.

Some checklists, of course, are personal and just for you or select people on your team. For example, there's no need to share your financial checklist with anyone except your investor, and you might not even want to share it with him. If you're confused about where to start, check Appendix B for a complete set of the checklist templates we use in our flips.

Target Neighborhoods

By now, we hope you've at least driven through all the neighborhoods you are considering for your first flip. Better still, perhaps you've toured an open house or two, preferably of flipped homes, to get a feel for the style of the neighborhood and the going prices for an attractive renovated home comparable to what you want to buy.

After you have assessed the available neighborhoods, write down your top three, and then list pros and cons for each one. If you are having difficulty deciding where to buy your first flip, this list should help you quickly see which locale might best serve your goals.

Financials, Budget, and Projected Profit

Keep these lists with you at all times. The biggest mistake new flippers make is ignoring their budget or convincing themselves their house really does need the $15-a-foot French oak floors when it would sell just as quickly with a $4-per-foot high-quality laminate. Keeping your budget near at hand will help you resist the urge to overspend. Every time you spend unbudgeted dollars, you'll see how it reduces your profit, and nothing can put a damper on an unwise decision quite like watching your profits slip away.

Schedule

Keep your schedule with you because you and your crew will be referencing it often. In fact, your contractor should have his own copy of the schedule so he will know how to line up his work crews. While your schedule should have a certain amount of flexibility built in to account for unexpected circumstances, it's a good idea to stick to it as closely as possible to keep your costs down.

Required Permits and Inspections

Ask your contractor to give you a list of the permits and inspections your property will require. He should take care of getting the necessary permits, but check to make sure they in fact have been obtained, then cross them off your list.

Assign a target date to each inspection and plug them into your work calendar. As the dates draw near, make sure your contractor will be ready for inspections as promised. If he is, call and make the inspection appointments immediately. Contractors often prefer to make these appointments themselves, because they already have good working relationships with the inspectors.

Contractors

Keep this list on your cellphone even if you're clinging to a clipboard to keep track of everything else. You need your contractors' names, phone numbers, and areas of expertise ready at hand, and nowhere is more near at hand than your own phone.

Whenever a contractor gives you a business card, transfer the contact information to your phone as quickly as possible. This will build a comprehensive list of local workers, along with their contact information and notes about their specialty.

Materials

There are so many different things you have to select and order for each flip that there's no possible way you could keep track of them all without a checklist. Treat your materials checklist as a road map that will guide you properly through the flipping process. Ask your contractors when they want the materials delivered then make sure those materials get there on time.

FLIPPER BEWARE

If you must add 3 or 4 extra days to your work schedule because you failed to order your materials on time, you're not just inconveniencing your contractors, you're costing yourself money. Delays add to your carrying costs. If you order materials late, you'll pay a hefty rush fee to get them to your site quickly. Workmen hate doing nothing, and if your poor materials management causes work stoppages, your workers could leave and go to another job.

Possible Pitfalls

Many things that can go wrong during the renovation of a house … most of which can be avoided through smart planning and good supervision, and some over which you have no control. When you are working with a contractor and crews for the first time, it's possible the relationships won't gel, and that can cause issues on the job. If a contractor or workman gives you attitude, take him or her aside and have a quiet chat. It's important that your crew respects your authority on the work site. If the bad attitude continues even after the chat, consider finding a new contractor or crew and letting the difficult one go.

Bad weather is responsible for creating many delays in flipping schedules. If you need to paint the exterior of your house and experience day after day of torrential rain, you'll have no choice but to keep postponing the paint job.

These delays are the reason we do contingency planning. We put extra dollars into the budget and extra days into the schedule to allow for all the things that could possibly go wrong.

When Things Fall Apart

No matter how carefully you plan a flip or how closely you stick to your budget and your schedule, things will fall apart on occasion. You might not get the house you wanted, or your house could be infested with termites or have hidden damage so extensive that you cannot justify the expense of the repairs.

Pick yourself up and move on to the next flip. It's a big task, but it's the only way to go. If you spend time moping about the what ifs, that's time that could be better spent planning your next flip.

If you lose a property to a natural or manmade disaster, file a claim against the hazard insurance you should maintain on all your properties, and once again, move forward. (For complete information on insurance needs, see Chapter 15.) There's always another flip waiting for you just around the corner.

The Least You Need to Know

- You'll improve your chance of success if you emulate the choices of successful flippers already working in your target neighborhoods.
- Spend time on comprehensive planning and on creating an accurate project budget and schedule to minimize headaches once the project begins.
- Checklists are a great way to manage a flipping project, and they ensure you have the materials you need when you need them, and are performing jobs in the correct order.
- Always make allowances for the unexpected.

PART 2

Selecting the Right Property to Flip

The choice of your first property plays a huge role in determining the ultimate success of your flip. You must learn how to spot trending neighborhoods and avoid neighborhoods where your finished flip is likely to sit on the market for months. Knowing how to use demographic data to target potential buyers and sellers will put you ahead of your competition from the start.

There are hidden gems in every real estate market; you must learn how to find them. The key to successful flipping is finding good properties at the right price and turning them into great properties. If you fight on the open market for every potential house that is avaiable, it might be a while before you are able to buy your first property. But if you know how to approach sellers of distressed properties and negotiate win-win deals with them, you will always have a ready source of properties to flip.

Location, Location, Location

The ultimate success or failure of your flip might well be determined by your first active step ... what property you buy, and even more importantly, where that property is located. Throughout this book, we preach that old real estate law: location, location, location. If you fail to truly appreciate the importance of location, then you more than likely will fail with your flip. By that, we mean you will either lose money on the deal or not be able to sell your renovated property at all.

It's simple. Buy a house to flip in a neighborhood people want and you'll enjoy success. Buy a house in a neighborhood people don't want, and it won't matter what kind of great job you do on your rehab. You could put diamonds in the door-knobs and still be forced to almost give the house away to unload it. Such a property won't leave you much room for profit, if any.

Let's look at some ways you can ensure you buy your first properties in desirable neighborhoods with a great chance of a fast sale.

In This Chapter

- Focusing on high-demand neighborhoods
- Finding a flipping hot spot
- Comparing pros and cons of neighborhoods
- Rating properties
- Maximizing profits

High-Demand Hot Spots

Depending upon where you live, the most popular neighborhoods for flipping can vary. In New York City, it could be vintage brownstones ripe for restoration on the Upper West Side. In New Orleans, nineteenth-century shotguns in almost any neighborhood of the city are hot, as long as they mostly survived Hurricane Katrina. In Los Angeles, midcentury modern homes in the Hollywood Hills sell almost as fast as they're flipped.

Research will reveal what neighborhoods are currently in high demand in your locale. While your Realtor can help you by providing sales data, the complete picture is not necessarily information you can find online. You have to do some detective work, which means driving neighborhoods, talking to other flippers, and talking to residents to get a feel for what is going on. You want to get an accurate picture of the demand for homes in the neighborhood you're targeting, and where you can push the price limits, as well as identify neighborhoods where price differentiations from one property to the next are very small.

From Cold to Hot and Back Again

When a bunch of homes sell in the same neighborhood in a short time period, it can suggest one of two things.

- In a mature, well-established neighborhood, it means demand for houses continues to be strong there.

- In an up and coming neighborhood that is not yet firmly established as a popular locale, those sales could indicate the area is about to get hot. That's a great time for a flipper to get into a neighborhood, because housing prices are still reasonable and have not yet skyrocketed due to burgeoning demand. It also means there are plenty of houses to use as comps to help you price your own house competitively.

> **FLIP TIP**
>
> Carefully watch the sales data in neighborhoods you're tracking. That data reveals when a neighborhood starts to trend upward, emerging as a great flipping location. However, the same data can also show when sales begin to slow down, signaling you to wrap up any flips you have underway and to not buy any more houses there. Why? In such a neighborhood, the odds of making a fast sale can greatly diminish once the area has reached saturation and starts to cool down.

Hot neighborhoods don't remain the same over extended time periods. If neighborhoods A, F, and L are hot this year, by next year the hot neighborhoods could be A, G, and M, with A stable and still popular, F and L trending downward, and G and M trending hot. Stay on top of these trends through research to know the best area to concentrate your flippable-house search.

Inventory doesn't stay the same, either. The availability of reasonably priced flippable houses shrinks to zero after a neighborhood matures into its rebirth. When an area first starts trending and flippers rehab many houses there, revitalizing the area, many long-term residents see what is happening and decide to stay in their homes and not sell. Others decide to sell, but overprice their homes in an attempt to cash in on the wave of popularity while it lasts. When either of these things happen, the supply of older houses to rehab will soon dry up.

The Flipping Cycle

The other element at play in a trending neighborhood is economic. When a formerly depressed area starts to get hot, houses there are plentiful and affordable. As renovated houses come on the market and sell for significantly higher prices than the previous average, it begins pushing all home prices in the neighborhood higher. Eventually, the average price to acquire a house becomes so high it pushes flippers out.

 FLIPPER BEWARE

When property acquisition costs become too high, there's not enough money in a deal to perform all the necessary repairs and still make a respectable profit on a flip. Even if you find a house you really want, make yourself walk away from the deal or you'll risk losing money.

This is a cycle that repeats again and again, from neighborhood to neighborhood. The most successful flippers stay up to date with this kind of information and use it to make smart decisions about where to buy their next property. Finding a neighborhood you like that's on the upswing then zeroing in on one house in that neighborhood to launch your flipping business, might require extra research and effort, but it's well worth it.

What's Ripe for Flipping?

There are several different factors that signal when a neighborhood is a good bet for flipping. We've mentioned high demand, but it's also important to know the number of houses available for sale there. If you find a desirable neighborhood but all the houses are overpriced, you can't work a deal there. If you have to pay too much for a house, you won't be able to make a reasonable profit and might even lose money on your project.

On the other hand, if you find a neighborhood that's starting to trend with a nice selection of reasonably priced properties, that can signal it's a good location to focus your efforts. When you identify a neighborhood like this, you might be able to work there for a couple of years or more before conditions change enough to make flipping a house more difficult.

Successful flipping is a matter of location coupled with great timing (and of course, good taste). When you find a neighborhood that's working for other flippers, swoop in and flip as many houses as you can there before moving on.

> **FLIP TIP**
>
> You might find it helpful to keep a laminated map of your city or town on the wall. Mark neighborhoods you are investigating, as well as houses you have purchased and are working to flip. A map provides a quick visual reference that helps you keep track of both your properties that are undergoing renovation, as well as areas where you are interested in buying properties in the future. You can also cross off neighborhoods that don't interest you.

We say this because when a neighborhood is hot, selling the flip is the relatively easy part, and that's what you want … for the sale to be fast and easy. Nothing is more disheartening than pouring your heart, soul, and most of your working capital into a flip only to have it sit on the market for weeks or months without a nibble, which will quickly stall out your business, especially if you are a new flipper with limited financial resources. Later in your career, you'll have the resources and experience to tackle more difficult neighborhoods, but you shouldn't start off with them.

Distressed vs. Up and Coming

As you gain more experience, you'll want to start searching for new neighborhoods on a more or less continual basis to keep your business running with little or no down time. You'll soon discover that there are entire neighborhoods in your town filled with nothing but *distressed properties*. Time, neglect, and changing demographics combine to relegate such neighborhoods to the dustbins of history. Believe it or not, distressed locations can actually become shining stars, but it doesn't happen overnight. Trying to save an entire neighborhood by yourself is something we don't recommend for beginners. It takes several flippers working together to turn the tide in a less than desirable locale. Start familiarizing yourself with all the available neighborhoods in your town and perhaps do some long-range goal setting to tackle a more difficult project later on.

> **DEFINITION**
>
> A **distressed property** has been allowed to fall into disrepair due to a combination of time, weather, vandalism, and neglect. Many distressed properties have been abandoned by their owners as a result of divorce, job loss, ill health, not being able to make mortgage or tax payments, or required repairs. As a result, the properties might be in foreclosure and available for a good price.

You might be confused at this point, thinking, "Hold on. You just spent the entire first part of this chapter stressing how important it is to buy a property in a desirable neighborhood. Why are you now talking about derelict houses that need thousands of dollars in repairs to even be habitable?"

That's a good question. We are not suggesting you buy a derelict house for your first, second, or even your third flip. We are saying that as you expand your business horizons, a distressed property in an upward-trending neighborhood might present a good opportunity for you.

It's possible to find distressed properties in every part of town, from Millionaire's Row to Skid Row. If everyone saw distressed properties only as problems to avoid, then the warehouse district of New Orleans, with its stunning lofts, elegant shops, and world-class restaurants would never have been dug out of the filthy industrial heap it had become. And a group of civic-minded Seattle residents wouldn't have devoted years of effort to rescuing north Capitol Hill by getting it designated as the Harvard-Belmont *Historic District*, thereby turning it once again into one of the city's premiere neighborhoods.

> **DEFINITION**
>
> A **historic district** is a group of properties, including residential and commercial, that have been designated by the federal, state, or local government as historically or architecturally significant or both. Property owners might have to follow strict guidelines when renovating a property located within such a district, but they might also be eligible for tax incentives to help pay for any approved renovations.

Every single city and town in America has a similar story to tell about old neighborhoods that were rescued by coordinated efforts at renewal. In fact, there are hundreds of examples in every state in which a group of citizens worked together to rescue and revive a once flourishing neighborhood that had fallen into neglect and disfavor. None of these turnarounds would have ever happened if someone hadn't been brave enough to take the first step in launching the revitalization efforts. Someone had to be the first to say, "this neighborhood is worth saving." Flippers can and do play significant roles in such efforts.

If you want to take advantage of distressed properties but don't want to devote the time it would take to save an entire neighborhood, another strategy is to drive through a great neighborhood street by street and see if you can find any distressed properties in need of rehab there. People who live in such homes have often been hit by illness, injury, a change in their life circumstances, or even just advancing age. Your offer to purchase their house as is could literally be a lifesaver for them. We'll discuss this and other techniques to find suitable properties in more detail in Chapter 8.

Another way to take advantage of a potentially lucrative trend is to identify up and coming neighborhoods. These areas have fallen into disrepute, but the revitalization process has started and buzz is building. Potential buyers are taking note, and interest in rehabbed properties is rising, but the area is not quite trending.

Such a neighborhood is not at the absolute start of its arc back into desirability, but neither has it been completely accepted as an ideal place to live just yet. Other flippers have already begun working there, which makes it easier for you to grab a piece of the action. However, there's still more work to be done to make the neighborhood truly desirable to buyers. This is one of the things we like best about flipping, the idea that we can contribute to the rebirth of a once fine neighborhood and help turn it back into something splendid again.

> **FLIPPER BEWARE**
>
> When you are researching neighborhoods, don't neglect to look up local crime rates. Almost every city and town now maintains an online database of offenses, sorted by type of crime. If a neighborhood you're considering has a lot of property crimes, such as burglary, car break-ins, and vandalism, keep looking. Of course, if there is *any* violent crime there at all, stay far away. All buyers are aware of the safe and not-so-safe neighborhoods in their town and prefer to avoid locations with high crime, particularly if they have young children. If you are not able to find your local crime database, call the public information office of the local police force, and they will point you in the right direction.

The safety of a neighborhood, both real and perceived, is critical to your success. You can rehab every house for 10 square blocks, but if the neighborhood is still subject to high crime and vandalism rates, you won't attract many buyers no matter how well you price your properties. Many different elements must come together to make a neighborhood desirable again, and crime control is one of the most important.

Trending vs. Stable

Another way to differentiate between neighborhoods is by identifying them as either trending or stable. Trending neighborhoods are ones that have a lot of buzz. People are suddenly talking about a trending neighborhood, and that raises both its profile and desirability. Stable neighborhoods offer fewer opportunities for flippers, because they are settled with not much turnover in home ownership. Their very stability makes them desirable locations, so keep an eye out because if you do find house you can rehab in a stable neighborhood, it's likely to sell quickly.

Trending neighborhoods with many rundown houses just waiting for your magic touch to bring them back to life are a virtual flipper's dream. When you find a desirable neighborhood with plenty of affordable houses that can be flipped, you and your team can stay busy for a year or more just flipping one house right after the other.

> **FLIP TIP**
>
> When it comes to deciding where to live, most people want to follow the crowd. While there are always a few pacesetters who want to do the opposite of what everyone else is doing, the majority feel most comfortable living near their peers. You can use this fact to your advantage by asking your buyers if they have any friends considering moving into the neighborhood. If they do, you might well have a built-in buyer ready and waiting to purchase the moment you complete your next flip.

City vs. Suburban

Whether you flip houses in the city or in the suburbs is an easy decision governed by both opportunity and proximity. We're firm believers in the idea that you should focus your efforts on properties that are located fairly close to where you live. In fact, we probably wouldn't flip a house if it was more than about 30 miles away from us. Remote flips cost more time, energy, and money than we want to invest. Consider, too, that you might have to pay your crew more money to cover their travel costs or hire a new crew that lives close to the site. By the time you add up the cost of gas, meals away from home, extra wages, and all the lost commuting time, you could be cutting deeply into your potential profit.

> **FLIPPER BEWARE**
>
> Flipping is a complex business with lots of details you must manage. If you get drawn into projects requiring too much of your time relative to the money you will earn, that can be stressful. Learn how to choose good projects right from the beginning, and be wary of doing too many flips at one time or taking on flips that are too far away and require a long commute to oversee.

If you live in the suburbs and those trendy downtown warehouses converting to condos are a 45-minute slog through heavy traffic, reconsider your investment. Look around and find something closer to home to work on. If you simply must have a piece of the warehouse action, consider hiring a project manager who lives near the worksite to oversee the project for you. That way, you can have your warehouse flip and keep your sanity, too.

The same thing goes for flippers who live in the city but are thinking about doing flips in the suburbs. Weigh all the costs, both in money and time, before making a decision about taking on a remote flip. There are great potential flips scattered all over every locale. If you focus on properties that are within a reasonable distance from your home, you might even be able to squeeze in an extra flip or two over the course of a year.

Urban vs. Rural

This match-up is almost a no-brainer. Remember we have said demand is one of the most important factors to consider when deciding where to buy your first property. How do you think demand for rural properties stacks up compared to demand for urban properties? There is no comparison.

It's very difficult to sell rural properties. Demand is intermittent, and it can literally take months or even years for the right buyer to come along. You simply cannot risk tying up your capital for that long.

Rating Property Potential

Many different elements go into rating the suitability of any given property for flipping. You must evaluate the following:

- Acquisition cost

- Location and neighborhood demand

- Condition of the house

- Cost and feasibility of any required repairs

- Time needed to complete the repairs and renovation and put the house on the market

- Price and availability of similar houses in the neighborhood that you can use for comps

And then of course, there's the most important question of all: can you make money on this flip?

Sometimes, all other things being equal, your choice might simply come down to a gut feeling, but it had better be a gut feeling backed by some great hard numbers. Perhaps one house might speak to you as another does not. That's fine, too. You can be a house whisperer as long as you make the finances work.

Avoiding Money Pits

All rundown houses are not created equal. Some will be easier to flip than others, but how do you tell which is which? This is where your general contractor earns his keep. The contractor performs a thorough inspection of potential properties and gives you his analysis of the pros and cons of each one.

If any of the following need repair or replacement, you might want to seriously reconsider your purchase unless you can make the numbers work. These are among the most expensive and time-consuming jobs you can tackle during a house flip.

- An in-ground swimming pool or hot tub
- HVAC system
- Roof
- Water heater
- Electrical box
- Foundation
- Extensive structural issues
- Significant termite or other pest infestation or damage
- Black mold or mildew
- Rusted-out plumbing pipes
- Out-of-date wiring and electrical system
- Standing water and other drainage problems
- Septic tank
- Driveways and sidewalks
- Fireplace

If your contractor finds problems with any of these areas, get a precise estimate of what repairs will cost. You might discover they are so expensive that there's no way to reasonably profit on the project. If that's the case, walk away.

Real problems can develop when damage exists in any of these areas, but it's not discovered before you purchase the house. Occasionally, this is due to carelessness or an oversight on the part of the contractor. More commonly, serious problems don't come to light until demolition starts on the house. When the walls are open, you'll see the rusted pipes that no one else suspected or the frayed wires that present a real fire hazard. It must all be replaced before the house can pass inspection.

FLIP TIP

If you have a problematic house that you don't feel good about even after you've completed renovations, get a home warranty for your buyers so if any hidden damage comes to light after the rehab, they can file against their warranty rather than coming after you.

We call such houses money pits, where flippers can lose their shirts because one problem after the other crops up during renovation, resulting in costs that spiral out of control.

If you are considering a marginal house, hire a home inspector before making your decision. Ask for a comprehensive inspection, specifically looking for any hidden damage. You'll be better able to make an informed decision once you have an official report on the home's condition. If you do go ahead and purchase and renovate the home, and something goes wrong after you've sold it, you'll have the inspector's written report as proof that you performed due diligence to verify the home's condition.

The Most House for Your Money

Every flipper dreams of a house in which renovations go as planned, there are no expensive hidden problems to wreck your profit, and no surprise expenses crop up along the way. You'll cross the finish line in budget and on schedule, and finally, the house sells quickly and for full price. That's the ideal.

When you are comparing several potential properties trying to decide which to buy, evaluate the following:

- Which house has the better floor plan and will be easier to renovate?
- Does one of the houses have more spacious bedrooms?
- Is there a half bath in addition to the main bathrooms?
- Are there bonus rooms you can repurpose to make the floor plan more appealing or add an extra bedroom?
- Which house has more closet space and better storage?
- Which house has the better master bedroom?
- Does the master bedroom have an en suite bathroom?
- Is there a finished attic or basement in one of the houses?

As you gain experience, you'll learn the little things that help a buyer decide to buy your house instead of another. Those same cues will guide you to buy the house most likely to sell.

The Least You Need to Know

- Location and neighborhood demand are the most important factors in the selection of your first property to flip.

- Purchase properties in neighborhoods that are just starting to trend upward for the best selection at affordable prices.

- Distressed properties can be excellent choices for your first flip.

- Avoid flipping rural properties because they can take a very long time to sell.

- Pass on houses with too many repairs because they can turn into money pits.

Finding Houses to Flip

Some aspiring flippers think it's a challenge to find a suitable house to flip. While we agree that housing availability differs from market to market, finding a house near you to launch your flipping career is not actually as difficult as it might seem. Your mom's neighbors might be retiring to Florida and looking to sell their home. A friendly Realtor could give you a tip, or you might read an interesting Craigslist ad about a house for sale. It's possible you could overhear a conversation while at the barbershop that leads to a great property. You can find leads and ideas to identify suitable houses in dozens of other ways if you just keep your eyes and ears open.

Information about potential houses is literally everywhere, but you need to be proactive. You could be standing in line at a sandwich shop and overhear a woman behind you discussing a house she knows is coming up for sale in a neighborhood you've been researching. If you remain silent, you could miss a great opportunity. You won't know any of the details you need to locate and investigate the property unless you introduce yourself and ask for the details. You must be ready to take advantage of any tips and ideas that come your way at any time.

In This Chapter

- Treat your Realtor right
- The importance of MLS
- Mine the classifieds
- Popular ways to find homes to flip
- Creative ways to find homes to flip

We have already briefly discussed a couple of the most obvious methods to find potential flips, but now we're going to explore them in depth. We'll also do a deep dive into all the not-so-obvious ways to find great houses and how you can ensure you're always in the loop when it comes to news about the local real estate market.

Relying on Your Realtor

Now is when your efforts to meet Realtors are finally going to pay off. No one knows as much about real estate as a successful Realtor. They live, breathe, eat, and sleep the housing market, Realtors keeping their fingers on the pulse of all local sales activity. They know the neighborhoods where flippers are working successfully, and which neighborhoods you should avoid.

Realtors are uniquely positioned to get information about upcoming properties before almost anyone else can. Sure, a banker or contractor might hear of the odd house, but the ebb and flow of available houses is not their everyday business like it is a Realtor's. The best Realtors have an almost instinctive feel for the market, sensing when neighborhoods are cooling down or are about to get hot again, and they apply their efforts accordingly. Realtors also know all the players in the field … the flippers, contractors, lenders, inspectors, and appraisers. They can recommend the best ones to work with and who to avoid.

Take some time to spoil your Realtor. He or she will be doing a lot of work for you and not always getting a paycheck, so treat your Realtor well and show you appreciate the hard work done on your behalf. If a Realtor works with three flippers, and one of those flippers is always doing little thoughtful things to show they appreciate the Realtor's efforts, which one of the three do you think is going to hear about the primo properties first?

How to Monitor MLS Listings

People in the real estate business monitor the Multiple Listing Service (MLS) almost as obsessively as a gambler watches a slot machine. The amount of data that flows through MLS on a daily basis is staggering. Realtors use it to monitor listings, take the pulse of a neighborhood they're watching, check on sales prices, look for comps to help them price new listings competitively, and search for properties for clients. MLS data contains gold nuggets you can use to find your next flip. But how do you get your hands on all that important information?

FLIPPER BEWARE

Don't treat your Realtor like your personal MLS service. Not only will you quickly lose your Realtor if you take up too much of their time with endless research requests, but they will warn their fellow Realtors to stay away from you as well. Performing research and compiling competitive market analyses takes time. Realtors are happy to do it when they have a realistic expectation of getting paid for their services by acting as the buyer's agent when you place an offer and seller's agent when you list your flip. Limit your requests to those pertinent to a pending offer or your listing that is about to go on the market.

Access to MLS data is another very good reason to work closely with a Realtor. The full MLS service is available by subscription only to licensed real estate brokers and licensed Realtors who also either own a brokerage themselves or work with a licensed broker. In order to qualify to sign up for the MLS service, a Realtor must also be a member in good standing of the local real estate board and pay quarterly dues there. If they don't have all these boxes ticked, they cannot get access to MLS.

We realize a lot of you might be data junkies who love nothing better than spending hours scrolling online through property after property, but access to MLS is not just a matter of, "Hey, I can go get my Realtor's license and sign up for Multiple Listing Service!" It's not that simple. Not to mention, all that time you spend online looking at other people's houses and dreaming is time you're taking away from your own flipping business.

Realtors guard their access to MLS zealously, because it's almost a hanging offense for them to get caught letting a non-Realtor surf MLS listings using their personal log-in.

FLIP TIP

If you still want to look at real estate data without having to bug your agent for it all the time, Zillow, Trulia, and Redfin offer quite a bit on their websites. Although their data isn't as comprehensive or complete as what MLS offers, you can still find the property's address and photographs, sales price, date of the most recent sale, the home's square footage, lot size, number of bedrooms and bathrooms, and any special amenities included for most properties. They also offer easy tools to find comparable houses in the surrounding neighborhoods of a target property.

There is also such a thing as clerical access to MLS intended for Realtor assistants, but it's limited in its scope and doesn't offer access to all the in-depth data a Realtor can see. Some people have suggested volunteering to help out in a Realtor's office for a few hours a week in order to gain clerical access to the MLS. If that works with your schedule and your Realtor is amenable to the idea, fine, but your time is better spent focusing on your flipping and letting your Realtor focus on using MLS to find properties and comps.

Even if you somehow had full access to MLS, learning how to use it to do competitive market analyses (CMAs) is another hurdle entirely. That is one of the jobs we recommend you leave in the capable hands of your Realtor. With their training and experience, he or she can monitor the market more effectively than you can, leaving you time to plan your next flip.

Watching the Classifieds

You can find intriguing properties in the newspaper, online classifieds, and Craigslist. Often, you will find people willing to make a deal just to get out from under a mortgage.

Many different life circumstances can make it imperative for someone to sell their house quickly. You can find most of the clues you need to track down such properties in the classifieds. As with all other forms of house hunting, you still must properly vet the house before you buy it. Make sure the neighborhood is good and that the house is free from significant damage before you invest. Just because you found the home in an unusual way does not exempt you from following your normal protocols to determine if it's a good deal or not.

Distressed and "As-Is" Properties

When families and individuals fall on hard times, it doesn't take long for their properties to become distressed, sometimes in almost every sense of the word. There are actually two different takes on the meaning of the phrase, "distressed property," and both of them are accurate:

- In the bank sense, a *distressed property* is any property that has gone into foreclosure.

- In the property sense, *distressed* can mean any property that needs significant repairs that the homeowner is unable to afford. Can you imagine living in a home with no working toilet, and not being able to fix it? This is the situation many families or elderly homeowners find themselves in.

You might be asking yourself, "But how can we tell if a property is distressed just by looking at the classifieds?"

One clue—the house will be listed "as is." No matter how or why it got there, that's the condition it's in now, and believe me when we say that for whatever reason, an as-is house is a distressed property. When you see those two little words in an ad, that's your cue that the property might be worth investigating. Just be sure to do all your normal research and due diligence, because an as-is house could well be a money pit. So go look at them all if you want, but only buy the ones that make sense financially.

Obituary Columns

It might sound macabre to recommend you read the death notices, but many a good property has been found that way. When someone dies, particularly if it is the family's breadwinner, the survivors might soon discover they must downsize by selling the family home.

Of course, you must be quite circumspect in how you approach a family still suffering from such recent grief. However, often survivors will welcome you because they feel overwhelmed by all they must do after their loved one passes away. Knowing that you are going to buy their home and they won't have to go through the stress of repeated showings and having to keep the home "visitor ready" all the time can actually come as quite a relief.

In these cases, reach out to the family in a caring way, offer your professional expertise, and also offer to help solve any problems related to their house they might be experiencing as a result of their loved one's death.

Estate Sales

If you are a fan of estate sales, there's one more thing the family might be selling that isn't all that obvious … the house where the sale is being held. Often an estate sale is the last family gathering before the home is put up for sale. Because of that, it's a very good time to approach the heirs and introduce yourself. Do not interfere with their sale in any way; you won't endear yourself that way. But do ask them if they plan to put the house up for sale, and let them know of your interest.

Give them a business card with your contact information and find out a good time to get back in touch with them. Often, the family will want to meet with you right after the conclusion of the sale, since all or most of the family members could be there helping out. Get in the habit of carrying your business cards at all times. Learn how to open up and speak with people you meet in your daily comings and going. You can get some great leads this way.

 FLIPPER BEWARE

> When the time does come to list a house that is part of an estate, it's a good idea to check with the family's probate attorney before you take the listing to make sure the heirs do in fact have the authority to sell the house.

If you see something you like at the sale, by all means buy it. It will serve as an icebreaker and confidence builder and prove to the family you're more than just a tire kicker.

Estate sales are often very emotional times for a family, and long-buried tensions might bubble to the surface at such times, particularly if the heirs don't agree on the disposition of their loved one's assets. Don't let yourself get caught in the middle of their feuds. Remain calm and neutral and give them the space they need to work out their differences.

Looming Foreclosures

Sometimes a family facing foreclosure is willing to sell their home for less than its appraised value just to get out from under a mortgage they can no longer afford. Just as with families who have lost a loved one, you can almost serve as a savior for families facing extreme financial difficulties. People in this situation will often be quite blunt in their classified ads. They will admit up front what is going on and ask if there's any buyer out there looking for a good deal who might be willing to buy their house quickly.

Go out and meet the family and inspect the property. If it meets all your normal criteria for a good property to flip, make them an offer they can't refuse. It can be a very good deal for both parties.

Courthouse Auctions

When you see television flippers sweating in the hot sun while an auctioneer rattles off bids on one property right after the other, you are watching a tax assessor's auction. Properties get auctioned on the courthouse steps either because the owner fell behind in paying their property taxes or they fell behind in making their mortgage payments, or they had a *mechanic's lien* placed against the property and the home went into foreclosure.

> **DEFINITION**
>
> A **mechanic's lien** is placed against a property by a workman who has not been paid for work done. If the homeowner still won't pay, the lien holder can file a court action forcing the homeowner into foreclosure to get his payment. When a house with a mechanic's lien is sold at a foreclosure auction, the workman's lien is the first claim paid off.

Foreclosed homes might have other liens against them— liens that you need to know about before you make a buying decision. If you want to buy a particular foreclosure, it's well worth the average cost of $100 or so to order a title search be done on the property. A title search will quickly reveal if there are any other outstanding liens against the foreclosed property, such as mechanic's liens or tax liens. This knowledge will help you make a truly informed buying decision, because you'll be able to factor in more accurate acquisition costs using that information.

Auctions are usually held on specific days of each month. Check with your local courthouse to find out when they are held in your jurisdiction. You must bring certified funds with you to the auction, such as a cashier's check or bank letter. You bid either by calling them out or by submitting them in writing. If you win a property, you must complete the purchase and pay for the property and any fees immediately after the auction's end.

These auctions are closely governed by the laws of each state. After all, it's a big deal to take someone's home away from them, and the whole process can be quite traumatic for the family losing their home. Be sure you are familiar with your local laws before attending your first courthouse auction.

Because families tend to stay in a foreclosed home until the last possible second, it's generally not possible to conduct a full inspection of the property, so this is really a buyer-beware situation. You could end up with either the deal of the century or the world's worst money pit.

Legal Announcements

Legal announcements include separations and divorces, and where there is a divorce, there usually follows a division of real property. And where there is a division of real property, especially under less than ideal conditions, opportunity arises.

As with a death in the family, don't go barging into a tense situation. You can send a letter expressing your interest to the parties' attorneys.

While you can sometimes find a good property this way, it doesn't happen all that frequently because the divorced couple could already have a Realtor on board. But it's still worth your while to check out the situation.

Other Techniques

There are many creative ways to look for properties other than just the old tried and true ways. Some of them might surprise you, but we've only included them here because we know for sure that they do work.

Cruising Neighborhoods

Sometimes, the best way to get a feel for a new neighborhood you are considering is just to hop in your car and cruise around. This technique has several distinct advantages. One, if you drive a block-by-block grid, you'll see exactly which homes are for sale and what they look like. Jot down their addresses so you can look them up when you return to the office and start figuring out a potential budget.

As you drive, you'll get a real sense of the neighborhood, and be able to see first-hand what sort of amenities it has—schools, parks, churches, groceries, shops, gas stations, medical care, emergency services, and so on. You'll also be able to see immediately if there are any obvious problems. For example, a neighborhood with a lot of graffiti and smashed mailboxes will tell you there's a problem with vandalism there, and you would perhaps be better off seeking a house in a different location.

The main advantage of cruising an entire neighborhood is it really does give you the 30,000-foot view. You'll get a very accurate picture of the neighborhood's character while cruising through, as well as a handle on its amenities and appeal. That will help you do a better job on your flip as you always want to match your rehab to the look of the neighborhood. Such familiarity will also help you when it comes time to sell the completed flip. With such an intimate knowledge of your location, you'll be far more precise in your pricing and marketing strategies.

Online Auctions

If you know anything about real estate, you are probably familiar with auctions held on the courthouse steps, where municipalities sell properties that have unpaid back taxes or foreclosures. Banks tend to auction off their REO properties in large hotel conference rooms they rent for the occasion. You might have even attended a few of these auctions. But did you know you can buy a perfectly acceptable house through an online auction as well?

Many flippers like online auctions because of their privacy and convenience. No standing on a crowded sidewalk, jostling for space with other bidders. No shivering in an overly cooled ballroom, once again trying to get comfortable in a cramped space crammed with hard plastic chairs.

With online auctions, you can buy a home from the comfort of your home office, sitting in your sweats and munching on wings if you like. You can search for properties by zip code, by price, by the number of bedrooms, or in any number of ways.

There are several online auction sites. Many charge a nominal fee to participate in the auctions; others are free. They provide full information about properties to be auctioned, along with photos. Many times it's even possible to tour an open house before the home goes up for auction, so you have a good idea of what you will be getting before you buy.

> **FLIP TIP**
>
> Popular online property auction sites include bid4homes.com, hudforeclosed.com and auction.com. Be sure to consult with your Realtor before bidding on a home on one of these sites. You'll want to make sure they are listed as the buyer's agent of record so they can collect their commission on the sale.

Sellers like online auctions because the listing fees are economical compared to regular auctions, and they only pay a commission if the property sells. They also like the idea that they can attract a wider audience than the typical courthouse auction can reach. While you might see several dozens to a couple hundred people at a typical courthouse auction, it's easy to reach thousands of potential buyers online.

Buyers like online auctions not only for the convenience, but also because you can run across some real bargains online. While that's not always the case, it's certainly worth investigating online auctions to see if you might get lucky and win some good properties.

Like regular auctions, the payment for an online auction is due in full in cash as soon as the auction is over. So make sure you have your finances lined up before you start bidding.

Rumors and Gossip

We're not suggesting you sit around the local coffee house with your head tilted toward the nearest table, but you should not discount the value of rumors and gossip as sources of information about upcoming properties. There's perhaps no means of communication in the world that works quite so well as a neighborhood gossip mill.

Neighbors, particularly in desirable neighborhoods, do keep up with what is happening around them. They know when someone is ill or has died, when there is a job loss or transfer to another city, and when there is a divorce. As a result, they also know when houses are going up for sale.

So how do you tap into this gossip mill? It's difficult to do for an entire city, but you can certainly manage it for one or two neighborhoods where you are currently focusing your efforts. Make a point of befriending someone in each neighborhood, and then call them every other week or so to touch base and catch up. These calls do not have to be long, 4 or 5 minutes will suffice. Be cordial, ask how they are doing, and ask if they know of any houses in the neighborhood that might be going up for sale soon.

If you dislike phone calls, get the person's email address and send them emails along the same line. If at any point, a person starts to seem resistant to your contact, thank them kindly and move on to another source for your information. You cannot beat information out of someone. They have to enjoy the contact and see it as a social rather than a business thing. That means you can never bombard them with phone calls or emails, or they will more than likely drop you immediately.

If you are able to buy a house as a result of one of these tips, be sure to reward the tipster appropriately with a nice gift certificate or fruit basket.

Neighborly Chats

At first, this might seem like the exact same thing as rumors and gossip, but it's really not. In the previous technique, you initiate the contacts and do the work to maintain them. In this version, the neighbors themselves initiate the contacts.

Usually what happens is that you will be working on a flip in a neighborhood, and one of the neighbors will start dropping by regularly. Now, you have to manage these contacts carefully. It's likely the person is dropping by for one of three reasons:

- He or she is nosey or lonely.

- He or she is interested in flipping houses.

- He or she wants you to buy their house.

If the person just wants to chat or learn how to flip houses by watching you and your crew every day, it could become a real problem. You should be friendly but firm about the fact that there is real work happening at your site, and it's potentially dangerous for noncrew members to hang around. You simply do not want this sort of person adopting you during your flip because it can become a nuisance and a real time-waster.

However, if the person is trying to ascertain if you would be interested in buying their house, that information will come out rather quickly. Get her address and phone number, give her your business card, and ask when is a good time to call and set up an appointment to tour her house. Then bid her a cordial goodbye and get back to work.

As the head of your own flipping team, you do have to carefully manage who stops by your worksites and how long you let them hang out there. If you don't, you could end up with a gaggle of onlookers interfering with your work and your crew, generally slowing down progress on your flip. Slowdowns cost you way too much money to be tolerated, so the moment a situation like this starts to develop, assess and handle it right then to keep it from becoming a problem.

Mailings

Though direct mail has fallen from favor over the past few years as a means of contacting customers, it's still a very effective way of reaching out to a particular neighborhood or demographic. Yes, it's definitely more expensive than an internet ad or email, but you'll also end up with a better customer, one who is more likely to respond to your offerings than some random person who opted into your email on a Facebook page. That's because mailings are sent to carefully selected demographics and addresses.

FLIP TIP

The average cost of a real estate mailing list is about $25 per 1,000 names. If you want to add demographic selections such as college graduate or income above a certain range, those cost an additional $5 to $10 each above the initial cost. You should also update your mailing lists annually to keep them performing optimally and to take into account any changes that might have occurred, such as a change of address, since your last mailing.

When you buy a mailing list, you can specify things, such as the minimum income you want your recipients to earn, their ages, current zip codes, and their household type (families with children, singles, retirees, and so on). You can ask that your postcard only be mailed to people who have already expressed an interest in real estate in an online survey you posted. Just know that the more specific and targeted the list you mail to, the more expensive each name on that list will be.

Also be aware that direct mailings are not a one-and-done affair. You build up your reputation among a select group of people by mailing them repeatedly over a certain period of time. That doesn't mean you stuff their mailboxes full of your postcards every week. They would just start tossing them the second they saw them. However, it does mean sending out cards in a neighborhood when your flip is ready to sell. If that sales mailing is the first contact you've had with this list, your response will be lower than if you've had three or four prior contacts with the group to build your credibility. Each new contact, particularly if they're spaced appropriately, builds the recipients' sense of familiarity with you and a comfort level that you are someone working in their neighborhood and communicating regularly with them. That raises your trust level significantly, and people like to do business with people they trust and feel like they already know.

The Least You Need to Know

- Your Realtor can be extremely helpful when it comes to finding properties to flip.
- MLS is a great tool to locate trending neighborhoods and properties, but only Realtors can actually use it.
- Classified ads can be an almost endless source of leads when you are looking for houses to flip.
- Don't limit yourself to the usual techniques when searching for potential flips. Get creative and try some of the usual techniques we outlined here.

Identifying Your Target Audience

The demographic profile of your ideal buyer will go a long way toward determining what kind of house you buy to flip, where you buy it, and how you choose to renovate it. A buyer's age, income, education, family size, and career all play a role in determining the buyer's housing preferences and desired location.

As a flipper, you must know this information to define and cater to your target audience. You must know what characteristics your buyers have in common to be able to fulfill their housing needs. Demographic data will help you do this.

For example, if you are working with families with children, buy a property close to good schools with a spacious den, two to three secondary bedrooms and bathrooms, a fenced yard, and kid-friendly finishes. You can design a house with a perfect family floor plan and features—everything a growing young family could want. However, if you bought that house in a neighborhood where the schools have a poor reputation, you will eventually sell it, but not to a family with school-age children because it's missing a key item on their check list—good schools.

In This Chapter

- What are demographics?
- How demographics can help you succeed
- Creating buyer profiles
- How lifestyles affect neighborhood choice
- Targeting your ideal buyer

Targeting young professionals? Elegant spaces in trendier neighborhoods with high-end finishes and a designer feel are the way to go. But you can lavish the slickest, trendiest, and most beautiful finishes available on a hip loft and still not be able to give it away if it's located across the street from a high school. Why? Because schools equal noise. Families with children can tolerate noise; they're used to it. But to young married couples just starting out, living across the street from yelling, cheering, and screeching tires, and with high wattage industrial lighting pouring through their windows is not their idea of fun.

Why does any of this matter? Because matching the location, look, and amenities of your home to what specific buyers want greatly increases your odds of a fast and full-price sale.

No matter which demographic you are targeting, do some research to verify what is currently popular with that group. While major style trends might resonate across all ages and incomes, particular age and income groups always prefer specific amenities related to their needs and interests. Your job is to give potential buyers what they want, so pay attention to trends, and watch your sales take off and average days on market drop.

Assessing Demographic Data

Assessing and analyzing demographic data can be a secret weapon in your business. Before we start discussing how important it is for a flipper to stay abreast of demographic trends, let's define *demographics*.

DEFINITION

Demographics is the study of human populations based upon various statistical characteristics such as age, income, and education. Demographics can be used to identify and target specific groups for marketing purposes.

It's not difficult to understand why the house that instantly appeals to a family with school-age children might not be as attractive to a retired couple, a single mom, or newlyweds. Each of these demographic groups has different needs based upon their life situations. If you study the groups and their likes and dislikes, you will soon understand the features and amenities that are most desirable and important to each. Understanding demographics and how they define audiences will help you plan and renovate more appealing houses that sell relatively quickly.

Now this doesn't mean that every retired couple wants a turquoise blue kitchen with retro enamel appliances. Individual tastes vary widely within each demographic group. But you can bet that most retired couples want houses with lower maintenance requirements than a suburban minifarm with one rolling acre of grass that needs cutting every week during the summer.

Think logically about what appeals to each demographic, and make every attempt to provide it when you select a house to flip and in your renovation planning. Do note that a good flipper will target multiple demographics that might buy his house to increase the chance of the quick sale.

Main Buyer Categories

As you become more familiar with the world of real estate transactions, you will begin to understand that there are certain demographics that tend to look for specific things when they are house hunting. In considering which way to take your business, you will soon focus on one or two groups. It might be a group with which you have much in common or just a group that appeals you to for whatever reasons. Here are some basic buyer profiles to introduce you to the importance of demographics in your business.

Families with School-Age Children

Families with school-age children look for the following: a large, well-equipped kitchens with nearby play space so parents can watch the kids as they prepare meals. Spacious den, plus a playroom, or finished basement, garage, or attic space that can serve as a playroom. Spacious secondary bedrooms that can hold two twin beds comfortably; adequate bathrooms, at least one with a tub where children can be bathed; indoor laundry room; fenced yard; childproof finishes; large master bedroom with en suite bath, preferably with his-and-her sinks; large walk-in master closet or his-and-her closets; a sewing or craft room for Mom and space for a mancave or retreat for Dad; at least a two-car garage; and a mudroom.

Families also require excellent schools, a good library, plentiful shopping, and medical care nearby. Bonus points if master suite is separate from children's bedrooms. This demographic tends to go for more traditional styles, such as colonial, Craftsman, Georgian, and warmer-toned neutral finishes that are easy to clean and maintain.

Trendsetting Newlyweds

They want everything they see on HGTV: granite or quartzite countertops and stainless appliances in a large kitchen whether they cook or not; luxurious master suite and bath with upscale fixtures, preferably porcelain, and a rainforest showerhead. His-and-her sinks in the master bath are more important than the overall number of bathrooms.

HGTV can take a large part of the credit for the flipping industry. Launched in 1994, the channel originally featured gardening and craft tips and home renovation shows, but as time passed, flipping shows edged out other content. That in turn, spurred more and more people to try their hand at flipping a house. With just shy of 100 million viewers, and almost 50 million tuning in during any given week, HGTV has become one of the leading cable channels. It appeals to a coveted demographic, educated, affluent, with time and money to spare. The median household income of an HGTV viewer is $85,600, significantly higher than most other cable channels.

Outdoor entertainment space is a must for trendsetters, but yard size isn't significant as long as there's room for a grill and some chairs. They're fine with a shared pool but care most about being in a hot location with nearby access to urban amenities, such as libraries, museums, live theater and music venues, great restaurants, and easily accessible public transportation. Green building with sustainable materials and eco-friendly finishes are important to this group. They also like ultra-modern design features, such as floating staircases and exposed mechanical elements. Period-wise they love ultra-modern, mid-century modern, Art Deco, and any style that smacks of Frank Lloyd Wright. They tend to like cooler tones, such as whites and greys with pops of bright color for accents.

Single Parents

They want what families with children want, with a few notable exceptions. They definitely want the kid-friendly house, fenced yard, and good schools. But if they've recently divorced, they might not be as insistent about all the extra features they once demanded. Adequate space is still definitely a desired feature. It's no fun having to cram two kids who once had their own bedrooms into one room, so look for affordable, clever floor plans that will give every member of the family their own private nook. If your client is a single mom, a low-maintenance yard might be a selling feature, with hardscaping and permanent landscaping and not much grass to mow. Some clients in this demographic might want proximity to entertainment venues. On the rare night off, it's nice for single moms and dads to be able to meet friends in the general neighborhood and not have to drive a long way just to catch a movie or go on a date.

Empty Nesters

This is the stage when people start realizing they don't really need all the stuff they've accumulated over the course of a lifetime. After the kids have left, empty nesters start to think seriously about decluttering and downsizing to free up more time and money for leisure activities. They want two to three bedrooms with a nice master suite, smaller kitchens—a smaller house overall, with fewer yard and household maintenance chores. As with single parents, a yard with attractive permanent landscaping, hardscaping, and not much grass will appeal to this demographic. Like trendsetting newlyweds, empty nesters want nice neighborhood amenities, perhaps including a country club and golf course, and great restaurants as they tend to eat out more frequently than other groups. It's also important to have quality health care and a hospital nearby.

Retired Couples

This demographic is eager to find one-story houses so they no longer have to navigate flights of stairs. They want wide halls so if they ever need a walker, they won't have to renovate the house to accommodate it. They need walk-in bath tubs with sturdy grab bars to reduce the risk of falls. If you can provide a large shower with a flat floor that can handle a roll-in wheelchair, that is a big selling feature with this group.

> **FLIP TIP**
>
> If you focus on neighborhoods that attract retired couples, be sure to add the amenities suggested here to your remodel. But never market your completed flip as if it were some sort of assisted living set-up. Retired couples know better than anyone the health challenges they might face as they age, but they don't like to be reminded of them. Point out the wider hallways, walk-in tub, grab bars, and so on, as desirable features, and let it go at that. These buyers know what they need in the house where they'll spend their final years, and will appreciate your thoughtfulness in providing it.

Style-wise, older couples tend to like grade-level ranch-style houses. If the house you buy is elevated and this is your target audience, consider adding a wheelchair ramp to increase your chances for a quick sale. An open concept is appealing because it makes it easier to get around the home.

This group likes softer colors, especially pastels, as that is what was popular when they were young adults. More than anything, retired couples want their houses to be practical and easy to care for. It is difficult for them to keep up with maintenance on big yards, so look for houses with relatively small lots to renovate. It's essential to have a good hospital and quality health care nearby, as this group uses the most health services of all the demographics.

Singles, Older or Younger

Many older single people completely change their lifestyles once their children have left home. Many find they no longer want a detached house with a big yard. This group tends to prefer condos or patio homes in gated communities where they feel safer living alone. They are often content with one to two bedrooms, or a bedroom and a study or office where they can put a sleeper sofa for when their grown children visit with their families. They don't mind two stories, and like the idea of living close to neighbors. They also tend to be more price-conscious and stricter about budgets than some other groups. Smaller kitchens are okay with them as long as there is adequate storage and space for a kitchen table and chairs. They might be content with a half bath downstairs and a full bath up. Younger single people select many of the same amenities, but for different reasons. They like smaller spaces because they don't yet own enough furniture to fill up a larger space. They like smaller kitchens for the same reason. They don't have much kitchen equipment and don't need an island, two sinks, double ovens, and so on.

Please note all these profiles are approximate. Just because we've said families with children tend to like more traditional-style homes doesn't mean you're not going to run into a family with children that wants everything space-age modern. These profiles are intended strictly as guidelines. As you work with buyers, you will start to develop your own profiles based on your own experience. Use these as a starting point.

Amenities, Shopping, and Services

Some of the most important factors that can influence the desirability of any given house are the neighborhood amenities, shopping, and services located nearby. No one wants to drive 10 miles to pick up a gallon of milk, or wait 30 minutes for an ambulance when time is critical.

When neighborhoods fail early on, it's often because developers didn't pay attention to the number, quality, and proximity of the everyday things we take for granted, such as having a doctor nearby, or a dry cleaner, hair salon, or movie theater. Families might feel excited about the gorgeous houses in the new neighborhood, but then start moving out as they realize a simple trip to the grocery is equivalent to a safari, and returning a book to the library takes a couple of hours out of their day. Your buyers *do* think about these things.

Keep in mind that no one neighborhood is going to have all these amenities unless it is a master-planned community. Even then, your buyer might have a particular need in mind that might require you to do some research. We're not saying you must take buyers' hands and lead them like children through the home-buying process. Instead, we're simply saying if you arm yourself with knowledge about what your target neighborhood has to offer, and know what it is lacking, that will help you get your clients in homes that are the best fit for their needs.

 FLIPPER BEWARE

The greatest flip in the world will not make up for a neighborhood lacking in the basic amenities. When potential buyers learn they'll have to drive 30 minutes or more round-trip to pick up bread or eggs or drive to the next town to find a dry cleaner or a dentist, that might wreck your sale.

Let's look at some of the most desirable amenities you should be looking for when you consider buying a house. As a flipper, you can do a lot to turn a lousy floor plan into something that takes full advantage of every square foot of available space. But you cannot singlehandedly install restaurants, doctors, excellent schools, grocery stores, etc., to make a neighborhood great. If you find a good house but its neighborhood is lacking many of these basic amenities, keep looking until you find a house in a more fully developed neighborhood. All those nearby conveniences will enhance the salability of your finished flip.

Schools and Churches

Neighborhoods with a great variety of schools and churches are like catnip to families with children. But it's not just schools. Every aspect of childcare is important, so check on the availability of excellent day care as well as schools all the way from pre-kindergarten to high school. Also become familiar with the availability of after-school care for working parents.

We say great variety of schools because not every family sends its children to public schools. Many prefer private schools, and families with strong religious affiliations might opt for parochial schools associated with their church of choice.

Speaking of churches, make sure your neighborhood offers a wide variety of services catering to all the major religions. Church attendance is a very important activity for families. They also like to take advantage of other church activities, such as vacation bible schools, picnics, and mission trips.

Although churchgoers certainly exist across the demographic spectrum, the largest group of churchgoers is families with children, so plan accordingly.

Hospitals, Medical Services, Police, Fire, and Rescue Services

Everyone needs readily available hospitals, medical and dental services for emergency care, preventive care, and routine checkups. Naturally, people in older demographics and families with children might be more concerned with the proximity of medical services, but that doesn't mean other demographics don't think about such services as well. We all require doctors and dentists at one point or another!

People also care about police, fire, and rescue services. Of course, no one ever wants to need such services, but when you do, it's best to have them nearby.

> **FLIP TIP**
>
> Sometimes, residents who live in highly desirable but remote neighborhoods subscribe to an air ambulance service to fly them to the nearest hospital when they need emergency care. If you're working in a small town with few medical amenities, check with your fire department to see if such a service is available. If it is, it's normally coordinated through local emergency services. A ground crew will rush to the scene, medically stabilize the patient, and transport him or her to a helipad where the air ambulance is waiting.

The neighborhoods you work in should have a good selection of primary care physicians with at least some specialists, and if not a hospital, then an emergency clinic. Families with children will need a pediatrician, and older couples might visit doctors who specialize in the care of older people.

There should also be a good selection of dentists and pediatric dentists, orthodontists, and oral surgeons.

People in all demographics want good police presence, a nearby firehouse, and rescue services that respond quickly to emergency calls.

Public Transportation

Sadly, many cities and towns in America—particularly the smaller ones—have little to no public transportation. The good news is that it only really matters to certain demographics. Younger eco-conscious people often want to ride public transportation to reduce their personal carbon footprint. Older folks might not understand what the fuss is about. Many baby boomers are so used to driving their gas-guzzling land barges that the idea of changing their routines is completely foreign to them. You need to know these preferences so you can cater to them.

Public transportation is usually readily available in larger cities and doesn't just serve the inner cities, but many if not most of the surrounding suburbs and bedroom communities as well. Check the neighborhoods you are interested in working to see if they have public transportation, such as a bus line, trolley, or commuter train so you'll be ready with the correct information if a potential buyer asks you about the availability of public transportation near your property.

Grocery Stores and Other Shopping

Every demographic needs groceries. Check to see what is available in the neighborhood you are considering. Ideally, there should be a superstore such as Fred Meyer or Target, along with a bulk shopping facility, such as Costco or Sam's Club. Every community has its own local grocery chains as well, where prices might be somewhat higher but the selection is more varied and more gourmet items are offered. For the health-minded, it's also great if there is a natural foods grocery, such as Whole Foods, Sprouts, or a community co-op or weekly farmers' market.

> **FLIP TIP**
>
> The more you know about the amenities and attractions that are available in the local neighborhoods, the better job you'll do of selecting and flipping houses. Just be sure when you select a property to keep one or two specific demographics in mind to guide you as you make your remodeling plans. This will help you formulate a targeted marketing plan when you place the property on the market.

If the area also has specialty stores, such as Asian, Middle Eastern, or Italian markets, or New York–style delis, so much the better.

If there are no malls with major retailers located nearby, check to see if there are clothing, shoe, and accessory stores for the entire family, as well as specialty shops, such as hardware stores, drugstores, garden supply stores, gift stores, card shops, liquor and convenience stores, and gas stations.

Restaurants, Theaters, and Other Entertainment Venues

While members of some demographics like to dine out more than others, all groups enjoy going out for a meal every once in a while. In addition to the usual pizza parlors, Chinese buffets, and Mexican restaurants, look for some good higher-end facilities suitable for celebrating events, such as birthdays, anniversaries, graduations, and promotions. Don't worry about fast food joints. We don't believe there is a town in America than doesn't have at least a half dozen or so.

Of course, dining out is not the only entertainment people seek. It's nice if there is a movie theater nearby and other enjoyable recreational activities, such as live theater, music and performance venues, museums, libraries, and even tourist attractions. Places that give people interesting things to do are always highly desirable, and the more variety your target neighborhood offers to potential residents, the better.

Parks, Hike and Bike Trails, Pools, and Sports Facilities

In addition to the typical indoor recreational activities, many people enjoy outdoor activities, such as cycling, hiking, walking, jogging, swimming, and team sports such as soccer, baseball, and volleyball. Facilities for these activities might be grouped in one central place, such as a municipal park or sports facility, or they might be spread throughout a neighborhood in pocket parks and neighborhood pools. Some malls offer athletic activities such as rock climbing or ice skating. Many people join gyms so they can participate in exercise and fitness programs even when the outside weather is bad.

Once again, the level of participation depends in some degree on the demographic, but active individuals who want sports and fitness amenities span all the age, education, and income groups. As with the other neighborhood amenities we've discussed, be prepared to answer buyers' questions about what's available and where it's located within the neighborhood.

Traffic and Commute Times

In the past, daily commute times of 2 to 3 hours round-trip were routine. No one thought much of it. You lived on Long Island and worked in New York City, and your wife would meet the train each evening with your ice-cold martini in hand. Or you lived in Plano and worked in downtown Dallas and listened to a book on tape or chewed your nails during the almost 2 hours a day you were stuck battling traffic.

The same story was true in large cities across the country. Jobs were concentrated downtown in the city center, and people lived in remote suburban communities and drove alone into the city, carpooled, or rode mass transit to work. The long daily commute was a normal and accepted part of life.

Then the price of gas began to rise and people became more eco-conscious and started valuing their personal time more dearly. Suddenly, a full-scale revolt against long commute times erupted, and people started eying shabby, rundown neighborhoods close to the city center. It's this change in attitude toward the daily commute, and increasing unwillingness to take it on, which is creating an ideal climate for flippers to work in.

> **FLIP TIP**
>
> Why have Americans rebelled against the long commutes that have so long been a part of our culture? There are several reasons, chief among them, the cost. According to the Brookings Institution, American workers spend an average of 4.1 percent of their income on commuting. For a family earning the median household income of $52,250 per year in the United States, that works out to $2,142 every year.

Matching Lifestyles to Neighborhoods

Now that you are more familiar with the demographic groups you might encounter when you are ready to sell your flip, it's time to think about another area where demographics can help. When you use buyer profiles to match lifestyles to neighborhoods, you will see a marked improvement in your success.

It makes sense to try and sell a larger home in a neighborhood with great schools to a family with school-age children. You wouldn't reach out to single people with that listing or to retired couples for that matter. Conversely, if you have refurbished a loft in a revitalized industrial area where the nearest school is 10 miles away, your first thought wouldn't be to show the listing to a couple with children. A single person or some trendsetting newlyweds offer your best chance of making a quick sale.

If you're saying to yourself, "Well, this isn't new information," it's not. Nor is it anything you might not already have thought of on your own. But we are asking you to think about the familiar in new ways to enhance your chances of success. Take all available information and put it together to create a more complete picture of your buyers, what their ideal homes might look like, and where they would be located. Think of all this as another technique that will help sell more houses.

Finding, Targeting, and Closing Your Ideal Buyers

Finding your ideal buyers can be a lot of work, but like any good thing, it's worth doing well. We maintain databases of buyers we have worked with before and often reach out to them when we have a new property ready to market. It's not so much that we are trying to sell them a new house, but to get referrals from them. Most recent homebuyers have friends who are also in the market for a new home, and often their friends want a house in the exact same neighborhood. We get great referrals this way, and many of them do buy one of our houses.

Establish a social media presence on sites, such as Facebook, Twitter, and Instagram, and use those platforms to announce when you have a new property available. We like how you can publish beautiful full-color photos of the properties along with brief and intriguing descriptions that will get your phone ringing. Don't provide too much information or people will just go straight to the house and bypass you. Provide just enough info to tantalize them and get a phone call coming your way.

Of course, you can go with the old reliable standby of running a classified ad, or better yet because you can add color photos, a Craigslist ad for your completed flip. Keep a weatherproof box full of flyers on the "For Sale" sign on your property. You'll definitely pick up some potential clients that way. Just be sure to keep the box full of flyers. If someone drops by and you are out of flyers, you could lose a potential sale.

Finally, use direct mail targeting the neighbors around your flip. In a trending neighborhood, many of the current residents might be thinking of trading up to a larger house or to a newly renovated house, which is what you are offering. Sending out a postcard with an attractive photo of the house to the neighbors is a great way to let them know you have a property available in the neighborhood that might be of interest to them. You'd be surprised how much business you can get from a simple targeted mailing.

Neighborhoods tend to define and attract their own buyers based on demographics matching up with the available amenities. This might seem like gobbledygook to you now, but as you become more experienced, all the pieces will snap into place and understanding the vital role demographics play in your business will become much easier.

The Least You Need to Know

- Buyer profiles can help you target buyers correctly.
- Knowing your local demographics is a smart way to identify trending neighborhoods.
- Many factors affect buyer preferences, and you should familiarize yourself with what influences your target buyers.
- A house that appeals to one particular type of buyer might not appeal to buyers defined by another set of demographics.

CHAPTER 10

Foreclosures: Yes or No?

Some flippers, particularly those who have been rehabbing properties for years, built their businesses around foreclosed homes bought at bargain prices. In the early days of flipping, this was the way to go. You could pick up attractive houses for $30,000 or less in many markets across the United States. That gave you plenty of room to make any necessary repairs plus add some nice upgrades, and still take home a healthy profit.

Like most good things, the ease of those early days didn't last. The 2008 housing crash pretty much flattened the real estate and flipping markets nationwide, and it took several years for them to recover. Some say the market is still recovering because banks have such large inventories of REO homes to dispose of.

In order to succeed with foreclosed properties, you must know the unwritten rules of the game, how to navigate hidden pitfalls and deal with the ever-growing slew of competitors who want to buy and flip the same properties that you are eying.

In This Chapter

- Finding foreclosed properties is fairly easy
- Competition to buy foreclosures can be intense
- Buying foreclosed properties requires extra vigilance
- Pre-foreclosures can be a better option for everyone
- Due diligence is especially important for foreclosed properties

This chapter will show you how to beat the crowd with a few savvy tips and tricks, plus smart strategies to cultivate friendships with lenders and courthouse clerks who can give you a heads up about desirable properties making their way to the auction block. We will teach you everything you need to know about buying and working with foreclosed properties, and how you can come out on top when flipping them, all without getting a pounding headache. Follow these strategies and you will soon be able to make flipping foreclosures a consistently profitable part of your business.

What Is a Foreclosed Property?

A property goes into foreclosure when the borrower fails to make three consecutive mortgage payments and is not able to meet the lender's demands for payment during the pre-foreclosure period.

There are two types of foreclosure, *judicial* and *nonjudicial*, but the end result is the same. The homeowner loses the property and the lender takes possession of it. Homeowners also lose the equity they had invested in the property. If they bought a house for $200,000 and put down 30 percent or $40,000, and have built up another $10,000 in equity during the period they lived in the home, that money is lost. The loss of equity combined with the damage a foreclosure does to credit scores makes it difficult for anyone who's been through foreclosure to buy a house again.

> **DEFINITION**
>
> A **judicial foreclosure** is a lawsuit filed against a borrower by the lender who holds the mortgage on their property after the borrower falls 3 or more months behind on payments. A court-appointed referee sends out a Notice of Foreclosure Sale announcing the time, date, and location of the foreclosure auction, giving the homeowner a certain period to redeem the home prior to the auction. The referee also conducts the foreclosure auction.
>
> A **nonjudicial foreclosure** is used in states where deeds of trust are issued to convey an interest in the property to a trustee (lender) who holds the deed as security for repayment of the mortgage loan. The deed contains a power of sale clause that gives the trustee authority to record a Notice of Default (NOD) with the county clerk when a borrower goes into default.

When you deal primarily in foreclosures, your life can be an up-and-down seesaw ride if you let it. You can make $50,000 on one flip, then lose $30,000 on the next. We want you to learn to control the process instead of letting the process control you.

Most homeowners don't even want to hear the word *foreclosure*, much less have a discussion about it. Initially, a foreclosed property tends to lower the appraised value of other homes in the neighborhood, making it more difficult for other homeowners to get the best price for their property if they happen to be selling at that time. Then, when flippers start to work the neighborhood, the unrealistic prices some of them are willing to pay for properties can have just the opposite effect.

 FLIPPER BEWARE

> When many houses are flipped and sold in one neighborhood in a short time period, homeowners and prospective buyers complain that the high number of sales combined with flipping activity in the neighborhood pushes purchase prices to unrealistic and unaffordable levels. Avoid working in neighborhoods where this has happened, because it will be more difficult to turn a profit on these houses, whether they're foreclosures or not.

On the other end of the deal, if you're a homeowner whose property is in foreclosure, that's really no fun, either.

Not surprisingly, more than 50 percent of the homes that entered foreclosure between 2007 and 2012 were located in poor or middle income areas. While houses at this end of the spectrum lost value the fastest during the 2008 housing crash, their sales prices recovered faster than average since the crash, meaning they were ripe for the plucking when the flipping reignited.

While such plums were plentiful for several years after the recovery, as flipping continued to grow in popularity, bargain properties became more difficult to obtain at courthouse auctions. Intense bidding by flippers who sometimes didn't truly know what they were doing often pushed prices past the point where a reasonable profit could be made.

How Do I Find Foreclosed Properties?

Thanks to the advent of the internet, finding foreclosed properties is easier than it has ever been before. Here are some of the most popular ways to find them.

Working with Your Realtor

There is a special MLS tool that searches for foreclosed properties in your area by zip code. Let your Realtor know you're looking and she can run a search for you and share the details of suitable properties. Of course, also provide the other parameters you want, such as price range, number of bedrooms, and so on. The list you get back will be tightly targeted to those specifications and can be very useful.

There should be plenty of houses to choose from. About 25 percent of the listed properties on MLS at any given time are foreclosures.

Searching the Internet

Of course, you can always search the internet yourself, but be aware, there are some scam artists out there who advertise foreclosed properties, take a fee from you to look at their listings, and then disappear. Or they'll send you old lists with properties that were auctioned off last year. Deal only with reputable, well-known names when looking for foreclosures, and that should keep you away from the scammers.

> **FLIP TIP**
>
> Here are just a few of the free websites that list foreclosed homes available for sale: auction.com, hudsonandmarshall.com, williamsauciton.com, usahud.com, bankforeclosureslisting.com, zillow.com/foreclosures, and homes.com/for-sale/foreclosures. All have filtered search so you can look for homes in your area by entering a zip code. Search through several because every site has different listings. You also get a free 7-day trial of foreclosure listings on paid sites, such as realtytrac.com. The paid sites do offer more complete information and often list foreclosed properties before the free sites have them.

You can find bank-owned or REO properties on a foreclosure site by using the term "REO" along with the zip code you are targeting in the search box. Doing so will return a list of bank-owned properties in your preferred neighborhood.

The other problem with researching foreclosures yourself is that the information provided on the listing might not be complete. For example, a listing might not provide the lien holder's name, which precludes you reaching out to the lender to make a deal.

If you're focused on foreclosures as a major part of your business, get in the habit of searching foreclosure sites daily to see what is new. If you only look once a week or so, you're going to miss some of the best deals. If you don't have time to do these searches yourself, hire someone to do them for you on a part-time contractual basis.

Other Methods

Read the legal notices in your local paper to find out when foreclosed properties will be auctioned at the courthouse. Note the names of local auctioneers who are running the auctions and then search their website for information on upcoming properties.

Some banks list their foreclosed properties in a special section on their website. If you know the names of the larger banks in your community, enter their name and foreclosures in a search and you should be taken to their current listings.

Many counties don't maintain publicly available lists of foreclosed properties coming up for auction. They either don't have the budget or the manpower to do so. However, they will email a list of properties that will be available a week or so before a courthouse auction to people who have signed up to receive that information. To get on the list, go to your county's website and follow the instructions to add your name and email to their contact list.

We also suggest you cultivate friendships with county clerks in the tax assessor's office, and at the local banks, credit unions, and mortgage brokers that make loans in your town. If you are always courteous, friendly, and treat people with respect, that will go a long way toward cementing good working relationships in important places. We're not promising you will automatically get insider information as a result of these friendships, but people like to do business with people they like. You will be working with these clerks, auctioneers, and lenders on an ongoing basis over many years. If you're an upstanding person with a well-earned reputation for honesty and producing quality products, and you are genuinely nice to the people you work with, only good things can come from that.

Buying Pre-Foreclosure Properties

We sometimes feel an underlying pang of regret when we are dealing with a foreclosure. It's not too difficult to figure out why. A foreclosure represents the death of someone's dreams, and we try to keep that in mind whenever we deal with families struggling to hang on to their homes and their credit scores.

Foreclosure is a huge stressor, probably one of the most upsetting life events anyone could ever go through. But knowing we can get in there when a house is in pre-foreclosure and help a family by buying their house *before* it's auctioned off is a big positive.

Pre-Foreclosure Defined

When a homeowner has missed three consecutive mortgage payments on their property, they enter a period called pre-foreclosure. They still own the home, but the lender has started the foreclosure process and has legally notified the homeowners that an auction is imminent.

FLIP TIP

Imminent means different things in different places. In New York, it takes an average of almost three years to complete a foreclosure, with the family still living in their foreclosed home for the bulk of that time. Contrast this with speedy Texas, where a home is auctioned off just 97 days after a notice of foreclosure is served! To look up how long it takes on average for a foreclosed property to go to auction in your state, go to http://www.marketwatch.com/story/how-long-a-foreclosure-takes-in-your-state-2012-12-03.

If the homeowner can come up with all the back payments plus late fees and other fees due and make a lump sum payment to the lender to bring the loan current, the property will go out of pre-foreclosure. Otherwise, it will proceed into foreclosure and be auctioned off to the highest bidder.

How a Pre-Foreclosure Purchase Works

When we buy a home in pre-foreclosure, we get a property at a good price and the family gets a way out of the jam they're in. You get the information about the pre-foreclosure from the lender, but that's it. You then work directly with the homeowners to put the deal together. Unlike an auction where you're required to pay the total cost of the home immediately in certified funds, you can get bank or private financing for pre-foreclosed properties you buy before they go to auction. The mortgage holder might even be willing to help the deal by lowering the amount of principal owed on the loan.

You might ask, "Why would they be willing to give a discount on the price of the property and take less money?" It's because lenders hate taking possession of properties. Their ledgers are backlogged with houses they have repossessed and now own, and in some cases, cannot seem to sell. Lenders would much rather sell a house in pre-foreclosure and take less profit than risk having the house sit on their books for months or even years, draining dollars from their bottom line the whole time.

 FLIPPER BEWARE

There is a lot of misinformation around about how to assume the loan on a pre-foreclosure and never actually talk to the lender or go through a credit check. This used to be possible on VA and FHA loans, but the rules have changed. Check with local lenders to see what's possible. If someone offers you a back alley deal on a pre-foreclosure, you'd better ensure you'll actually own the home or the payments you make will just be fattening the bank's pockets and increasing equity for the property's actual owner.

Homeowners who find someone to buy their house while it's still in pre-foreclosure get to walk away without a foreclosure or bankruptcy on their credit history and maybe even a little cash in their pockets to get a new start. Flippers who also are Realtors can help them find a new place to live that's a better fit with their economic situation. They also get to leave the constant stress of struggling to make ends meet behind them and start over again with a clean slate, so we all win.

Another great benefit of doing foreclosures this way is that you get to skip the hassle of jostling with other determined bidders at courthouse auctions. Those auctions take place rain or shine, hot or cold, and you have to stand there and endure the crowds and whatever the weather conditions might be just for a chance to bid on a house that might have a pack of other flippers furiously on it bidding, too. In a pre-foreclosure sale, you are essentially the only "bidder."

Don't Believe Everything You See on HGTV

With programs that make flipping seem fast, fun, and a sure-fire road to riches, HGTV has drawn many new people into the field. Many aspiring flippers think they know all they need to know from watching television, so they don't bother to learn anything about their new profession before they start. They go into flipping unprepared, lacking knowledge of the basics, and woefully short on skills. They haven't spent time cultivating those essential contacts in the business as we've discussed, nor have they built teams. As a result, some new flippers are not all that knowledgeable about what they're doing, and believe me when we say everyone knows it after just one meeting with them.

Inexperienced flippers create problems industrywide, some of which, such as jacked up prices, could negatively affect your business. So before we go further, we want to take a moment to tell you that you should feel proud you're taking the time to read this book before you launch your flipping business. It means you have focus and that you're serious about achieving success.

These days, thanks to the fast-buck crowd, competition for foreclosed properties is beyond fierce. During a heated auction, purchase prices can quickly escalate past your bid limit if there are determined but inexperienced flippers with no project budget wildly throwing out big bids as fast as the auctioneer can call them. It bears repeating: when you pay too much to buy a property to begin with, it's almost impossible to earn any sort of reasonable profit on flipping the house, so why bother?

> **FLIP TIP**
>
> Too many bidders targeting the same house at an auction can mean the property sells for an inflated price. If you're the unlucky "winner," it will make it difficult to turn a profit on the flip. If you find yourself snared by one of these fast-moving auctions with bids flying back and forth, stick to your predetermined budget to keep yourself out of trouble. Don't make an error in judgment because you got caught up in the excitement of a bidding war.

Often, you have no idea what you're getting when you buy a foreclosure. Most previews are limited to a quick walk around the outside of the property and a glance through a few darkened windows to get an idea of the interior layout and condition. Once you buy a foreclosed property, you might discover that in a final pique of anger, the family that lost the home basically trashed the place. Or, perhaps they left it in such filthy condition you'll have to spend a wad of cash to get it cleaned and made safe before you can bring in your work crews. Chances are you didn't factor extreme cleanup costs into your budget.

That said, look at the ways we've discussed to do foreclosures that can eliminate many of the problems that can be associated with them. Many foreclosed properties are beautiful houses that will present few if any problems during the rehab. You just have to be at the right place at the right time to get your hands on them. That is a matter of preparation, practice, good timing, learning from your failures, and a little bit of luck.

Pros and Cons of Foreclosed Properties

Some flippers won't work on anything but foreclosed homes, while others won't come near them. We can see advantages to both points of view.

We will flip a foreclosure if it's in the right neighborhood and we're able to buy it at a price that gives us room to do a great job and still make a healthy profit. You have to decide for yourself where you will focus your efforts and if rehabbing foreclosures is right for you.

Now let's take a look at the pros and cons of flipping foreclosed properties.

Cons	Pros
Can turn into a money pit	Potential for higher profit
Available primarily in poor-to-middle class neighborhoods	Easier to sell cheaper properties than high-end ones
Fierce competition to buy can drive prices too high	If you get one at a good price, you're going to make bank
Courthouse auctions are madhouses	You know insider ways to find foreclosures and can skip the auctions
People in foreclosure can be difficult to deal with	You can help homeowners in distress solve their problem
Must pay total amount due in certified funds immediately after auction	You can get financing if you buy homes in pre-foreclosure

Be aware that market conditions vary from state to state. If you're working in a state, such as California, that has an oversupply of foreclosed properties, you're likely to get a much better deal on a foreclosed property than you'll find in a state, such as North Dakota, which according to realtytrac.com, has the lowest foreclosure rate in the nation. When there are not that many foreclosed properties for sale, the ones that do go on the market tend to sell for higher prices.

FLIP TIP

Don't buy the very first foreclosure you run across at an auction just because you can. Follow the same guidelines for purchasing property we've discussed since the beginning of this book. You still need to buy low and sell high; the property should still be located in your target neighborhood; and it shouldn't be a complete tear-down.

Before you decide whether or not to flip foreclosed properties, familiarize yourself with local ordinances governing foreclosures, and meet with a few lenders to see if they have protocols they want buyers to follow when bidding on foreclosures. Attend a few courthouse auctions strictly to observe, not buy. Make a note of the most active bidders and their bidding styles. After the auction is over, introduce yourself. You're going to be seeing a lot of each other if you do decide to flip foreclosed properties, and as we've mentioned before, it's always best to be cordial to your competitors.

Foreclosure Auctions

The big day has come. You are going to your first foreclosure auction to bid. You have your financing lined up, certified check in hand, and all the hope and excitement in the world. If you followed my advice and have already attended a few auctions without bidding, you should feel relaxed, because you're already familiar with the players and the process.

Before you go to the auction, research available properties that meet your specifications that you could possibly buy and flip. Select three to five homes to bid on even if you only have funding to buy one. You're not going to win every home you bid on, so if you lose the house you were set on and don't have a backup already selected, you'll have to wait until the next foreclosure auction, which could be weeks away, to try again.

Prior to the auction, you should perform *due diligence* on all properties you are interested in bidding on. That means title searches to make sure the property is not encumbered. Even though you cannot get inside occupied properties, a thorough inspection of the outside of the house with your contractor to make sure there are no obvious structural problems or damage that could be expensive to repair. Know the average days on market for houses in that neighborhood, and the average sales price for houses comparable to the one you are considering buying. In other words, you are ready to bid knowledgeably on properties you have thoroughly vetted prior to the auction.

DEFINITION

In the world of real estate, **due diligence** is the research and analysis of a real property in preparation for a business transaction, such as an offer to buy a house.

If no bids are received at the opening amount, the property is legally transferred to the bank and becomes an REO or real estate owned property. Sometimes a lender will accept an offer lower than the opening bid to keep a house off their books and save money over the long term.

> **FLIPPER BEWARE**
>
> The opening bid on most foreclosed homes at auction is the unpaid loan balance for that home. When houses are sold this way, it's called a value-based bid. Beware of total debt bids. That means that you, as the buyer, are obligated to pay not only the total amount due on the property, but also any fees, interest, and so on, that have built up over the course of the loan and the foreclosure. In many cases, a total debt bid can actually push the price of a foreclosure well beyond its market value, which means no one can flip the house profitably.

Avoiding "Gotchas!" on Distressed Properties

If buying a house is a straight line from Point A to Point B, then buying a foreclosed property might look more like a squiggle. You should exercise due diligence before buying any property, but must be doubly cautious when it comes to purchasing foreclosures.

Perform a property inspection to rule out structural or other forms of damage. It can be difficult to do such inspections if a foreclosed property is occupied, because it's unlawful to disturb the people living there. This means you will not be allowed to inspect the inside of the home.

You can tell a lot about the inside of a house though by the way the outside is maintained. If the yard is mowed and everything looks neat, chances are the inside of the house is in decent shape as well. The converse is also true. If the yard is overgrown, roof shingles are missing, and gutters hanging loose, it's more likely the inside is in rough shape, too, and will require significant work before you can start your rehab.

> **FLIP TIP**
>
> Pay for a professional title search to make sure the foreclosure property you are considering has a clear title and no large outstanding liens. Yes, there will be times when you order a title search and don't get the house, but think of it as a cost of doing business. Title searches protect your interests and let you know which houses you just need to walk away from as fast as you can.

For example, did you know if the IRS has a standing tax lien against the house when you buy it, the lien transfers to you, the purchaser? You will be obligated to pay the former owner's tax debt. While that might seem outrageous to you, the debt is attached to the house, not the person who owed it. *Nothing* overrides an IRS lien, so if you buy a house and then discover a lien, you just have to pay up. The costs can be substantial, wrecking your profit potential not only on the house you just bought, but perhaps putting your entire business in the hole financially. You must be very careful when house hunting in this minefield. There are bargains to be had for sure, but you could also lose the shirt off your back if you're not careful.

The Least You Need to Know

- Carefully consider all the ramifications before deciding if you want to flip foreclosed properties.
- Attend a few auctions before you are ready to buy to familiarize yourself with the process.
- Before bidding, order title searches on foreclosed properties that interest you to make sure they are unencumbered.
- Buying properties in pre-foreclosure can save you a lot of time and money.

CHAPTER 11

Buying Your First Property

The long-awaited day has finally arrived. You've read and studied; you've toured many different neighborhoods and chosen the one where you want to focus your flipping efforts. You've made sure buyer demand is high there, inventory is relatively low, sales are hot, and the area is trending up.

You've selected a Realtor and contractor to work with, and maybe even already found a private investor or gotten yourself prequalified for a loan.

Congratulations! Now it's finally time to go buy your first house to flip.

But don't break out the champagne and glasses just yet. There are still steps to take and guidelines to follow if you want to give yourself the best chance of profitability and success.

In this chapter, we'll take you step by step through a smooth transition from aspiring house flipper to the proud owner of your first renovation-ready property.

In This Chapter

* Buying the right house at the right price
* Bringing your team together
* Calculating costs and potential profit
* The significance of the 70 percent rule
* Crafting the right offer

Working with Your Realtor and Contractor

Meet with your Realtor to discuss what you're looking for in an investment property. Make it clear that you are buying this house to launch your flipping business, and you want a house you can rehab and sell for a nice profit within a short time period.

Ask your Realtor to research available properties in your target neighborhood. Choose a neighborhood with a favorable average days on market (DOM). You don't want to do your first few flips in a locale where the average DOM is 165 days when less than a mile away there's a comparable neighborhood with a DOM of just 47 days. The second neighborhood is where you *should* be working, and your investor will thank you for thinking of important details like this, especially when so many new flippers don't.

The math is simple. The longer your house sits unsold, the more interest, taxes, and maintenance costs build up, and the lower your profit will be. Finding a high-demand neighborhood where houses sell faster than average is a key step toward success.

Next, research the going prices in your target neighborhood for a typical 3-bedroom, 2-bath. You'll notice a theme here, that every single step of your flipping journey should be researched and carefully planned. While we like spontaneity, at the beginning of your flipping career, impulsive, ill-considered decisions can wreck your business and your dreams.

FLIP TIP

You need two to three comparable sales in your target neighborhood within the previous 6 months to know how to price your house. Set your price no higher than the most expensive sale, but only do that if your property has similar square footage and upgrades to justify a premium price. If you price your flip a couple of thousand under the market, buyers will be interested faster. If you can't find enough comparable properties in your neighborhood, it will be more difficult to set a sales price, because you won't have sufficient data to guide you.

Go tour all the properties on the list your Realtor provides for you and select your top two to three. Order title searches on those, and call your contractor to schedule a walkthrough and inspection at each house.

Be courteous. If you plan on visiting an occupied foreclosed home, have your Realtor call the selling agent so he can let the occupants know that you are coming and that you will be conducting a walk-around on the outside of the property.

If one of your top property picks is unoccupied, it should go higher on your list. When you can conduct a complete inspection to determine the actual physical condition of the entire house inside and out, you can make a more accurate estimate of what repairs are needed. Seeing the inside of a house can also spark creative ideas about how to renovate the space. This is far preferable to buying a house almost blind, which is what happens when you and your contractor are not able to conduct a thorough inspection of the premises due to occupancy issues.

Working with Your Investor on Board

Meet with your investor to discuss financing for the house you are about to buy. Provide your investor with as much information as possible about the particular home that's your number one. Print out and bring the MLS listing and any other information you have available about your target property. Bring your budget, including your estimate of the purchase price of the house along with any needed repairs and upgrades you have planned. Tell him about the neighborhood and why you chose it, and discuss the sales prospects for the property.

You have many decisions to make. Would the investor prefer to pay all cash for the property? Does he want you to take out a *bridge loan* to purchase the house and then just provide the funds to repair and renovate it? Or perhaps the investor has another way to finance the purchase. The two of you must answer these questions before you make the purchase.

> **DEFINITION**
>
> A **bridge loan**, also called *gap* or *interim financing,* is a short-term bank loan meant to provide financing during a period between two separate transactions. In flipping, the two transactions are the purchase of the house to be flipped, and after the rehab is completed, the sale of that same house. Bridge loans normally come due after 6 to 12 months.

Remember this is a mutually beneficial relationship. Private real estate investors like to feel confident you will deliver a good return on their investment. Being calm, in command of the facts, confident, and knowledgeable about what you want to accomplish will go a long way toward allaying any doubts they might have. After all, if you have never flipped a house before, the investor is taking a huge risk on the unknown when he hands over a wad of his cash to you. It's your job to do everything you can to prove to your investor over the ensuing several months that you are worthy of that confidence.

> **FLIPPER BEWARE**
>
> Be cautious about using bridge loans. The fees are high and the bank requires you to secure such a loan with real property, usually your house. If the flip fails, you could be in danger of losing your own home when the bank calls the loan due after 6 short months.

Whatever deal the two of you agree upon, be sure to get all the details in writing. Both you and the investor should sign two copies of your working contract and each keep a notarized copy. This way, there will be no confusion down the road when it comes time to disburse the proceeds of the property sale. All the shares and percentages should be specified in the contract.

Evaluating Profit Potential

In my opinion, evaluating the potential profit you can make on a particular flip is one of the most important components to ongoing success as a flipper. But you would be surprised how many new flippers gloss over this step. They are so bedazzled by the huge profits bandied about on television that they fail to accurately assess all the costs involved in flipping a house. They seem to be of the opinion that if they flip a house, they will automatically make money. That's just not true.

Many flippers actually end up losing money, sometimes quite a bit, on their first flip. The reason almost always can be traced back to a lack of adequate research and preparation, and a genuine misunderstanding of how to properly build a budget for purchasing and renovating a house.

Many inexperienced flippers leave entire categories of expenses, such as taxes, real estate commissions, and holding or carrying costs, out of their profit calculations when purchasing a home to flip. After the flip is completed and sold and all the actual costs deducted from the proceeds, the flipper could discover he's left with little or nothing to show for all the months of hard work. Or, he might actually still owe money over and above what was made on the sale of the house. This is such a discouraging experience, so different from what was expected based on watching flipping shows on television. Because of the pitfalls many first-time flippers encounter that undermine their chances of success, many join what we call the "one and done" club. They flip one house, they lose money, and they quit the business.

While no one can ever truly say with 100 percent certainty that they are going to make such and such amount of money on a flip, you can make sure that you have planned and prepared properly, and wait to buy a house until you find one that is in your target neighborhood and priced so that you can fix and resell it for a profit. If you do this, you will have already put yourself a category above most beginning flippers who barge into the field without bothering to do any research first.

Defining a Target Price

Most flippers use something known as the *70 percent rule* when trying to figure out if a house is a good deal and can be successfully flipped or not. We're only talking in terms of the numbers here, not all the other factors and intangibles we've been discussing that also play a role in shaping how desirable your finished flip is to potential buyers. Just in terms of the hard numbers, to make sure you end up with a profit, you should follow the 70 percent rule and know your home's *ARV.*

DEFINITION

The **70 percent rule** is a formula flippers, Realtors, and investors use to determine if a house is suitable for flipping. You should pay no more than 70 percent of a home's after repaired value (ARV) to acquire the home. The 70 percent rule helps you calculate the maximum amount you should pay for a home if you want to make money on the deal.

After repaired value (ARV) is what a property will be worth once all the necessary repairs and optional upgrades have been made. It's vitally important to know your approximate ARV on any property you are considering so you can determine if you'll make a profit from flipping that house.

Here's how to figure the ARV and use it with the 70 percent rule to determine if a house is a good deal or not. No matter how much you like a house or how great a deal it might seem to you, if you cannot make the numbers work, you shouldn't do the deal. Move on to the next house and make a deal there.

Make sure the numbers you are working with are accurate. It helps to err on the side of caution. If one heating contractor says a replacement furnace will cost $4,000 and another quotes $5,000, use the $5,000 figure to be on the safe side. This is not padding your budget. This is putting safety bumpers into it.

You know your purchase price, and should know your ERC or estimated repair costs. By running comparables, you can get a good idea of what the house will sell for after you rehab it. That is your ARV or after repaired value. Multiply the ARV by .7 (in other words, 70 percent), then deduct the estimated repair costs. The resulting sum is the maximum amount you should pay for the house to end up with a profitable deal at the end.

For example, say your ARV is $200,000 and your repairs and renovations are estimated to cost $40,000.

$$\$200,000 \times .7 = \$140,000 \text{ - the } \$40,000 \text{ ERC.}$$

That leaves you a total of $100,000 you can actually afford to spend to buy the house. You can fudge $1,000 or $2,000 on either side of that number, but go much more and you can end up with a loss once all the bills associated with the flip are paid.

A lot of people try to talk themselves out of using this tried and true rule. They convince themselves they don't really need the full $40,000 in repairs, or they can actually pay $120,000 for a house even though the formula says $100,000. But in reality, you often need even more money to fully repair a house, even with a substantial contingency budget built in, so we don't recommend scrimping on any part of this formula. And remember, if you are willing to pay $20,000 over the recommended formula price just to land a house, you will be doing the renovation mostly for grins and giggles. There won't be much of a profit left to divide when you are done because you sank most of the profit into an overly expensive purchase price.

Now you're probably asking yourself where you're going to find a $100,000 house in a neighborhood of homes that routinely sell for $200,000. We assure you, they are out there. If they were not, there would be no such thing as the flipping business. But it does take hard work, lots of research, persistence, and patience to find these gems. That is one of your primary jobs as a flipper, to keep a steady stream of flip-worthy homes coming in so you can keep your team members busy and happy.

> **FLIP TIP**
>
> Time management is an integral part of the flipping business. Unless you have a project manager, it's one of your primary jobs. If you complete a successful flip but don't yet have the next one lined up, you're going to lose your contractor and work crews to someone else's job. They can't afford to sit around waiting and earning nothing while you lollygag about looking for your next flip. Always think ahead to stay on top in this business.

If you tweak the numbers just so you can justify making a deal, you're going to wind up in a hole financially speaking or else make way less on the flip than you promised your investor you would make. Believe me when we say it's never a good idea to disappoint your investor. If they find out you've given them inaccurate numbers just to land the financing, they'll never give you another penny. Nor will any of their investor friends, because bad news really does travel fast.

You cannot fool the numbers. Sooner or later inaccurate or fudged numbers are going to trip you up. If the hole you dig yourself is deep enough, one bad flip might even end your flipping career.

Assessing Your Risk Tolerance

Flipping is an unusual business in that it demands seemingly contradictory personality traits. On the one hand, you must be conservative with your numbers to avoid getting yourself into trouble. Yet, sometimes you just have to go with your gut instincts and dive head first off the end of the pier to make a deal come together.

Where conservative traits are needed is in the realm of budgeting, spending, and investment. Where a perhaps more adventuresome spirit is called for is in deal making, decorating, and marketing your flip. You have to figure out your own risk tolerance to know the path that best suits you.

We love flipping because it can be a lot of fun, and bring in great financial and social benefits. It's a busy job and you never get bored. It provides a great mix of indoor desk time and outdoor active time. To me, there's nothing more rewarding than watching a rundown house come back to life, except selling that house to a family overjoyed that they've finally found a house they love at a price they can afford in the neighborhood they want. That's a priceless moment and as a flipper, you get to experience it over and over again. It's the main reason we do it, that and the great return on investment we can earn when we do a flip correctly from start to finish.

But it's only fair to mention, there can be a downside to flipping. It's more than just a business filled with risks. It's also a stressful business. You're a little like a general during a battle. You have all these chess pieces moving about the board, and you have to keep up with all of them. If you neglect one, then that part of the flip could suffer or fall apart.

 FLIPPER BEWARE

> If you're a person who dislikes stress and hates taking risks, perhaps you should reconsider your decision to try flipping houses. Even on the best days, flipping has inherent risks, such as the possibility of losing money instead of earning some. And as for stress, it's pretty much constant until you get that check in your hand at the sale. Then, you divide the proceeds, and it starts all over again. If this doesn't sound like something you would enjoy, perhaps it would be best to pass it by.

For example, if you keep forgetting to order the flooring because you're so busy lining up repairs for an unexpected major plumbing problem, when your contractor tells you he's ready for the floors, you won't be. Then you'll be scrambling around and telling yourself it's alright to go with contractor-grade flooring from a big box store that can be delivered the next day. You might have kept the project on track timewise, but when you go to sell the property, the cheap flooring will turn off your target customers. And believe us when we say your prospective buyers will be aware of almost every corner you cut in your rush to finish on time. Today's buyers watch the same television shows you do and are difficult to fool.

If you're beginning to think that in many ways, flipping houses is like juggling plates, you're not too far off the mark. But if you do manage to keep them all up in the air, at the end of the flip one of those plates might be stacked with money!

Setting Limits on Spending

As we've discussed, it's difficult to put an exact amount on the total cost of a flip due to so many factors contributing to the final cost. However, you can go a long way toward insuring profitability by being responsible and adhering to the spending limits you laid out in your original budget.

One place where it's essential to maintain firm spending limits is at a property auction. It's far too easy to get caught up in the excitement and overpay for a hotly contested property. Remembering that you have to pay for the property in full at the end of the auction should help mitigate any urge to overspend you might feel.

> **FLIP TIP**
>
> If you have trouble keeping your paddle out of the air at an auction, bring along an auction buddy whose only job is to keep you within your spending limits. It can be an enjoyable and very effective way to ensure you don't blow your budget in the heat of an auction.

Any deviations from your budget should be due to additional expenses, such as unexpected repairs (which should actually be covered under your contingency budget) and not because you decided to switch from the $7-per-linear-foot laminate to the primo $10-per-foot stuff simply because you like it better.

Managing your budget is the area of flipping that requires the most self-discipline, especially if you like to shop. You will not be able to buy everything you see, no matter how much you love it. Buy the best materials you can for the budget you have allocated and be done with it. If you're really successful with flipping as a result of being so budget conscious, once the flip is sold, you can afford to go back and buy that material you loved so much and have it installed in your own house!

The Art of the Offer

All your research and hard work have brought you here. Now it's time to review the due diligence you've performed to make sure the numbers work with your prospective flip. Then you'll be ready to make an offer on your first house!

Contact your Realtor and tell him you want to place an offer. Provide the address of the property and how much you want to offer. Specify if you're making an all-cash offer or if you will be using financing. If you're financing, tell your Realtor how much you want to put down. He needs this information in order to write the offer and present it.

Be prepared to write a check for the deposit or *earnest money* if your offer is successful. Your Realtor must deliver this check to the seller's agent within 24 hours of the contract being signed, or you could lose the house.

> **DEFINITION**
>
> **Earnest money** is a small deposit made to confirm that a person placing an offer on a home is serious about buying the house and acting in good faith. If they follow through and the house goes to act of sale, this money is applied to the sales price. If the buyer defaults on the sale, they lose their deposit, which goes to the seller as compensation for their property having been held off the market. Typically, earnest money deposits are 1 to 2 percent of the total purchase price of a property.

Tell your Realtor if you have any wiggle room on the price. For example, you offer $100,000 to begin with, but the 70 percent rule indicates you could safely go up to $110,000 and still have a successful flip. Tell your Realtor about that extra $10,000 sitting in your back pocket. They won't always spend it, but if they need it to secure the purchase of your house, it saves time if you've already authorized them to negotiate for you within that limit.

We've seen offers where the Realtor being able to negotiate on behalf of a flipper saved the sale. While other Realtors are on the phone with their clients trying to see if they can shake out another $5,000 to $10,000 to work with, your Realtor will be able to quickly seal the deal because they're able to respond quickly to a fast-moving and highly competitive negotiation.

This is where an experienced professional Realtor can really shine, in securing a highly desirable property for you that many people wanted. If you are not a Realtor, or don't have one on your team, you will always come out on the bottom of complex negotiations because you haven't got the experience, contacts, or negotiation skills to close a deal on a hot property quickly.

 FLIPPER BEWARE

Many new flippers, particularly those from the building trades, believe they can save big bucks by not using a Realtor. Your expenses will be lower if you eliminate them, but we can tell you flipping teams without a Realtor don't fare as well. A Realtor brings you the best deals and can wrangle a purchase offer like no one else, because that's their business. Their knowledge and experience keep you from wasting money and making mistakes, and they should be paid for that expertise.

Sometimes, your financial arrangements will allow you to make a full-price all-cash offer. Sellers place a premium on all-cash offers because they go to act of sale faster, and there are no worries about financing falling through. Generally, you will have to obtain financing, and your Realtor will end up negotiating strategic offers until an agreement is reached. It's natural that you want to pay the least you can for the property and that the seller wants to sell for as much as he can get. You'll meet somewhere in the middle, and your Realtor will facilitate this. They can also tell you when a seller is being hopelessly unrealistic about the value of his property, and when it's time to walk away from negotiations.

Of course, the dynamics and procedures change if there are multiple bidders on a property. If a house is highly desirable, a lot of flippers will place offers, and the bidding will be more urgent. In this situation, come in as fast as you can with an all-cash full-price offer if your investor has already authorized such a move. However, only go forward if the numbers work with the 70 percent rule. If a negotiation flies past your maximum bid, no matter how much you want the house, walk away.

Getting Ready for Your First Act of Sale

Once you have a completed sales contract signed by all the parties, all that is left is to wait for the act of sale. Then you will be able start working on your first flip.

While you are waiting, you must take care of several chores in order to be fully ready when the first workday arrives. Let's review them now.

Insurance Coverage

Contact your insurance agent and ask what sort of insurance you need. If you have financed your purchase, you will not even be allowed to complete the act of sale if you don't have hazard and property insurance in place on the house you are buying. Some companies won't issue policies on houses that are being rehabbed due to an elevated risk of theft and vandalism on such projects.

Once you do find an agent willing to write a policy, make it substantial enough to cover the entire replacement cost of the structure and all the materials you put into it. If you should suffer a total loss, such as a floor or fire, this type of policy will cover all your losses.

If your house is going to sit vacant for a while, be sure to keep it fully insured. It's still subject to most of the same hazards as occupied properties.

Don't forget make sure your contractor carries workers' compensation insurance to provide for any workers who might get injured on your job.

Financial Matters

The handling of finances can vary from flipper to flipper and investor to investor. Some investors are comfortable handing over a lump sum amount to a flipping partner and don't want to hear another word until the profits are ready to be paid out. Others dole the money out a few hundred at a time and want to personally see all the bills and write out all the checks. Your situation will likely fall somewhere between these two extremes.

Some accountants recommend opening a new checking account for each new flip, to easily keep all the expenses associated with that house in one spot. Others argue that's a lot of extra work, and any good CPA or bookkeeper can sort out the expenses with proper receipts. Meet with your financial team members prior to the act of sale to see how they prefer to manage the handling of money, bills, and expenses on your flip.

Of course, if you financed the purchase of the property, use this time to complete the loan process so that you will have the necessary funds to go to the act of sale.

Getting Your Team Ready

Don't wait until the night before work starts on your flip to let your team know you expect them on the job. Contractors and work crews are all very busy most of the time, especially if flipping has become popular in your location. Consult with your contractor as soon as your offer on the property is accepted. Let him know the date of the act of sale and together, create a work schedule for the project. By giving him a 4-week heads up, you're allowing plenty of time for a reasonable schedule to be established and followed as work proceeds on your flip.

Ordering Materials

Meet with your contractor to determine which materials will be needed on-site for the start of the work. Review your schedule and make sure you and your contractor agree on what materials will be needed when. To reduce the risk of theft, only order materials that will be used within 24 to 48 hours. Leaving expensive items, such as uninstalled appliances, lying around your property for several days is an invitation to thieves, so manage your materials schedule very tightly, and only order things as they are needed.

The Least You Need to Know

- This is the time when you will truly activate your team.
- Know the potential for profit and a quick sale before you buy a house.
- Never spend so much money buying a house that you have no chance of making a profit on the flip.
- Don't neglect the required due diligence on a property.
- Base your offers to buy on the 70 percent rule to maximize your chances for success.

CHAPTER 12

How Much Are You Willing (and Able) to Do?

First-time flippers who are long on dreams and short on cash think they can do most of the work on a rehab themselves. While it's easy enough to wield a crowbar during demolition or pick up a paintbrush, most jobs should be left to professionals. Too many renovations have turned into money-sucking disasters because a flipper tried to handle a job above his skill set and ended up ruining something. It's faster and cheaper to call in the pros from the beginning and let them do the job right.

Don't forget that whatever repairs you do personally still have to pass inspection, so if your workmanship is shoddy or you try to get away with using sub-par materials, that can come back to haunt you and cost you even more cash before you're done.

Plan your repairs and renovation carefully. As you inspect the house, take note of any work you can do but check with your contractor. Some don't appreciate a flipper mucking around, gumming up the job with amateur efforts. Others are more open to help, but only if you actually know what you're doing.

Remember, time is money. If you're busy tiling a bath when you could be out looking for your next flip, you're losing money.

In This Chapter

- The art of the thorough inspection
- Plan everything before you start work
- Choosing a flipper-friendly contractor
- The importance of careful budgeting
- Should you always hire professionals?

Assessing Repair and Renovation Needs

One of the jobs you must tackle soon after you close on your first house is performing a thorough inventory of the repairs that must be made to the property, as well as any new features and amenities you want to be part of the renovation.

You already have an idea of repairs needed from the pre-purchase inspection. Now go back with your contractor again, and dig down to the basics. You must accurately determine your repair and renovation costs before you start the flip, and the only way to do this is with a thorough inspection. If your inspection is hurried or slipshod, you could watch your profits disappear as your costs escalate upon finding more hidden damage. This is the nightmare scenario everyone fears, the scenario that makes many aspiring flippers a "one and done" flipper with thousands of dollars in debt to pay off. A hurried inspection leads to inadequate planning and budgeting, and then unexpected problems crop up and put the entire project into the red.

This is exactly the opposite of how you want things to go on a rehab. Good preparation now will reduce the risk of you ever finding yourself in this situation.

> **FLIP TIP**
>
> Make note of all necessary repairs as you walk the property, so that you can check your list against the bid your contractor gives you, to make sure all the repairs you want to make have a bid on them.

Presale inspections, particularly of foreclosed properties, are not done under ideal conditions, so it's easy to miss things. You must inspect the property now to know what must be done. This second inspection always reveals more than the first and helps you prepare a more accurate working budget.

Start on the Outside

First, assess what repairs are needed to the exterior of the home. Here are some things you should note:

- How does the roof look?

- Are there loose shingles?

- Is the soffit and fascia in good shape or rotted out?

- Are the gutters and downspouts free of rust and firmly attached to the house?

- Do the exterior spigots and lighting fixtures work? How about the siding, stucco, or bricks? Are they in good shape, or do they need replacing?

- Is the garage door intact and easy to open and close? Does it have a working automatic garage door opener?

- Does the exterior trim of the house look good or does it have areas of dry rot?

- Is there any obvious termite damage anywhere?

- Does the house need to be repainted?

- Check the porches, stairs, and stair railings, along with any decks or any other exterior features of the house or yard. Make note of every thing that needs repair or replacement.

Now move on to the yard and landscaping. Note the following:

- How does the lawn look?

- Is the grass okay or does the yard need new sod?

- How about the flowerbeds and trees?

- Do you need to replace the mulch in the gardens?

- Are there any dead trees that must be removed or overgrown shrubs that need trimming?

- Does the fence require repair or replacement?

All these jobs must be included in your overall repair estimate.

FLIP TIP

If your concrete features, such as the driveway, sidewalks, and patio are structurally sound, but look grungy because of stains, you don't always have to replace them. First try pressure washing. If that doesn't get rid of the stains, hire a professional to resurface the driveway. You can save about 40 percent over the cost of replacing these features when you resurface instead. They will end up looking brand new.

Now check the hardscaping and note the following:

- Are there cracks in the driveway, patio, sidewalks, or walkways that need repair?

- Is the damage so bad that the entire feature must be removed and replaced?

- Does the concrete require pressure washing?

- Are there landscaping features, such as pools, fountains, or garden statuary that need repair or replacement?

You should also remember to include some budget to enhance your property's curb appeal with new flowers, shrubs, mulch for the gardens, and so on. You can find a complete checklist with all interior and exterior items in Appendix C.

Once you have the answers to all these questions, you'll have a good idea of what you need to spend to get the outside of the house looking great again.

Check Out the Inside

If you purchased a home that only needs a standard cosmetic upgrade, you just made your life a lot easier. For a flipper this means completely new kitchen and baths, including new appliances, plumbing fixtures and sinks, new cabinets, countertops, new flooring (carpet, laminate, or vinyl), paint, new lighting fixtures, and if needed, new doors and windows.

In many cases though, your interior is also going to require some repairs or major construction in addition to a cosmetic polish. For example, if you bought an old house chopped up into many small rooms, you might want to remove a wall to give the living area a more open feel. Removing a wall and installing a load-bearing beam in its place is an expensive proposition, but that one change can definitely increase buyer interest and also allow you to charge more for the finished flip.

> **FLIPPER BEWARE**
>
> If there is "popcorn" on the ceilings and your house was built prior to 1978, be aware that the texture probably contains asbestos. In 1978, ceilings made with asbestos fibers were banned, because asbestos is a known carcinogen. If the ceiling is intact, it poses no danger and can be left as is. However, popcorn ceilings can kill a sale, so it's better to hire an asbestos abatement professional to remove the ceiling and have it retextured with one of the smoother patterns now in favor.

Follow a checklist much as you did for the exterior:

- Walk through room by room making note of the condition of the walls, floors, ceilings, doors, baseboards and trim, lighting fixtures, and so on.

- Open and close every door to make sure each one fits snugly within its frame, but doesn't stick.

- Turn on every light, flush all the toilets, and test every faucet and drain.

- Look for water stains that could indicate a leak.

- Don't forget to check the attic, basement, and garage, if the property has them, and also look over the insulation, electric panel, ductwork, pipes, and wiring.

- Inspect all the mechanical elements of the house as well, including the furnace, air conditioner, and water heater.

Make note of any problems you find.

Replace all light switches, electrical outlets, and faceplates throughout the house. These get grubby from years of use, and it is a waste of time and can even be dangerous to try and clean them. It makes no sense to spend all the money on a complete rehab if you're going to overlook one detail that can make an otherwise spectacular flip look off. No one is impressed by a beautiful room that has a dirty light switch.

Develop a Renovation Plan

The next step is developing a renovation plan for the house. Many flippers skip this step. They repair and replace but leave the original floor plan and room configuration. When you've been rehabbing houses as long as we have, you'll realize there are some really weird houses out there, so weird you wonder what the guys who built them were smoking. You question how people ever lived in such strange spaces, and know most modern families would not, so you make a renovation plan.

We've seen "bedrooms" so tiny you couldn't fit a bed in them, only a crib, and hallways so narrow you practically have to fold a mattress in half to get it into a bedroom. Many older houses have four to five bedrooms upstairs, but only one downstairs bathroom. That was a popular Victorian arrangement. Or they have a master bedroom, but no master bath. That's just how houses used to be built, but modern buyers see these oddities as real deficits and pass over houses where they haven't been corrected.

These are things that, as a flipper, you will instantly know have to be corrected if you are going to get top dollar for your house. This is where your renovation plan comes in.

What form your renovation plan takes is up to you and your contractor. Many contractors are comfortable just talking about what is needed, with perhaps a sketch drawn on a fast food napkin to guide the way, but we don't recommend working this way until you have become very familiar with how your contractor works. Others insist on having a set of blueprints.

FLIP TIP

If you hire an architect to draw plans for your rehab, make it clear you are commissioning the blueprint only and that your contractor will handle the permitting and oversight of the construction. Having an architect do those jobs is more expensive than having your contractor do them.

If you're going to have blueprints drawn, hire a draftsman or an architect. Architects are more expensive to use, averaging $130 per hour versus $100 per hour for draftsmen. Plans drawn by a draftsman must be approved by both a licensed architect and a structural engineer before they can be used to build or renovate a structure, so that is an added expense on the back end. If you are doing a high-end flip and really want to attract buyers who will spend high six-figures to low seven figures for a renovated house, you definitely should consider investing the money to have an architect draw your blueprint.

Get Multiple Bids

Now that you have an accurate idea of what needs to be done in your house, it's time to find out how much it will all cost. It's fine if you haven't yet actually settled on your contractor at this point. You're brand new and it's reasonable for you to want to get a fair price on the labor and materials required to complete your rehab. Interview several contractors to see which one you work with best and who gives you the most attractive bid (which might not always be the cheapest one).

Get bids from three different contractors for all the work needed on your property. About 50 percent of the bid your general contractor provides is for labor and 50 percent is to cover the cost of materials. And of course, his profit is worked in there as well.

One important tip when choosing a contractor … select someone who's open to working with flippers. Some are not. They take your job, but give you nothing but attitude the whole way through. Needless to say, a less than friendly contractor can ruin what should be a positive experience. Take your time to choose a contractor you like and feel comfortable with. And if you hire someone and are not pleased with either the quality of his work or how the two of you work together, don't be afraid to part ways with him and hire a new contractor.

> **FLIP TIP**
>
> When your contractor assesses the cost of repairs, have him price the cost of replacing everything in the house, even if you have no intention of doing so. This can protect you down the road. If you have written estimates for all repairs in hand and then find hidden damage during demolition or rehab, you already know the price to repair it. This prevents a contractor from taking advantage of the situation by tacking on a few hundred or even a few thousand dollars to an urgent job he knows must get done.

You might be surprised to see the range of bids you receive for the same job. Some contractors are just more expensive than others. Find one you like that you can afford, and hire him.

What Materials Will You Use?

When it comes to the creative part of your design, you can let your imagination soar and do a majority of the work yourself. You have your own unique vision and should be the person who selects materials and finishes to help bring it to life. This is one of the most enjoyable parts of the flip to me, bringing the color and design scheme together to create a particular look and feel for the interior and exterior of a property.

But if you might don't understand how to select a new furnace, water heater, or electrical panel, you can leave the selection and purchase of technical items to your contractor. Just make sure he stays within the allocated budget for the items he buys.

Repair and renovation costs can vary greatly depending upon the materials you choose. If you need 1,500 square feet of carpet and have allocated $3 per square yard for a medium-grade carpet, let your contractor know so he doesn't buy a $4-per-square-yard carpet instead. Your contractor, needs your budget numbers and the quality of materials you want to use in the rehab before he can give you an accurate estimate for the job.

Starting out, many flippers ask a contractor to use investor-grade materials, the typical sort of light fixtures, appliances, carpet, tile, cabinets, and plumbing fixtures you see in every *tract home.* That might be okay with potential buyers if you are working in a middle class suburban neighborhood and they're just looking for a clean, attractive, and affordable home. But you can hurt your chances of a quick full-price sale by being too cheap with the materials you select on more iconic homes, such as old Craftsman models, or vintage one-of-a-kind homes in historic neighborhoods. If you have a house like this, then you must choose higher-end materials that suit both the house and the neighborhood or run the risk of not selling the finished home. All those gorgeous houses you love on HGTV were not made irresistible to buyers with $99 vanities from a big box store.

> **DEFINITION**
>
> A **tract home** is one of many similar homes built on a large tract of land subdivided into small lots. Because developers use only four or so floor plans for an entire community, even if it has thousands of houses, tract developments became infamous for having a cookie cutter look.

Obviously, a kitchen with top-of-the-line appliances, a farmhouse sink, designer faucet and lighting, solid wood cabinets and floors, and top-grade granite countertops is going to cost a lot more than a kitchen with builder-grade appliances, standard lighting and sink, vinyl flooring, Formica countertops, and particle board cabinets. You might be able to do the less expensive one for $15,000, while the designer kitchen could cost as much as $50,000 to $80,000 or even more.

Why would you ever choose to do the $80,000 upgrade? Because the two kitchens will attract different kinds of buyers, and there's a place in flipping for both of them. Just make sure the materials you choose fit your project. If you are too tightly focused on the bottom line and mistakenly put the $15,000 kitchen in a house and a neighborhood that clearly calls for the $80,000 kitchen, then your savings will get eaten up while the property sits on the market as puzzled buyers pass it by.

If you're still unsure which way to go in materials selection, visit open houses for flipped homes in the same neighborhood as yours to check out the kind and quality of materials your competitors are using. Don't copy their designs or choices, just get an idea of what they are using in their flips. This research can serve as a very valuable guideline until you become more familiar with choosing your own materials.

Estimating Costs

Now that you have gathered all the information you need, it's time to estimate the cost of the repairs and renovation. You've already done most of the work. You should have all the estimates for materials from your suppliers—flooring, appliances, plumbing and lighting fixtures, paint, landscaping, and so on. You also have an itemized bid from your contractor that outlines what the contractor is going to repair and renovate, and what materials he is going to use to do it. Add these together and you'll have a fair idea of your total costs to rehab the property. Now add 10 to 25 percent and you will have a realistic budget.

Why add so much money to the budget when we already have everything covered? The entire additional amount is allocated to a single line item called contingencies. Every flip has them—the unexpected repairs you don't discover until you start the demo, the bad weather that threw your schedule off by 6 weeks and doubled your carrying costs—how are you going to pay for them unless you already have money allocated to do so?

Flippers who don't budget for contingencies are flippers who lose money. One surprise repair can turn a flip where you expected a $20,000 profit into a money-losing proposition. It can signal an abrupt end to your flipping career, because who can afford to lose thousands of dollars on a flip? So be sure to budget for contingencies on every flip you do. If you get wildly lucky and don't have to spend any of the contingency money, it just adds to the profitability of the project.

 FLIPPER BEWARE

Be sure the bids you receive from your contractors are itemized, detailed, and complete, including breakdowns on the cost of materials and the exact types of materials that will be used. If you accept a bid that is not specific, you are giving the contractor room to make more money by using cheaper materials. That can happen when you don't insist on a detailed materials list along with the bid.

Once you agree to the contractor's bid, sign a written contract so both of you know what the agreement is. If disagreements arise down the road, it's much easier to clear them up if you have a signed, detailed contract in hand.

Use all this information to draw up a project budget, and stick to it! You already know there will be unexpected expenses, sometimes increasing your costs by as much as 25 percent. But if you're smart, you already have that 25 percent contingency figured into your budget.

DIY vs. Hiring Professionals

We discussed this briefly earlier in this chapter but want to explore the topic more fully. Some new flippers are convinced they can maximize profits if they do most of the work on a flip themselves. Like Tom Sawyer, they host a party to get their flip painted, but how many of your friends know how to properly paint a home interior, much less an exterior with its scary heights and different textures? Not many.

If you were buying a new house, wouldn't you want a home with a great paint job inside and out? Would you be willing to settle for a house that had streaks on the walls and uneven coverage, with paint splotches splattered across the floor? Most of us would choose the professional paint job every time.

Yet, even knowing this, newbies who are trying to do a flip on an overly tight budget somehow manage to convince themselves that they can get away with doing most of the work themselves.

The simple truth is that DIY work is often not done well. Buyers insist on professional standards and so do building inspectors, so how do you think you are going to get a pass on this?

The larger problem is that what you believe is saving you money can cost you more. If you and your friends do a terrible paint job, the money you spent on the job is wasted. Now you have to go buy *more* paint and supplies and hire a professional painter to correct the bad paint job. Oh, and correcting mistakes costs more than having the job done by a pro in the first place.

 FLIPPER BEWARE

Many of the jobs associated with rehabbing a house are dangerous. If you're afraid of heights, stay off ladders, and if you value your limbs and don't know how to use power tools, leave that to the pros, too.

Let's imagine you are the best trim carpenter in the history of the world. Maybe you even made a good living as a trim carpenter before you decided to try flipping, so you are determined to do your own carpentry on your flip. That seems reasonable, but if you spend all your time on the job doing trim carpentry, then you are no longer flipping, and the rest of the project can slide away from you while you are otherwise engaged. You could hire a project manager to oversee the job for you, but if you are counting every penny, that's not a practical solution.

Some of you might think that the flippers on HGTV do a lot of their own work. That's how it appears, but remember, the director tells the star to turn on the saw for a 30-second shot. Then it's turned off and the real workers come finish the job.

We can tell you from our own personal experience, how it appears on television is not necessarily how it happens in the real world. Find a contractor you like, do all the planning and oversee the job, but you let him and his crews do the work.

We are not saying you can't do any work on your flip, just that if you do, do it professionally and be careful of how much time and attention it takes from other critical aspects of your work.

Dividing the Labor

As you prepare your list of repairs and renovations, try to assess if there are any jobs you can do to save money. But we have a big caveat. Tackle a job if you have enough skill to produce professional results.

For example, if you have masonry skills and know how to use a wet saw, your help could make the work go more quickly. But if you are all thumbs with a hammer and frightened by power tools, your presence on the job as a "worker" will slow things down.

Almost anyone can do jobs such as mowing the lawn and tearing out old cabinets or tile. It's a good way for you to pitch in if you really want to help and need to save on labor costs.

Any job that requires specific skills and training, or that requires a licensed person to perform the work should be left to professionals. If you've never laid tile; hung siding; replaced roofing shingles; or installed underground pipes or a window, a sink, light fixtures, or a door, leave those jobs to those who actually know how to do them correctly, first time and every time.

What Can You Actually Do?

Like most jobs associated with flipping, deciding what jobs you can actually handle is a task best managed with a list. Talk to your contractor for ideas.

It's easy to find things you can do. For example, if you've purchased a sight-unseen rehab, only to discover the tenants wrecked the place before they left, hauling out all the trash and cleaning up is a perfect job for you, family members, and friends. It's tough work physically speaking, but you don't have to have a license in trash hauling to be able to do it.

Or, try sprucing up the yard, trimming shrubs, weeding the gardens. During demolition, you can help tear out cabinets, remove old tile, unscrew switch covers and faceplates on the electrical outlets, or any other job your contractor suggests that will keep you productive but also out of the way.

> **FLIP TIP**
>
> A house undergoing rehab is a worksite. Like any other worksite, there are inherent dangers. Keep safety a top priority during your flips, both your own and that of the contractors and work crews. Sometimes, being mindful of safety means staying out of the workers' way and letting them do their jobs without interference from you.

If you're stumped for ideas, sit down and list your skills. If you can use some power tools safely and comfortably, list that. But don't be surprised if your contractor doesn't want your "help." In the time it takes you to measure and cut one board, an experienced pro might have measured and cut four.

What Must You Hire Out?

No matter how skilled you think you are, leave work involving plumbing and electricity to professionals. These jobs must be performed by licensed master plumbers and electricians, and will be inspected by someone who is also a top-level pro in the field. Your half-baked duct tape job is not going to get you a green pass card saying your home is ready for move-in, so don't waste time trying to save money in these important arenas.

Also, consider hiring out other skilled work such as carpentry, masonry, tile work, flooring installation, any work that requires a specific set of skills to be performed by an experienced craftsman who can deliver a high quality job.

The Least You Need to Know

- Start with a complete overall plan.
- Let your contractor help you estimate costs accurately.
- Be realistic about your own work skills.
- Save plumbing and electrical jobs for the pros.
- Always put extra money in your budget to cover the cost of unexpected contingencies.

PART 3

Demolition and Renovation

Every part of the flipping business is interesting, but perhaps none is so intense as the demolition and renovation of a property. It's amazing to watch the transformation of a house from a rundown heap of bricks to an eye-catching home that hopeful buyers battle to win. It's almost like giving the house CPR as it rises from the ashes of ruin and is restored to life, ready to welcome in a new family. As a flipper, you have the privilege of watching these amazing transformations first hand. It's an enormously satisfying experience, and the fact that you also get paid to do it makes flipping a near-perfect job in my opinion.

CHAPTER 13

Permit or Perish

First-time flippers sometimes make the mistake of not getting the permits they need before starting work on a house. They might believe that because they own a house, they can do anything they want to it. This is not true.

Building codes were established to protect the rights of home-buyers and to keep them safe from accidents and potential dangers caused by shoddy or substandard workmanship. Permits are the way that everyone involved—the flipper, the contractor, the inspector, and the home's future owners—all know without a doubt that the repairs and renovations on a home meet the precise standards set out by the codes in that particular municipality.

It's the building inspector's job to ensure all applicable codes are followed and that work is done professionally using quality materials. If it's not, your house will not pass inspection and you will be unable to offer it for sale or allow it to be occupied until the required repairs have been made and all substandard work and materials have been brought up to code.

In This Chapter

- Defining building codes
- Why are building codes necessary?
- Other required approvals
- What permits do you need?
- Where you get permits and how much they cost

You must obtain a permit for all the work you plan to do on your flip. There are no exceptions to this. Unless you think an inspector telling you to tear out your gorgeous but unpermitted new $25,000 bathroom might be fun, better make sure you have all your permits lined up before you swing that sledgehammer.

As you read this chapter, remember the information provided here is general. Building codes do vary, sometimes significantly, from locale to locale. Review your local codes before you start your first project, and make sure all jobs associated with your flip have the proper permits in place before you start the work.

What Are Building Codes?

If you are not familiar with the construction trades, it might be difficult for you to understand why building codes, permits, and inspections are required. In the early history of the United States, a number of tragedies occurred in substandard buildings—some resulting in great loss of life. In the aftermath, shoddy building practices were blamed for the collapsing buildings, for substandard wiring causing disastrous fires, for people being trapped in burning buildings because there were not adequate fire exits, among other problems. This list of accidents continued to mount until it became a full-fledged public scandal. Citizens demanded reform and demanded protection from builders who took their money and delivered poor quality work.

Some of the loudest voices demanding reform came from insurers who were tired of paying out claims on poorly constructed buildings. They called for building standards to be enacted and enforced in order to reduce the number of claims. They were deeply influential in helping enact the necessary legislative reforms to ensure minimum building safety standards nationwide.

Building codes emerged from these scandals. In 1905, the National Board of Fire Examiners approved the first National Building Code. It was quite comprehensive and professionally done. Many state legislatures adopted it for their own use. It was intended to protect public welfare, enforce a high standard of safety and quality in building, and put an end to the tragedies that had claimed so many lives. And it worked.

> **FLIP TIP**
>
> King Hammurabi of Babylon enacted the first known building code in 1758 B.C.E. It stated that if a builder built a house for a man and the house was not strong, and collapsed and killed its occupants, the builder would be slain as a punishment for bad workmanship. Needless to say, builders in ancient Babylon crafted only high-quality dwellings after this code was published and enforced a few times.

Building codes set out minimum standards for construction and materials that must be used to build residential and commercial buildings. They are detailed and precise. Though they do vary somewhat from state to state, county to county, and town to town, all building codes define what steps must be followed during construction and what materials must be used to make a building safe for habitation and public use.

Modern building codes are rarely just one rule or one document. They can be comprised of a complex series of legal documents specifying requirements for the construction of any given building. There are separate codes covering the installation of plumbing, natural gas lines, electrical systems, mechanical systems such as HVAC and fire alarm systems, along with a code laying out the general safety and quality requirements for the construction of the overall building itself.

Although building codes are now monitored and enforced at local levels, most states do maintain licensing or proficiency standards for building inspectors. While not every state requires that building inspectors be licensed, all do require proof of proficiency in their area of specialty. Almost every municipality that administers and enforces building codes requires that its inspectors to be licensed or possess demonstrable expertise in the type of construction they inspect.

Two Potential Speed Bumps

Before you apply for your permits, we need to discuss a couple of other subjects—design review boards and zoning compliance. What if you invest thousands of dollars to get all your permits approved, only to find out the neighborhood design review board doesn't like your design and won't approve it? Or, what if your plans violate neighborhood zoning ordinances? Better to find out now so you can bring your plans into compliance and get approval prior to spending money on building permits you cannot use.

Design Review Boards

Design review boards are a group of neighborhood residents that review, and approve or disapprove, all plans for building and renovation in their community. They ensure all building activity complies with their covenants. Their oversight helps maintain the community's specific look and feel and also helps to maintain consistent property values.

If you're working in a seaside community where the covenants specify that residences cannot be any taller than 15 feet to preserve water views for as many people as possible, you won't be able to get a second story addition approved because that would interfere with someone else's view. Even if you already have your two-story plans approved by your local municipality, it won't do you a bit of good because the authority of the design board in this instance supersedes the authority of the permitting office.

Design boards control everything from the color you can paint your house to the type of roofing, shingles, and siding you use.

> **FLIP TIP**
>
> It's especially important to get approval for your renovation plans if you are working in a neighborhood designated as a historic landmark area. There are very specific design requirements for such neighborhoods. In order to preserve the harmonious and historic appearance of the area, no deviation from those requirements is allowed.

Check with the community association in the neighborhood where you are working and ask about their review process. Not every neighborhood has design review boards, but if yours has one, you absolutely must work with them and get their approval for your plans prior to applying for any necessary building permits.

It's impossible to list all the requirements for the tens of thousands of such boards that exist in America. Before you go to the trouble and expense of applying for building permits, make sure the plans you submit to get your permits have already been reviewed and approved by the presiding design review board.

Zoning Compliance

You also need to check that your demolition and renovation plans comply with local zoning ordinances. Before you have your work plans drawn up, check the local zoning laws to make sure your proposed work will be allowed.

Many local zoning boards offer online applications to speed the approval process. Each community is governed by its own zoning laws. It's up to you to find out what those laws are and to make sure your project is in compliance with them. Contact the zoning board prior to starting any work to determine what the local process is, and what you must do to ensure your project is in compliance prior to applying for your building permits.

It's far better to address potential zoning problems at this stage, before you invest time or money in plans or actual work. This is far preferable to discovering later that your addition must be torn down because it violates local zoning ordinances.

What Permits Are Required?

The number and type of permits you need depends on the type and amount of demolition and work you plan to do. At the very least, every house needs a building permit and permits for any planned electrical, plumbing, or mechanical work. If you are making significant structural changes to the property, such as moving a load-bearing wall, then you'll need a special structural changes permit. If you're making any additions to the building, you must apply for a new construction or an additions permit. All renovations will require a renovation permit.

Permits required can also depend upon the amenities you are adding to your house. For example, if your house has natural gas, then you'll need a permit to install, repair, or replace the natural gas lines and any appliances, such as an oven or a water heater that will be attached to them. Obviously, if the house you are rehabbing has no gas, you won't need this permit.

No matter where you live, you'll be required to hire a licensed plumber to perform any required work on your gas lines. Building codes do not allow amateurs to work on any installation, such as a gas line, that if improperly done presents an imminent danger to the occupants of a residence and those nearby.

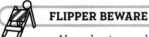 **FLIPPER BEWARE**

> *Never begin any demolition or construction until you have your building permit in hand. Never!* The penalties for doing so can be severe, the fines steep, and a building inspector will always catch you. Play strictly by the rules when it comes to building permits and you will be fine.

Once your plans are approved, you'll be granted the required permits. For each one, you will be given what is known as a *field card* that must be prominently displayed on the house you are renovating. These cards contain your permitting approval information. The reason you must ensure they are visible and instantly accessible at all times is so that any municipal inspector who happens to stop by your worksite can instantly see your construction has been approved and legally sanctioned by the governing municipality issuing permits in your area.

DEFINITION

> A **field card**, also called an *inspection card* in some locales, is a card that contains all the information about your permit. It must be prominently displayed on your worksite to prove that the work underway is legal and being performed under the oversight of the local permitting authorities.

Permits are more than just pieces of paper giving you permission to go forth and build. They are actually legal documents providing you with official approval to perform the scope of work you submitted with your permit request.

Once all planned work covered by a permit is complete, you must call an inspector to approve the final work and issue a certificate of completion or occupancy. No one can move into the house, nor can the house be sold until this certificate has been obtained to show that all work was performed up to code.

General Building Permit

The first permit you must acquire is a general building permit. Before you go to the courthouse and fill out the required forms, look online to see what you must submit with your request. Some municipalities require only one set of blueprints; others want two. You'll save time and an extra trip by finding out ahead of time what you need to bring with you to apply for this permit.

> **FLIP TIP**
>
> When your permit is issued, you'll be given a date by which work must start, usually within 3 to 6 months, and also a date by which work must be completed. If, due to unavoidable circumstances, you do not start or complete the work by the deadlines listed on your permit, you must apply for an extension. This extension requires filling out more applications and paying additional fees, so it's a good idea to stick to your originally assigned dates if you can. Permits might also expire if you suspend or abandon the job for longer than 180 days.

Also ask for an estimate of your fees. Some places have online worksheets you can use to estimate fees. It's important to know ahead of time how much money to set aside because you must pay all the required fees in full at the time of application. Fees can range from a few hundred dollars up to several thousand dollars, depending on the size of the home you are building. General building permits are charged on a sliding scale. Permits for larger homes cost more than permits for smaller homes.

You are required to submit final drawings and blueprints showing exactly what you plan to do, along with the address of the property. They must cover the full scope of planned work and be sufficiently detailed for the inspectors to be able to fully understand your objectives.

> **FLIPPER BEWARE**
>
> Never submit incomplete or unclear plans. They will be returned to you for correction, and you will have to start the process all over again from the beginning and pay the fees again, too. Avoid wasting time and money by always being completely prepared before you apply for a permit of any kind.

The length of time required to get a building permit application approved varies widely. In some small municipalities, it can be approved in a day or two. In cities, such as Los Angeles, where building and rehab activity is intense and inspectors are chronically overworked, it typically requires 3 months to get a building permit, but it can take up to a year!

Electrical Permit

Check with your local jurisdiction to see what type of electrical work and installations require permits. Requirements do vary from town to town and state to state. Generally speaking, if you are doing any work on your home's electrical wiring, conduits, electrical boxes, or fuses, you are required to get a work permit and should hire a licensed electrician. Permits are also required for adding additional wiring, outlets, switches, or light fixtures, wiring in a garage door opener, and installing or altering low voltage systems such as fire alarms, home sound installations, or computer systems.

Permits are not usually required to replace light fixtures, broken outlets, switches, or to install appliances drawing 30 amps or less of power such as a dishwasher or garbage disposal. You also don't need a permit to install coaxial television cable or to replace an existing doorbell. However, do check with your local jurisdiction about requirements in your area.

FLIP TIP

Some jurisdictions allow for a homeowner to do minor electrical work if he's occupying the house. However, most places require a licensed electrician to perform all electrical work in order to enforce consistent safety and quality standards for electrical installations.

Electrical permits call for two to three separate work inspections:

- The first is performed when all the wiring and electrical boxes have been installed but before insulation is added or walls closed in.

- The second takes place after the electrical mast, electric meter base, and service panels have been installed. Some places perform the first two sets of inspections together.

- The final inspection takes place after all electrical work on your flip has been completed.

Like building permits, fees for electrical permits are due at the application time. Unlike building permits, you do not have to submit any drawn plans of your planned electrical work along with your application.

You are required to notify the jurisdiction within a specified time period when your electrical work has been completed. A final inspection will be scheduled and performed before you receive final approval of the work.

Plumbing Permit

Like electrical permits, plumbing permits require most work to be performed by a licensed professional plumber. Plumbing permits are required for the following:

- Replacing a water heater or underground pipes

- Total repiping of the house

- Changing or replacing any pipes that run inside a wall, ceiling, or floor

- Plumbing in any new appliances, such as a dishwasher or an icemaker

- Adding any new plumbing fixtures, such as a sink, toilet, or tub

- Emergency repairs

- Replacement of damaged or leaking pipes

- Relocation of any existing plumbing

Permit fees are calculated depending on job size and complexity, and are due upon application for the permit. Plumbing permits are easier to obtain than general building permits. You can usually get your permit the same day you apply for it. Blueprints are usually not required when applying for a plumbing permit for a single-family home. Like all other permits, your plumbing permit must be visibly displayed on your worksite.

Once again, it's up to you to call for an inspection once the work is completed. After the work has passed inspection, you'll receive your certificate of approval.

Mechanical or HVAC Permit

Mechanical permits, also known as *HVAC permits* in some locales, are required whenever you are going to do work on a property's heating or cooling systems, ventilation systems including bathroom vents and kitchen exhaust fans, or wood stoves or fireplace inserts. A mechanical permit is also required to install pipes for natural gas. Generally speaking, you are not required to submit blueprints to obtain a mechanical permit.

If you're installing a wood stove or a fireplace insert, it must be compliant with Department of Environmental Quality emission standards or you will not be allowed to install it. Check for this when you are buying the stove or insert. It will save you time and money to buy a compliant product to begin with.

While only a licensed plumbing contractor is allowed to install natural gas piping, homeowners are allowed to perform most other mechanical installations themselves. As always, check your local ordinances before proceeding.

As with the other permits, call for an inspection when the work is completed so you can get your final approval.

Where to Get Permits

In the past, a homeowner or contractor always had to apply for any required building permits in person. In most communities, the permit office is located in the county courthouse. Check your community for the location of your permit office.

> **FLIP TIP**
>
> Having trouble figuring out the location of your local permit office? Go online and search for building permits with your zip code appended to the search. This search will return the correct link to your local permit office. Even if the permit office doesn't have an online application form available, you'll be able to use this trick to find out where you need to go to apply for your building permits.

Today, in many municipalities it's possible to digitally scan building plans and upload them to an online application site. You can then do everything required to apply for a permit online—fill out the forms, pay the application fees, and provide digital copies of your construction plans.

Many architects and draftsmen supply digital copies of plans to clients since so many communities now offer online permit applications. Ask if digital plans are available for your job and the additional fee to get a digital copy. Contractors also use digital plans in laptop or tablet construction apps to manage their jobs. As project leader, a digital plan is a handy thing for you to have at your fingertips, too.

Time Required to Obtain Permits

Getting required permits can be a lengthy process. Most locales make every effort to provide permits within 5 to 30 business days, but it can take much longer, sometimes several months if you live in an area where there's a lot of building and flipping going on. General building permits require the most time for approval, as a committee of experts must review your blueprints for structural integrity along with code and zoning compliance. Some less complicated permits, such as for minor electrical or plumbing repairs, can actually be obtained in a single day.

You might be required to change your building plans to comply with some aspect of the code. The new plans must be reexamined and you could be required to pay additional fees before your permit can be approved. Any of a dozen or more different snags can interrupt or slow down the process.

Some municipalities pile so many requirements on top of the basic building permits that it can take years and thousands of dollars to obtain any necessary building permits. They can require environmental studies, shoreline impact studies, soil subsidence studies, water quality studies, or any of a dozen other studies before granting your building permit request. A soil subsidence study alone can easily run into the thousands of dollars—tens of thousands of dollars if you live in an area where the soil is unstable and you must hire a geologist.

Needless to say, when communities enforce such complex and demanding rules for building, it has a depressive effect on how much building or flipping goes on. The whole process is somewhat self-defeating when it becomes so complex, but if you live in a community where the process is this convoluted, you just have to deal with it.

> **FLIP TIP**
>
> Tired of dealing with your local permit office? Consider hiring a permit service to do the work for you. Since they work with permitting offices daily, they can sometimes help guide a complex permit application through the process a bit faster. See below for more information on permitting services.

You must be able to start and complete your flip within a reasonable amount of time. If permit requirements make it impossible to do so, consider moving your business to a nearby location where regulatory requirements are not so burdensome.

Once you submit all the required paperwork and fees, the clock will start ticking toward approval. If you are lucky or live in a smaller community that has fewer permit applications to handle every day, your permit might come through in a week or less. If you live in a large city, acquiring building permits can take a month or sometimes more. General building permits require the most time for approval. Most of the other permits—plumbing, electrical, and mechanical—can be acquired in 1 to 2 days.

Call your local permitting office (usually located in your county courthouse) and ask the average length of time required for building permits. Factor this time into your work schedule.

In areas in which permit approvals take longer than average, consider ordering and paying for some basic items now, such as plumbing and lighting fixtures, cabinets, and countertops. We suggest this because the cost of materials can escalate rapidly. If your permits take 3 months for final approval and you order and pay for at least some of your required materials now, you might end up saving yourself several hundred dollars.

Don't store materials that will not be used for several weeks or months on the job site. Doing so presents too tempting a target for thieves who cruise construction sites at night looking for things they can easily steal and sell for cash.

Costs Required to Obtain Permits

The cost of permits can vary widely from one locale to the next. In some places, you'll pay just a few hundred dollars. In larger cities, permit costs can range into the thousands of dollars.

> **FLIP TIP**
>
> According to homeadvisor.com, the average reported cost of building permits across the United States is $911 per project. They say most homeowners spent between $398 to $1,456 dollars on permits, but the price can go up to $3,000 or more in states with high permit fees. Whatever the cost, factor it into your expenses when drawing up your budget.

Ask what forms of payment are accepted. Some permit offices only accept cash while others will only take credit cards.

Calling for Inspections

Inspectors do not magically know when you have completed permitted work. It's up to you to call for an inspection as soon as work is completed on each part of your project that requires a permit. Some municipalities even have time frames for ordering inspections, such as requiring you to call to schedule your inspection within 24 hours of completing the work.

Inspectors make every effort to comply with inspection requests in a timely manner, but when things get busy during the summer, it can take a few days to get to you. Always allow a minimum of 1 business day between the time you call for an inspection and the time you request for the inspection to be made. Inspectors will not always be able to make it at the time requested. Just make a note of when the inspector says he will arrive and make sure that you or your contractor is there to greet him.

Many contractors like to deal with inspectors themselves. If they've been in the business awhile, they have long-standing relationships with inspectors. Sometimes new flippers are overly eager or assume too much, and can impede the inspection process.

If your contractor wants to handle inspectors on his own, don't be alarmed as it can save you some time. Another benefit is that if you receive a violation notice, your contractor will know exactly what must be done to take care of it.

Generally speaking, the owner of a house is required to apply for building permits. The only exceptions are if your contractor applies or you use a permit service to handle your requests.

Using a Permit Service

If all this talk of permits has your head spinning in confusion, you're not alone. Many people use a permit service to obtain the required documents simply because applying for and getting building permits can be a little like trying to find a piece of cheese in a maze, only someone keeps moving the cheese.

People who run permit services are experts in every stage of the permit process. They have managed hundreds or thousands of permit applications from start to finish, saving homeowners time, effort, and frustration as a result. They submit your applications and blueprints, stay on top of the process, and notify you if any additional information or any changes are required.

Yes, to use such a service is an added expense, but they can save you time. Since time is money in the flipping business, the service can end up paying for itself. Because they are well-known in the permit office and maintain good relationships with the people working there, permit services are sometimes able to expedite the permitting process in ways that you never could.

If you want someone else to handle your permitting, do an online search for construction permit services with your zip code appended. That will give you a list of the permit services serving your area.

Notice of Violation

When an inspector finds one or more areas of work that are not up to the local codes, he will give you or your contractor a notice of violation. The notice lists all the violations separately, along with what you must do to fix them.

Depending upon your locale, you might be required to apply for a separate permit and pay additional fees in order to correct the violations. In some places, violation notices are called *orders of correction.*

The violation will contain a deadline by which time all violations must be corrected. In some locations, if you cannot complete the corrections on time due to needing to order a part or some other valid reason, you might be granted an extension of time to complete the required repairs and corrections.

If you ignore a violation notice and let the deadline pass without correcting the problems, you'll be fined and the municipality may choose to take you to court if inspectors consider the violations warrant such action. In some places, code violation fines are cumulative and increase daily until the violation is corrected.

Building inspectors are serious about ensuring homes are up to code. As an ethical flipper, you should follow all local ordinances governing permitting of renovated houses. If you do receive a violation notice, make the repairs quickly to minimize downtime and reduce costs that could accrue due to the delay.

Consequences of Unpermitted Work

The consequences of unpermitted work are costly. It makes no sense to rehab a house without proper permits. You can destroy a project and lose all hope of any profit when inspectors learn you don't have your permits. And believe us, they *will* find out. How could an inspector possibly discover you don't have the required permits? They are on the lookout for unpermitted work. An inspector visiting a nearby house could drive by, and not see your field cards. A quick tap on his laptop and he will know if you have obtained the required permits or not.

But let's assume no inspector is driving around the neighborhood where you are working. What about a disgruntled neighbor who sees you working on your renovations? Or a former employee unhappy that you let him go? A quick call to the city permitting office to report your work can have an inspector on your doorstep in a matter of hours.

When an inspector discovers you have unpermitted work, you will be required to tear out, tear down, and remove any work you have done that is not properly permitted prior. That's a huge price to pay for skipping one vital step in the flipping process.

The Least You Need to Know

- Permits are required for almost all construction and renovation projects.
- Check zoning laws and your neighborhood design review board to make sure your project is compliant before applying for your permits.
- Set aside sufficient time and money to cover the permitting process in your planning stage.
- Handle any violations notices promptly.
- Use a permit service to pull your permits if the process is too confusing to you.
- If you skip the permitting process, you do so at your own peril. Violations fines can be steep, and you might even be forced to remove all the improvements you have already completed if they were performed without a proper permit in place.

CHAPTER 14

The Quick Makeover

On occasion, you might be lucky enough to find and purchase a house that doesn't require an entire renovation. If a property is located in a trending neighborhood, is in decent shape, and has good bones, a quick facelift might be all you need to pump up the price and get a fast sale.

The rehab could be something as easy as fresh paint and carpet, or new countertops and cabinets, to give the place an attractive sparkle that says, "Buy me!" Or maybe it's just the outside that needs some TLC, and new mulched gardens with bright blooms, eye-catching shrubs, and an accent border will add the curb appeal you need for a speedy sale.

However you decide to proceed with your quick makeover, remember to follow all the guidelines we've already discussed about planning: team building, financing, scheduling, and buying in the right neighborhood. Just because you anticipate a flip is going to be a fast turnover is no excuse not to work smart and give yourself the very best chance to succeed.

For some aspiring flippers who have a little capital of their own, redoing a quick fixer-upper can be a great way to ease into the business. You don't have to deal with the hassles, headaches, and expense of a full demo and rehab, so you can

In This Chapter

- Small updates can equal big improvements
- Fast affordable fixes
- Prioritizing upgrades for maximum impact
- The importance of landscaping
- Dealing with construction debris

flip the house faster than normal. If you buy at the right price in a high-demand neighborhood, then spend maybe $10,000 to $15,000 on upgrades, you should be able to move the house very quickly for a $15,000 to $20,000 profit.

Here's how you do a quick makeover. You might not even have to do any real repairs or demolition!

You Still Need Permits!

Before you start work on your fabulous find, review Chapter 13 to see if any of the work you have planned requires a permit. If it does, drop everything, and go apply for the required permits now. Remember, in most jurisdictions you don't need blueprints to apply for electrical, plumbing, or mechanical permits. These permits also tend to be easier to get than general building permits, and the approvals are faster. You just have to remember to apply for them as soon as you know they are needed.

Call and schedule an appointment with the permit office without delay. If you live in an area where it's possible to apply for permits online, take advantage of the ease and convenience of that system to get the ball rolling on your quick makeover as soon as possible.

 FLIPPER BEWARE

We continue to be amazed by the number of new flippers who completely ignore the issue of work permits. Don't be one of those guys. You can literally lose thousands and thousands of dollars if an inspector discovers you are performing unpermitted work and orders you to tear it out. Don't work without a permit! It's not worth the risks.

If you're unsure about whether or not something requires a permit, you can wait until you walk through the property with your contractor, as long as that meeting is scheduled rather quickly. You don't want a hot property to sit off the market any longer than is absolutely necessary.

Your contractor will be able to quickly tell you what work requires a permit and will probably be happy to file for the permits for you. If he volunteers to do so, accept his offer with gratitude. Just remember, you still have to pay for the permit fees. Your contractor might be the world's nicest guy, but he's not going to pay your permit fees unless he's 100 percent certain you will reimburse him immediately.

Once you have all the required permits in hand and posted prominently on the home's exterior, you can begin any work the permits cover. Until then, limit yourself to planning, cleaning, painting, planting flowers, or any little job that does not require a permit.

Assessing What Is Needed

By now you know the drill. Walk through the property with your contractor to assess what needs to be done and what upgrades, if any, you want to invest in to boost the home's value. Make your lists. Draw up your schedule and your budget, order your materials, line up your permits and work crews, and get to work. Ideally, you should be able to get the house on the market within 2 to 4 weeks at the most.

Since you'll be working with a more limited budget, you'll need to prioritize your upgrades, focusing first on things that will bring maximum impact with a minimum investment.

Some of you might be wondering, why wouldn't you want to go full bore on every flip? Because it's not necessary. Let's look at it another way. If you were given your choice of the following two diamonds, which one would you choose?

The first diamond is worth just $3,000 and it's buried less than a foot down, easy digging straight through soft soil. You could basically plunge your hand into the dirt and grab it.

Now the second diamond is worth $10,000, but it's buried 20 feet down under bedrock and hard clay, and no one quite knows where it's actually located. So you might spend weeks digging and digging and get all the way down there and still not find it, but man, you really want it, so you keep digging while the clock is ticking.

Again, which one would you choose? We would grab for the easy $3,000 diamond every time. In the time it takes to retrieve one $10,000 diamond, you might have found four or five of the $3,000 ones, and you'll end up making more money for way less work.

We look at flipping houses the same way. We've done million dollar flips and brought home 6-figure paydays on houses that were hotly contested in bidding wars. But each one of those premium properties took several months of hard work and effort from a lot of people. We are not opposed to the hard work at all, especially when the payoff is so handsome. But when you can turn a nice smaller profit with a minimum of work, why wouldn't you? Why make it harder than it must be?

> **FLIP TIP**
>
> The nice thing about cosmetic makeovers is that you and your friends and family can safely do much of the work yourselves, which is a good thing when you're first starting out in flipping and perhaps short on funds. Whatever task you take on, just be sure to focus on doing a good, professional-quality job. For example, if you've never pulled up carpet before, watch some online videos to learn about the proper way to do it without damaging the subfloor.

Flipping is not an easy business, and sometimes you put a lot of time and hard work into a flip only to have it sit on the market for months without a nibble, costing you money every day. It happens to all of us at one time or another. No one is immune to the vagaries of the real estate market: changing tastes in homes and neighborhoods or shifts in interest rates that boot some prospective buyers right out of the housing market. When we can find a house that will put a quick few thousand dollars in our pockets without too much effort on our part, you can bet we're going to pounce on it. You should do the same.

Quick Updates with Big Results

Our hearts always beat a little faster when we find a house that will only require a few cosmetic fixes to become, literally, a hot property. We know there's money to be made there. But before you put in an offer, do your due diligence just as you would do for any other house you are considering flipping.

As we mentioned briefly in the opening of this chapter, the house must still fit *all* your other search criteria. If it doesn't, you can lavish all the care and attention in the world on it, and still have a more difficult time than usual selling it. No amount of paint or decorating can fix a dull neighborhood, a bad floor plan, or postage-stamp bedrooms and tiny closets.

That's why we mentioned the house should have good bones. No matter the style of the house— ranch, Craftsman, mid-century modern or something else—the floor plan should make good sense, with rooms flowing one into the other in an orderly way. If you find one of those houses where the master bedroom sits off the kitchen, or a tiny kitchen with no pantry opens into the living room instead of the dining room, you can scratch your head, ponder what the architect was smoking when he designed the place, and move on.

In order to fix a house with what we call a disastrous floor plan, you have to make major structural changes to better apportion the available space. As we're sure you can imagine, that's an expensive proposition and time consuming, not to mention it requires a whole other permit to do.

There are many things you can do to upgrade a house inexpensively, but to our way of thinking, these are the fastest and most affordable fixes that can provide big results in terms of return on your investment and increased salability of a house. All these tricks produce a noticeable improvement in the way the house looks, and none of them cost much.

Paint New paint inside and out makes a house look and feel brand new. Do paint the entire house. Doing just one or two rooms will make all the other unpainted rooms look bad in comparison.

New electric outlets, switches, faceplates, and covers You can change all the switches and outlets in a house for a few hundred dollars. That's important because painting without switching out the electrical trim can leave your switch plates and outlet covers looking dingy and dirty in comparison. For those of you thinking you can just spray some cleaner on them and have at it, uh, no. Liquid and electricity do not go together. Don't ever try to "clean" your electrical outlets. If they look gross, replace them. While you're at it, instead of just replacing the old covers with the same old thing, upgrade from the 39¢ option to the $3 option and choose from a variety of stylish finishes, such as brushed aluminum or bronze, to add an inexpensive designer touch to your house. But only do this if it fits in with the overall design of your rehab.

New kitchen sink and designer faucet   For a few hundred dollars, you can give an older kitchen a stylish upgrade just by replacing a grungy old sink and faucet. Add an in-sink water filter for about another $120 dollars to really add some class and functionality to the new look.

Repaint the front door   Choose a bright color, such as red. Just make sure whatever color you choose complements the paint on the rest of the house. A bright entrance is a cheap upgrade that can do wonders for a home's curb appeal, particularly if you plant flowers of the same color in the front gardens.

Recaulk   Let's face it. Caulk rots. It degrades and starts to look bad faster than almost anything else in a home, but it's a necessary evil to keep water from leaking around kitchen and bathroom fixtures. Wherever you see caulk in the home, along the bathtubs and shower seams and around the kitchen sinks or windows, replace it. But don't just caulk over the old nasty chalky stuff that's already there. That just creates more problems and can even encourage the growth of mold. Apply a caulk remover gel and let it sit, preferably overnight. Use a caulk remover tool to lift the old caulk from the joints. Never pick at caulk with a knife or other sharp tool. You could end up damaging the surrounding wall, tile, or yourself!

> **FLIP TIP**
>
> One of our favorite tricks is to add a decorative ceiling fan in the den or master bedroom. Ceiling fans look great and help reduce energy bills by keeping cooler air circulating throughout the home. They are available in a variety of styles to fit every kind of décor. You can have one installed for under $200.

New light fixtures   This is another affordable fix. You can replace every fixture in a 3-bedroom home for $1,000 or so. We know it's tempting to buy at the big box stores, but find a lighting wholesaler and open an account there. You'll get a much wider selection of styles, generally a higher-level of design and good prices if you stick to sale items. You can go wild and spend $5,000 on one chandelier, but there goes your profit. What you're aiming for is attractive, eye-catching, and different than what buyers will see in 99 percent of other flips in the area, but still affordable.

Crown molding   If you're rehabbing an older home in one of the ornate or classical styles that features formal living and dining rooms, you can add a touch of affordable elegance with crown molding in those two rooms. Crown molding used to be a major pain to install, strips of heavy plaster of Paris moldings that were nonetheless quite fragile and very difficult to lift and secure to the ceiling. Now it's made from extruded foam covered with a light coat of plaster that you paint over. It's light, easy to handle, can be cut with a hand saw, and installs very quickly.

These are just a few ideas to get you started. As you gain more experience in flipping, you'll create your own cool quick fixes to tempt buyers into writing out a deposit check.

The goal of any quick update is to make big, noticeable improvements in the appearance and attractiveness of a house without making an equally big investment of either time or money to do it. If the floor plan is good, then your addition of new carpet, paint, light fixtures, and some landscaping will make the house look like a showplace. If the floor plan looks like a pretzel with a case of the bends, no amount of icing is going to make that particular cake look tasty to buyers.

If you think about it, people only buy really bizarre houses or houses in bad locations, such as backed up to a railroad line, when they've been priced out of the normal housing market. Such misbegotten properties almost always have to be deeply discounted in order to sell, and sellers often take a loss just to get rid of them. No matter how attractive a price may be, don't make their problems yours by buying such a house. Remember, you might be able to fix the house to a degree, but you cannot fix an entire neighborhood, nor ask Amtrak if they would mind moving their tracks so the train won't shake your house quite so hard.

Cleaning Up

Even if the previous tenants of your recently purchased property were very neat people, houses do get dirty and worn-looking over time. Paint starts to chip or streak, humidity causes the silver backing to peel from bathroom mirrors, stained woodwork fades, grout darkens with grime, and things just start to look shabby. Dirt and dust drift into every little nook and even a weekly dusting and running the vacuum across the carpet is not quite enough to renew a home's fresh look. The house might even *smell* old and fusty.

So what can you do? We've found that one very inexpensive way to renew the appearance of a home is with a little something called elbow grease. That's right. Giving a property a good old-fashioned deep cleaning right down to the dust bunnies in the corners is a great way to instantly make it look more attractive. And the great news is, if funds are tight, this is definitely something you and your buddies can tackle together.

Don't neglect the outside. Gardens get overgrown, lawns get patchy, ivy goes wild and threatens to swallow the house whole. Take a little of your ambition outside and clean up the yard while you're at it.

A thorough cleaning might not seem like much, especially when compared to whatever cosmetic upgrades you are planning to do, but it can work wonders. Add a coat of paint and some smart staging and your house could be ready to list.

Just be sure to do all your deep cleaning before you start work on the actual upgrades. You don't want to be stirring up a lot of grit right after you've installed new laminate flooring or countertops.

Minor Repairs

As you inspect the house to determine what needs fixing, you might run across several minor repairs that must be done before you can list the house. For example, nail holes in drywall. We're sure you've read about putting white toothpaste in nail holes, but that's not a good idea. All your repairs should be done properly and to professional standards. Nail holes need to be filled in with *spackle*, sanded down, and the entire wall painted.

> **DEFINITION**
>
> **Spackle** is a quick-drying plaster-like compound used to fill in cracks and small holes in drywall and plaster. It can be sanded and painted to match the color of the repaired wall.

As you work your way through the house, you might find a closet or built-in bookcase missing a shelf, or perhaps the mirror on the medicine cabinet is cracked. You might run across a light fixture that is shorted out. The doorbell could be broken. All of these things are relatively minor and inexpensive to fix. None of them require any permits to do the work. If you're handy with a power drill and screwdriver, you should be able to do most of them yourself. Or, of course, let your contractor give you a lump sum price for all the minor repairs, and have the work crews do them.

Paint, Flooring, and Countertops

We've already mentioned paint as one of our favorite quick and affordable fixes. It's particularly effective when you redo the flooring and countertops after you paint. Those three upgrades can combine to make any house look almost new from top to bottom.

That's not just our opinion. Do an online search for affordable ways to upgrade a house, and practically every time the number one result is going to be new paint. A fresh coat of paint is by far the easiest, fastest and most affordable way to make a slightly rundown house look new.

Even if you're getting your paint at a big box store and paying retail prices instead of going through a wholesale paint distributor, you can still paint a room for an average of $150 to $200, and that includes two coats and all the brushes, rollers, painter's tape, and drop cloths you'll need.

FLIPPER BEWARE

Paint is one item where you definitely do not want to buy the cheapest available. Painting is a lot of work and requires precision. Wouldn't you hate to spend 3 or 4 hours painting a room, only to look up and see the walls are streaked and unevenly covered because you bought cheap paint? Spend a few dollars more per gallon to buy a quality brand that will cover the walls completely with one streak-free coat.

While we always prefer to hire out all the jobs on a flip, another nice thing about painting for a new flipper is that it's truly something you can do yourself or with the help of friends and family members. Just make sure you're all being careful and taking the time to do a precision job. That means taping your trim, windows, and doors to avoid getting paint on them, and putting down drop cloths to protect your floors or carpet. The only time you don't have to worry about the floors is if you plan to replace them, but if this is the case, just make sure to complete all the painting *before* you have new floors put down. Having to clean paint splotches from a beautiful new floor before you can show the house is no fun.

Using laminate flooring is almost a no-brainer these days. We use it in most of our flips. Real wood floors are too expensive to use except in high-end houses, and low-end flips tend to be all carpet with a cheap sheet vinyl in the kitchen, baths, entrance hall, and utility room. Laminate comes in a huge range of colors, styles, and quality. As with paint, don't buy the cheapest. Select flooring that complements your cabinets and wall colors, nothing that will clash.

FLIP TIP

Make sure that whatever flooring you install in the bathrooms is slip-resistant. More than a third of household falls take place in a bathroom. You can help reduce the risk by installing floors designed to help people stay upright even when there's water on the floor.

New countertops will complete the illusion that a house has had a near-total makeover. If you want granite, pick one of the more affordable styles, such as Uba Tuba. If you go for Formica, which is out of style at the moment, select a pattern that looks like granite. We definitely would not put Formica in a higher-end house. It could impede a sale.

If you want to splurge and give the look of a designer kitchen, install stainless steel countertops with a wood block prep area. That will make your kitchen look like a real cook's kitchen and appeal to buyers who do a lot of entertaining. You will also be able to ask a higher price for a house that has stainless steel countertops in the kitchen. It's a trending style at the moment.

Plumbing Fixtures

New plumbing fixtures are a sure-fire way to tempt buyers, but they're a step up in terms of expense. A new toilet, tub, sink, faucets, and showerheads for two bathrooms can cost upwards of $3,000 to $5,000, or even more if you're not careful. There are spa bathtubs that cost $10,000 all by themselves. Add in another few thousand for tile and flooring, and you can see why bathroom upgrades cost so much. But even though they do cost a lot, bathrooms and kitchens are the two areas of a home where you can get almost dollar for dollar value out of the upgrades you install.

Once again, go for something middle of the road that looks classy but won't break the bank. Standalone tubs are in demand right now, but they cost two to three times more than a tub that slides in next to a tiled enclosure.

Farmhouse and apron front sinks are hot for kitchens, but there is nothing wrong with a high-quality stainless steel sink, either. They seem to be a timeless element in modern kitchens, and the good news is that they are almost maintenance-free.

We will say that when we do quick flips, we try to avoid replacing plumbing fixtures if at all possible. It's not just that the fixtures themselves are expensive, but that it's messy, time-consuming, and fairly costly to have them pulled out, carted off, disposed of, and new ones installed in their place. Suddenly, instead of a quick fix, you're talking about a major upgrade with a major price.

Lighting

Instead of replacing all the lighting in a house, consider just replacing strategic, high-visibility lights, such as the dining room chandelier or the kitchen lighting. Those are lights that everyone who visits your home will see almost instantly, so you want them to have some dramatic impact and make a style statement. If you have to trim your lighting budget, do it in rooms other than these two focal points.

FLIP TIP

Use economies of scale to save money in lighting. You can frequently get significant savings on lighting fixtures if you buy a case of them at one time. Now, of course you're not going to want to sink a wad of cash into a case of chandeliers that might be gracing your garage for years to come, but certainly you can buy in bulk for basic fixtures that go in bedrooms, hallways, utility rooms, and so on.

Or, consider replacing all the exterior lights. If it's inadequate, do a lighting plan to add new fixtures and increase nighttime visibility in the yard. New exterior lighting not only adds a safety element to your home, but can also dramatically affect how the house looks from the street. Study the current trends, set a budget, and see how far the dollars will take you. As always, try to get maximum benefit for your investment by taking advantage of sales and discount buys.

New Appliances

When you start talking about replacing all the kitchen appliances, you're getting into some serious expense. If all the appliances look good except for one, replace just that one, being sure to match the exterior finish to whatever is already in the kitchen.

A new stove, dishwasher, and refrigerator can cost $3,000 to $10,000, depending on the amenities and brand you choose. Only go for designer brands if you are working in a high-end home you can sell for six figures. Otherwise, choose a good middle-grade quality appliance.

Power Washing

Power washing is a fast and easy way to spruce up the exterior of a home. Brick and stucco houses tend to grow moss or green algae along the foundation lines in humid climates, and concrete driveways and sidewalks gather a variety of stains over the years. All this grunge combines to give a home a weathered, rundown look.

 FLIPPER BEWARE

If your house has wood that is dry-rotted or has termite damage, don't power wash it. A power washer can blow damaged wood into a pile of splinters in a heartbeat. Instead, have your contractor replace and prime the wood first, and then get the power washer in to put a new shine on things.

You can hire a guy with a power washer anywhere in the country. For under $200, he can remove all grunge and grime and get things looking new again.

Landscaping

Don't make the mistake of spending all your rehab budget inside the house. Make sure to leave some money for landscaping, because the outside of the house is what people will see first. If it's not attractive, they might never bother to stop and check out how great the interior looks.

A little landscaping goes a long way to renew the curb appeal of a house. For $20 or $30, you can buy a bounty of flowering plants to put in front gardens or along a walkway. For another $100 or so, you can add colorful shrubs for harmony and balance that takes outdoor living to another level.

If you have no clue about which plants grow in your climate or what looks good together, consult with your local nursery for ideas and suggestions.

Trash Removal

When you complete your quick cosmetic makeover, you'll have a fair amount of trash and construction debris that needs to be removed from the premises before you can put the house on the market. You can certainly rent a dumpster, but for small jobs, that's like using a nuclear bomb to kill a mosquito. Why pay several hundred dollars for a dumpster that holds 6,000 pounds just to remove a few bags of trash?

Some contractors like to remove trash several times a week to keep it from building up. They have their work crews throw it in the back of their trucks and take it to a local dump. That can certainly be an economical way to handle trash, but dump fees do build up over time and you might suddenly find yourself with a bill for several hundred dollars.

Our favorite solution is to buy something called a Bagster. It's available for just $29.95 at all hardware stores. You might be asking yourself how a mere "bag" can hold construction debris. Not only can a Bagster hold it, it can hold up to 3,300 pounds of it. It's big enough to accommodate a full sheet of drywall or plywood, or anything else you need to remove from the premises of your property.

FLIPPER BEWARE

Bagsters are strictly for picking up trash, no garbage. Never put any garbage in a Bagster, especially not food. The low, open design of the bag will attract critters and create a big mess on your lawn.

Just place the Bagster on the curb like you would a garbage can, and instruct your crew to place all trash and construction debris there. Provide a separate garbage can for them to place food items and garbage. And if you're really ecologically minded, add a collection bin for recyclables, such as aluminum cans and plastic water bottles.

Pickup prices vary from community to community, so call ahead to get pricing. It usually costs no more than $199 to pick up the first bag. The pickup price per bag is cheaper if you have two or more Bagsters picked up at the same time.

There are a few things you cannot put in a Bagster, such as old televisions, but they will accept most common construction debris. If you are unsure about a particular item, call the company for guidance.

The Least You Need to Know

- Follow the same guidelines for success as you would on a full rehab.
- Try some quick fixes first to see if they bring enough improvement to put the house on the market.
- Look for strategic combos of fixes that will make it seem like you spent a lot more than you did on the rehab.
- Quick makeovers are a great way to start out in the flipping business.
- Be sure to make arrangements for trash removal when the job is done.

CHAPTER 15

The Demolition

The big day has finally arrived. You have your plans, permits, financing, and work crews in place. Now all you have to do is tear out the old to make room for the new.

There is a lot more to demolition than just wildly swinging sledgehammers and crowbars to rip through drywall like you see on television. Not only can that hurt more than it helps, but if you do your demolition without proper planning and preparation, it can create dangerous and even potentially deadly situations.

Yes, demolition can be dangerous. You don't see all the careful prep work that must be performed before they start the cameras rolling on a TV demolition. If you mistakenly start your own demo without first taking steps to remove all possible hazards, you'll soon discover just how dangerous it can be.

There are precise steps you must follow in the correct sequence to perform a demolition correctly. And there are other tasks you must take care of as well, such as getting the proper insurance for your house while it undergoes renovation and making sure you have somewhere to put your demolition debris.

In This Chapter

- Demolition requires careful planning
- Proper work order is key
- Assessing interim insurance needs
- Crew problems
- Handling weather delays
- Getting ready to renovate

Here are some practical tips to do a clean demo every time. This chapter will help you make the most of your demolition dollars and avoid common problems and accidents through careful preparation, paying good attention to safety, and following a well-planned demolition schedule.

Before You Start

Of course you want to jump in and start tearing out drywall and ancient paneling, but hold on. A demolition requires careful planning before you begin work.

You must take into consideration any unseen hazards, such as frayed electrical wires, rotten floorboards, or rusty nails. Asbestos and lead were used routinely in home construction in the past. If you're going to demolish structures that could expose your crew to either of these two dangerous substances, you must take special precautions.

 FLIPPER BEWARE

> Many older houses contain asbestos, which can cause cancer. Before its dangers were known, it was used in roof shingles, siding, textured ceilings, vinyl tiles, insulation and many other items. Asbestos was banned in home building in 1977, but is present in millions of homes built prior to the ban. If asbestos materials are in good condition, experts recommend leaving them alone. The danger comes when asbestos is improperly removed. It releases microscopic fibers into the air, which are then inhaled. If you do need to remove asbestos, hire a qualified asbestos removal expert, as it is a hazardous job.

Then there are design considerations. For example, if you remove the original knotty pine or birch wood paneling in a mid-century modern ranch, or even paint over it, you could be knocking off a big chunk of value from your home—several thousand dollars of value. The same is true if you do ill-considered demolition in any desirable vintage home, no matter what its style or period.

Before you tear out anything, look at what you have in the home, and compare it against the standards for that style of house. If you're not sure what is and isn't authentic, call in an expert consultant. The few hundred dollars it costs will be offset by the premium price your flip will command if you restore it faithfully to the design glory it had when it was first built.

It's About More Than HGTV

If you watch a lot of flipping shows on TV, you are familiar with what we call the HGTV look. No doubt it's gorgeous … open concept floor plans, granite countertops, stainless kitchen appliances, laminate floors, sleek bathrooms with huge walk-in showers and vessel sinks, all pulled together with a neutral palette accented with bright pops of color. It works in many different styles of house, creating an inviting interior that can have buyers scrambling to pull out their checkbooks.

The HGTV look is beautiful, but it might surprise you when we say it doesn't belong in every rehab, particularly not in certain vintage rehabs currently in high demand, such as mid-century modern and Craftsman homes. Most people who buy period properties want the original features that came with the home. That means steel kitchen cabinets, paneling, and stone fireplaces in mid-century modern homes; gingerbread trim, leaded glass doors and crown molding in Victorians; and tapered columns, coffered ceilings and built-in book cases in Craftsman bungalows. Too many flippers just rip everything out without stopping to consider what potential buyers might value and want to keep in the house so that it stays true to its design roots.

In my experience, people who bid high and often to get their hands on a faithfully restored mid-century modern ranch or ornate Victorian masterpiece are not going to bid quite so high or so often, or perhaps at all, if you have significantly altered the original aesthetic of the home by using modern finishes that clash with the architecture.

Everything Old Is Desirable Again

You might be asking yourself why any of this matters. Within the past decade, there has been a true renaissance of appreciation for vintage homes. The mid-century design aesthetic with its pastel bathrooms, chrome accents and wood paneling everywhere is currently ultra hot, so if you've bought a house of this style, it's a better idea to restore it than to renovate it.

> **FLIP TIP**
>
> Not really sure what authentic mid-century modern décor and finishes should look like? Visit retrorenovation.com, a popular blog that helps people who own mid-century modern homes find just the right finishes for an authentic renovation.

The same is true of other distinct styles of period homes. People who are fans of those styles buy them for their authenticity and because the houses appeal to their individual tastes. If you've gone in and torn out all the original finishes in such a house and replaced them with standard modern finishes, you've removed the very things many buyers look for in such homes, and perhaps some of the biggest potential selling points of your property.

So, before you tear out, remove or destroy anything in your house, do some research first. There are great-looking modern rehab options that blend wonderfully well with each style of beautiful vintage homes. Consult an expert and do a little research, and you'll know how to proceed.

Insuring Your Project

Insuring your house is a necessary and important step. However, insurance is a complex subject, and laws regulating policies vary from state to state. We will discuss the highlights and offer some smart tips to help you save money, but you truly need to discuss your insurance needs with a local agent who is familiar with the house flipping business and what insurance options are available for flippers in your area.

As we discussed in Chapter 11, you should have bought an insurance policy for your house before you went to the act of sale. Now that the actual demolition and renovation are about to get underway, it is time to revisit your insurance to make sure you have adequate coverage for every possible contingency.

What Kind of Insurance Do You Need?

High-quality vacant house policies vary as to what they cover. Be sure to ask for vandalism and malicious mischief coverage if you can get it. This is the most frequent cause of loss on a flip project. You also need coverage for theft of materials from your worksite, and of course, you need liability coverage in case anyone gets injured on your site. Make sure your contractor and all your subcontractors carry workers' comp insurance.

There are many different issues you should discuss with your agent before you buy insurance. You might need to change the type of policy you have, or expand your policy with additional riders or extensions to make sure you are fully covered for the entire replacement value of the repaired and remodeled home. Your insurance agent can best advise you as to which policies best suit your needs.

Insurance companies can be picky about insuring flips due to the increased liability associated with vacant houses, particularly those undergoing renovation. Some underwriters won't insure houses that you plan to flip at all. Or they might require you to move all your other insurance business, such as car insurance, to their agency before they will consider underwriting your flipping projects.

FLIPPER BEWARE

If you plan to store expensive tools or building materials, appliances, plumbing and light fixtures, and so on, on your premises as you work on the rehab, remember to buy a separate policy to cover the possible loss of these materials in the event of a fire, natural disaster, vandalism, or theft. Vacant home insurance will not compensate you for the loss of these items. A basic policy only covers damage to the actual structure, not contents.

Vacant house insurance costs significantly more than regular homeowner's policies because insurers categorize uninhabited houses as "attractive nuisances" with a built-in appeal to vandals and thieves looking for their next target. The rate of claims filed for vacant properties undergoing renovation is significantly higher than claims filed against homeowner's insurance for properties that are primary residences, so the added cost is directly correlated to the added risk. Your costs can rise further if your house is located in an area with many vacant houses, or where a high number of claims for theft or vandalism associated with vacant houses have been reported.

What About Homeowner's Insurance?

Some of you might be asking, "Why can't I just buy regular homeowner's insurance that covers the contents of the home?" Since you are not living in the home, you cannot ethically obtain homeowner's insurance.

Some people try to trick an insurance company into giving them a homeowner's policy when they don't actually live in the home. We've seen online flipping blogs claim that if you stage the home with at least one furnished bedroom and a table with at least one chair, that will somehow "fool" an insurance company into believing the house is occupied. Not a chance! Insurers will cancel the policy as soon as they learn a home is unoccupied. And believe me, they will find out. They always do.

This falls under the heading of "false economies," or trying to save money in not-so-smart ways. If you have to make a claim, that means the insurance company is going to send an underwriter to investigate the claim, and that means they'll find out you lied about living in the home, which means they are not legally obligated to pay you anything. Do yourself a favor and take this "bright idea" out of your toolbox.

Some flippers do choose to live in their homes while they are rehabbing them. While that's not something we would recommend, particularly if you have small children, many do it as a way to save money when they're first starting out in the business.

If you *do* live in a home during rehab, then you can legitimately purchase homeowner's insurance to cover the house while you are working there. You must let the agent know you are rehabbing the house, though. That can determine what coverage you can buy when the agent knows you're only living in the home temporarily.

Is There Any Way to Save Money on Coverage?

There are several good ways to mitigate some of the higher costs associated with vacant house policies:

Buy a policy with a much higher deductible. Yes, it costs more if you do file a claim and must pay out the first $5,000 before insurance kicks in, but you'll save enough on insurance premiums over time to cover that larger deductible if you ever file a claim. Higher deductibles can save you thousands compared to policies with lower deductibles such as $500 or $1,000.

Buy a named perils policy, where you select the type of hazardous events for which you want coverage. Named perils coverage can be significantly less expensive than open coverage that covers almost every type of event, natural or manmade, that could damage a property. You select the perils you want covered based on your assessment of risk. Everyone should elect to cover typical casualties, such as damage from fire, lightning, hail and windstorms, then discuss with your agent what other perils are worth covering. For every peril you add, your costs will rise. The bad news is if you forget to include a certain event, you're out of luck if that event occurs. For example, you might not think of drains backing up and flooding your house, but they do. If you have not specifically named flooding from backed-up drains as a peril, none of your damage will be covered.

Consolidate all your insurance coverage with one agency. When you move your car, health, personal homeowner's or renter's, along with any other policies you might have, to one agent, you can get as much as a 10 percent preferred customer discount on ALL your policies, including your vacant house insurance.

Buy what is known as a *Builder's Risk insurance policy.* These policies cost 1 to 3 percent of your total construction budget. With the increasing popularity of flipping, these policies are crafted to the time schedules and insurance needs of flippers and are available just about everywhere. You can pay for a policy on either a month-to-month or annual basis. Month to month saves money in that you're only insuring your property for the time you are actually rehabbing and then marketing it. An annual policy does the same, but you must pay the entire year's premium at once, which can be a big chunk of money.

> **DEFINITION**
>
> A **Builder's Risk insurance policy** insures against accidental loss or damage from a covered cause to equipment, supplies, and materials being used in a construction or renovation project.

When you sell the house, you'll be reimbursed for unused time on the policy. Once your house is sold, Builder's Risk coverage ends. Be aware such policies only cover actual new construction, not an existing structure. If your flip burns down, you will only be reimbursed for new portions of the house. These policies also cover the loss or theft of building materials on the site, and even insure building materials on their way to the site.

Other Types of Policies

Here are some other types of coverage you might also want to consider. Discuss what you want covered with your agent and ask them to recommend the best policy to cover your specific needs.

Liability coverage   Absolutely essential to protect yourself from claims and lawsuits filed by anyone who gets injured on your property.

Agreed loss settlement   A clause in an insurance policy that agrees to reimburse you for the total replacement cost of your house in the event that it's completely destroyed. You and your agent determine this figure when the policy is written. It's not cheap, as we are sure you can imagine, but well worth every penny for the peace of mind it provides.

Property damage coverage   A separate policy that would reimburse you in the event that items and materials stored in your rehab while you're working get damaged, destroyed, or stolen. Many flippers forget to obtain this coverage, which is a shame because these types of smaller incidents are responsible for the majority of insurance claims on rehabs.

You might have to hunt to find the right agent and policy to cover your individual needs and business circumstances, so don't give up just because you get turned down a few times. You will eventually find someone who wants your business.

Comprehensive Coverage

As your business grows, ask your agent about a comprehensive policy, sometimes called an *umbrella* or *investor's policy*. Instead of insuring individual houses as you buy and rehab them, you purchase a policy that covers all properties you buy. This eliminates the repetitive hassles you might have to endure with insurance companies every time you buy a new house to flip.

In order to obtain such a policy, some insurance agencies might require that your business be set up as an LLC or corporation. Availability depends on insurance and tax regulations in your state. Because these policies are designed to cover multiple properties valued in total at a certain amount, say, up to $2 million, they are naturally expensive to buy. But the insurance cost per property is lower.

It is important for you to make clear to your insurance agent you are flipping homes. Some won't write comprehensive policies for houses that are owned for less than 60 days.

Doing the Demolition

When you do a demolition, it's important to follow certain established safety practices to reduce the risk of injury to your crew and unexpected damage to your property. Consistent use of personal protection equipment greatly reduces the risk of job site injuries. Having the proper demolition tools is essential as well.

You must also follow a certain order of demolition, both for safety's sake, and also to keep things organized and flowing smoothly on your worksite.

All the Right Equipment

A safe demolition starts with having the right equipment, not just tools, but also safety gear to protect the crew doing the work. At the minimum, each crewmember should wear the following personal protection equipment: a hard hat, shatterproof safety goggles, leather gloves, steel-toed boots, and high-quality respirator masks to prevent inhalation of potentially dangerous airborne particles. Don't forget earplugs to protect your crew from hearing loss. Power tools make a lot of noise, and long-term exposure to loud noise damages hearing.

> **FLIP TIP**
>
> It's rare that a demo goes down to the studs in every room of the house, which means many rooms will need protection from the dust and dirt a demo generates. Buy some painter's canvas drop cloths or a roll of heavy brown kraft paper to cover surfaces, such as floors and countertops to keep them safe from dust and debris created by the demolition.

Some crews, particularly those in warm climates, might be careless or inconsistent about wearing safety equipment. For your own protection, insist they follow safety guidelines. You'd be the first person sued if a worker suffered a preventable injury due to a failure to wear proper protective gear.

Demo tools include crowbars, sledgehammers and regular hammers, jackhammers, saws, chisels, and other tools as needed. All tools should be clean and well maintained with sharpened blades. Check to make sure safety devices, such as shields and fences on power tools have not been removed or disabled.

If you cut through concrete, wall off the area with plastic sheeting, and use a wet saw to reduce inhalation of silicon fibers. Insist all crewmembers wear protective respirators.

Unseen Hazards

The number one rule of demolition is to absolutely make certain that electrical power to the house has been turned off prior to starting work. Tape over the breakers and put a big sign on the electrical box saying the only one with authority to turn them back on is you. If power tools are needed, they can be run off a generator. Can you imagine what would happen if a crewmember swung into a wall with an iron crowbar and hit a live wire? Not only would you have a possible crew fatality on your hands, you might also have to deal with a resulting fire.

As the demolition progresses, you might find other dangerous situations you must handle promptly. For example, when you tear out drywall and wooden studs, cabinets, or built-in bookcases, you will find many nails and screws sticking up out of the wood at odd angles. This is hazardous. Let every crewmember know they must remove all nails from debris before it's loaded into the dumpster. You don't want anyone stepping on a rusty nail.

Order of Demolition

After you have made certain the electric power is off, next remove any cabinets, countertops, appliances, plumbing fixtures, or lights you plan to replace. Make sure all this material is carried to the dumpster promptly to maintain a clean worksite. You might be able to sell some of your used materials, such as an old porcelain tub, cabinets, or stainless steel sink still in good condition. Have the crew put those to the side in a designated spot, such as the garage, until you can get them listed for sale. This might seem like a waste of time, but if you can make an extra $500 to $1,000 by selling components from your house, it will certainly help with the bottom line.

Next, rip up old carpeting and other flooring. Be especially mindful of sharp carpet tack strips when removing carpeting. They hurt! Remove floor and bathroom tiles, and also take out the old back splash.

Tear out any drywall you will be replacing. In some older houses, you'll be removing plaster and lath, which is a series of thin strips of wood nailed close together which form a foundation for an overlying coat of plaster. Also remove any insulation from exterior walls, especially if it is degraded or has been in an area subject to leaks.

Once the drywall or plaster is gone, remove all nails, screws, electrical wiring, switch plates, electrical outlets, and plumbing pipes. At this point, all the walls in the areas you are renovating should be open and free of any items that could pose a hazard. The idea is to leave a totally clean space for your crews to work in. This provides a safer worksite, and also speeds the work since your crew doesn't have to waste time cleaning or moving things around just to get their work done.

Now is the time to remove any old equipment, such as a furnace, water heater, or air conditioning unit that is no longer functioning. Have them carried to the dumpster, along with any ductwork that is being replaced.

After you have removed everything that needs to go, rent a shop vac and thoroughly clean the interior of the house to prepare it for your rehab crews.

Weather Watch

There's a reason most rehabs are done in the spring, summer or fall. Awful weather that delays or shuts down your rehab can strike during any season and in any part of the country, but snow, chill wind, and bitterly cold temperatures make winter a less than ideal time to flip a house. Just getting to the job site on icy roads can be a challenge in winter conditions.

That's not to say you cannot rehab a house during the winter months … just that you must be aware that weather delays can hamper your progress when snow is falling and the roads are a mess. At any time of the year, severe thunderstorms, tornadoes, flooding, extreme heat, or any extreme weather condition can strike, effectively stopping or delaying work on your project.

Handling Unreliable Crews

Most contractors and work crews are great. They get to work on time, work hard, and do a quality job. But every once in a while, you might run into a contractor or crewmember who is disruptive, disrespectful, angry, or downright rude.

Even if you received reliable recommendations for your contractor and work crews, interviewed them first, and determined they would be a good fit, sometimes it doesn't work out that way on the job. Sometimes, a contractor is an outgoing sort who is able to put on a good show during an interview, but in reality, he is scattered and disorganized, and has trouble consistently meeting deadlines. Or he could be the world's greatest contractor, but going through a divorce and custody battle that has completely disrupted his work performance.

Work crews can wreck your schedule by getting to work late, not showing up at all, working slowly and indifferently once they do arrive, doing poor quality work, or, worst of all, being dishonest … ready to grab anything on your site that's not nailed down.

The point is you don't have to tolerate any of this behavior. You're at the beginning of your flipping career and you need the best performance out of everyone. You cannot afford to let their problems and failures become your own.

FLIPPER BEWARE

> If you do have to fire someone, be extra vigilant for the next few days. If the person threatens you, report it to the police. It might be worth your while to hire an overnight security guard if you've had crew difficulties. Sometimes, someone who has lost a job will try to retaliate. You can prevent trouble by keeping a night watchman on your worksite for a week or so after the termination.

If an employee steals something, terminate them immediately. Be careful of confronting them yourself. Call the police, tell them the evidence you have, and file charges against the employee.

For other issues, take the person causing problems aside and explain your concerns. Use specific examples of incidents and behavior that do not meet your expectations. Allow them to respond. Perhaps they will have an explanation and promise to do better. But if you just get silence, a stubborn insistence that nothing is wrong, or a lot of attitude, set a time limit, such as a week, and explain that if things do not improve by then, you will be letting them go. People are unpredictable, but if you stay calm, you can keep the situation from getting too tense.

If you don't nip problem behaviors in the bud, things can get out of hand quickly. Disrespectful crewmembers can wreck a rehab. You must demonstrate at all times that you are in charge. You're the one signing the paychecks and should demand respect. If your crew doesn't give it to you, find yourself another crew.

Even if you lose a few days or a week from your overall schedule by firing a contractor or a crew, that's okay. You should have a few extra contingency days in your schedule anyway. It's more important to work with reliable and courteous team members than to absolutely nail your ideal deadline.

It's worth noting that as you get more experience, and build a strong and cohesive team, your odds of running into crew problems will go down to almost zero.

Dealing with Demolition Debris

Every demolition and renovation creates a mountain of debris. The key to managing debris is to not let it build up. Have a plan before you start work so that the moment the first debris is carried out of the house, you will have a place to put it.

The best way to handle the large quantity of debris a demolition creates is to rent a dumpster and have it delivered to your worksite. Before you rent, check with the county or city for any regulations concerning dumpsters. In some locales, you need a permit for a dumpster, particularly if it will block a public access throughway, such as a sidewalk.

When you rent a dumpster, get its dimensions and make sure you have enough room in your driveway or another location accessible to the delivery truck to place your dumpster. A 30-yard dumpster requires a space 22 feet long by 8 feet wide, plus you need additional room to open the rear door so you can carry debris right into the dumpster.

> **FLIP TIP**
>
> Keep your dumpster securely covered with a tarp when not in use. This keeps rain out—important because water soaking into materials, such as drywall and wood, can add hundreds of pounds, effectively reducing the amount of debris you can load. A tarp also keeps unauthorized people from using your dumpster to discard their debris and also prevents garbage from being tossed in overnight.

Also known as a *roll-off container,* a dumpster is a large portable metal trash bin that is delivered to your location. One end features a hinged door that swings open for easy loading. When it is full, call for a pickup and the dumpster is hauled away and taken to an authorized dumpsite to be emptied.

Dumpsters are available in several different sizes ranging from 10 to 40 cubic yards. The maximum weight limits vary with the size dumpster you rent, but typically, most companies that rent dumpsters allow no more than 14,000 to 20,000 pounds of debris per dumpster. Dumpster weight limits must conform to road regulations and the maximum load capacity of the trucks that haul them back and forth.

Check with several local companies to get the best price. Most renovations require at least a 15- to 20-yard dumpster. If you're renovating an entire house, you'll probably need a larger size, 30 to 40 yards.

Dumpsters are rented for 7- to 10-day periods, so don't have one delivered before you are ready to start filling it. Costs vary according to location, but on average, renting will run in the neighborhood of $250 to $500 per week for a large dumpster. Try to find a company offering all-inclusive prices. Some companies offer lower upfront rental fees, but then tack on high per-ton landfill fees, which can add $200 or more to your final bill.

> **FLIPPER BEWARE**
>
> Most construction debris can be put in dumpsters. However, you cannot place hazardous waste, garbage of any kind, batteries, tires, or automotive fluids in a dumpster. If someone is injured by hazardous material you put in a dumpster, you will be held liable. Be sure to let the rental company know if you have a lot of dirt or concrete to dispose of as these are handled in a different way.

Also be mindful of weight. If you exceed the weight limit for the size dumpster you have rented, you will be charged a hefty overage fee, ranging from $40 to $100 per extra ton.

Prepping a Demolished Space for Renovation

Once you have finished your demolition, you still have work to do before you start your renovation. First, give your house a thorough cleaning. You are about to bring items, such as new cabinets, fixtures, and flooring, into the house and you don't want something, such as a nail carelessly left on the floor, damaging your expensive materials.

> **FLIP TIP**
>
> Have your materials delivered as close as possible to the day you will actually use or install them. This keeps your work space open, reduces the risk of accidents, and also lowers your potential loss in case of fire, theft, natural disaster or vandalism.

Check your schedule and make sure you have all your materials ordered and scheduled for delivery in the correct order. You don't want everything to arrive all at once, particularly if your house is on the smaller side. Your crew will be tripping over the materials and maybe even each other. You don't want workers having to waste time digging through a mountain of flooring material and cabinets looking for one light fixture.

The Least You Need to Know

- Planning is essential for a safe demolition.
- Make sure your crew wears personal protection equipment during the demolition.
- Rent a dumpster to collect demolition debris.
- Handle crew problems swiftly and decisively to maintain a good work environment on your job site.
- Allow for weather delays in your demolition schedule.

CHAPTER 16

The Renovation

Weeks of preparation have brought you and your team to this point. You are finally ready to start the renovation and infuse your house with new life, energy, and style.

The renovation, or as some prefer to call it, rehab, is where all your hard work and planning really start to pay off. For the first time, you'll be able to see "the house in your head" as it takes shape in front of you.

This is where you will really cut your teeth as a flipper. You'll be managing a budget, cash flow, selection and ordering of materials, and required equipment and supplies, along with scheduling of the crew and delivery of materials. It's a lot to manage, especially for someone new to the business. We can only assure you that as you become more experienced, things will flow more smoothly and big projects will seem less daunting.

Renovation is actually our favorite part of the entire flipping process ... well, that and depositing the check with our profits in the bank. This is where you can really have some fun. It's great going from showroom to showroom looking for just the right plumbing fixtures, faucets and showerheads, kitchen appliances, cabinets, countertops, tiles, lighting, paint colors,

In This Chapter

- Choosing the right materials
- Money-saving ideas
- Handling structural problems
- Doing things in the right order
- Cleaning up

and flooring. It can even be enjoyable to select new shingles and siding, if that is part of your rehab, and to select a new high-efficiency furnace or air conditioning system.

However, the most fun of all is seeing all these elements coming together to create an attractive and compelling house that practically begs for an offer.

Here's how you can make sure your renovations go smoothly.

Selecting Materials and Finishes

Your materials and finishes shape what your completed flip will look like inside and out. More importantly, those choices will determine what the completed flip will feel like, as well as what sort of energy potential buyers will pick up the moment they walk through the door.

Picking out the materials and finishes is really enjoyable. It's almost as if you are selecting various building blocks that when stacked together, will create a particular desired result.

On occasion, we will consult with an interior designer to make sure our choices are appropriate for that particular house. For example, if we are redoing a Queen Anne–style Victorian, we might ask a designer who has expertise in period rehabs for advice to make sure the look we have in mind and the materials and finishes we choose are authentic to the period of the house.

> **FLIP TIP**
>
> If you are truly unsure about how to start selecting finishes, don't be afraid to ask for advice. Most showrooms employ designers who will help you make choices that work well together. If you buy a certain amount, the design service is free.

Right from the start of any flipping project, it is important to ensure the design choices you make for the interior of the home match the style of the outside of the home. Can you imagine how disconcerting it would be to walk up to a sleek modern house that was all redwood, steel and glass on the outside, only to go inside and find early bunkhouse style with exposed rustic beams, wagon wheel chandeliers and knotty pine paneling? You would almost feel like you had fallen into a time warp.

Start with your paint color. For walls, select a neutral palette that will appeal to a wide range of people. The most popular choices are a warm palette that features a pale beige or ivory wall, or a cool palette that features a cool grey or white wall. People can decorate however they want when they start with one of these basic palettes.

Use a *color wheel* to help you select accent colors that complement your basic wall paint color choice. Or ask someone in the paint department for guidance in picking colors that go together well.

DEFINITION

A **color wheel** is a circular diagram in which primary and complementary colors are arranged sequentially in a circle. It is arranged so that complementary colors lie directly across from each other on the color wheel. They are invaluable in helping you select paint colors that work well together. You can buy color wheels at art supply stores and some paint stores.

You don't have to use your accent color as a wall paint. It will look just as good used as cushions on a sofa or vases on a counter as it would on the wall. The idea is to create a pleasing palette of colors that evoke positive feelings when potential buyers walk through the door to view the house.

FLIPPER BEWARE

Even if deep purple and lime green are your favorite colors, don't inflict them on potential buyers. You are rehabbing a house with the idea of selling it quickly and making a profit, not working on personal expression. That means you should select neutral colors that appeal to almost everyone, not unusual colors that could cost you a sale because it's difficult for people to imagine themselves living in a space decorated with jarring colors.

Once you have your basic paint and accent colors selected, choose all other materials to complement them. Select materials that work together to tell a complete story inside your house. Every finish you choose, every cabinet, tile, appliance, bit of carpet, and light fixture adds a little piece to the overall picture. As the creator of this tableau, it is your job to make sure the elements you choose work together to tell a compelling story that adheres to a strong and easily identifiable theme.

Vintage Materials

Whether you're doing a period rehab or simply want to add a unique flavor to your flip, using vintage materials can bring an element of class and nostalgia to your build.

We go through periods where one vintage material or another are in high demand. Several years ago, Victorian claw-footed bathtubs were hot. At the moment, old barn doors and recycled barn wood are trending, particularly since so many flipping and design shows have been featuring barn doors as room dividers, closet doors, and even entry doors.

The use of vintage materials is generally reserved for higher-end projects that have the potential to bring a substantial return on your investment. You won't have room in your budget to use such materials in a modest flip.

FLIP TIP

When you're hunting for vintage materials, don't overlook estate sales, particularly those in rural and semirural areas. You never know what treasures you will find in an old barn and can usually pick them up for a reasonable price. Keep an eye on craigslist.com for upcoming estate sales, where families are trying to unload a lifetime of goods after the passing of a loved one. For the most part, don't waste time on garage sales. They're not ideal for finding vintage building materials.

Visit local dealers when you're looking for a particular vintage item. They can tell you what is available and what sort of price range you're looking at. Over time, once you develop a good working relationship, they might even call you when they know a piece that might interest you comes in.

Just be sure that whatever you buy is in fundamentally good shape and can be renewed with something as simple as a good sanding down and a fresh coat of paint or stain. Avoid using vintage materials in situations in which structural integrity is required. It's best to rely on new materials for jobs like that.

Smart Ways to Save

When you're rehabbing a house, you walk a fine line between wanting to save money, and needing to achieve a certain look and style that are desirable to buyers. Unfortunately, you cannot create the sort of high-end look buyers favor with low-end materials. It just won't happen.

Of course, many home buyers, particularly first-time buyers, are happy to get a home of any kind and would be thrilled to have a house with all-new appliances, paint, and flooring. But the influence of TV on the tastes of American buyers is pervasive, so don't be surprised when even buyers looking for an affordable bargain home still want it to look like it could appear on the cover of *Architectural Digest*.

Savvy Shopping

You can get at least some of that designer look for a more affordable price by savvy shopping. Visit a granite countertop outlet and ask about *stone remnants*. Even though you cannot get a kitchen countertop from a stone remnant, they are large enough to do a countertop for a bathroom vanity or fireplace surround. You can add a lot of style and class to your rehab with stone remnants, and best of all, it will save you 50 percent or more over the regular cost of granite countertops.

DEFINITION

Stone remnants are pieces of granite, quartz, or any other countertop or flooring material that are left over after a custom order has been cut from a large slab of granite.

Check out the scratch-and-dent selection of appliances at your local big box store. Look at your kitchen layout and figure out if any of your appliances have sides hidden against walls or cabinets. If so, look for appliances with dents on the side you know will be hidden. The warranty on these cosmetically damaged appliances is the same, and the scratch or dent will not adversely affect the performance of the appliance. You will save an average of 20 percent over regular price and can sometimes negotiate an even bigger discount by buying all your appliances in one store.

FLIPPER BEWARE

This might seem obvious to you, but trust us when we say it's not obvious to everyone. *Do not* buy appliances with cosmetic damage that will be visible after installation. No one wants a brand new kitchen with a stove that has a big ding on the front.

If you want to save even more money, follow the sales, or have an assistant do it for you. All stores, whether wholesale or retail, have sales of one kind or another running regularly. Get on the email notification list for any wholesaler you do business with, and review the sales in the Sunday newspapers for retail stores so you can be aware what's on sale that week.

When you see a sale for products you know you are going to need, buy then to save money. Even if you have to stick the boxes in your garage for a few weeks, it will save you significant money when you buy materials on sale.

Bulk Purchases

Once you reach a certain level of success in your flipping business, you could find yourself working on two or more houses at the same time. Many wholesalers and even big box stores offer additional discounts for purchases made in bulk.

This technique works best if the houses you're rehabbing are all of a type, from the same design period. If you select a look for the interior of one house, it will work with your second and third similar houses as well.

Bulk purchases don't work as well when you go from rehabbing one period of house to another. For example, if you found a screaming deal on surplus farmhouse sinks, those would look great in a Pennsylvania Dutch house or a log home with a more rustic interior. But a farmhouse sink would look out of place in a contemporary or mid-century modern home. In other words, no matter how great a deal you find, don't buy it if you cannot use it.

Take advantage of bulk purchases when you can. However, don't just buy up a bunch of stuff to "save" money with no real purpose in mind. If you can't have all the material you buy delivered right to your various worksites, then you'll have to rent a storage unit. Doing so will eat up any money you saved very quickly, and soon, it could start digging into your profits on an ongoing basis.

Structural Issues

The first thing you must do is repair any problems with the basic structure itself, such as sagging floors, a leaking roof, cracked foundation, moldy basement, and so on.

If your home inspection showed the house was structurally sound and the walls were in good condition, you can skip this step. Your walls should only be awaiting a fresh coat of paint.

FLIPPER BEWARE

We often encounter aspiring flippers who believe every house must be demolished down to the studs simply because that is what they have seen on television flipping shows. You should never demolish or remove anything from a house that is in good condition and usable. That's just throwing money away. Only open a wall if you have major plumbing or electrical work or repairs to do. Plumbers and electricians appreciate the easier access an open wall gives them.

If you do have to open walls, remove the insulation so that all wiring, switch plates, electrical outlets, and junction boxes, as well as all plumbing pipes and HVAC ductwork are exposed.

Generally, you would have an open ceiling only if you had to find and repair a leak and replace any sheetrock or insulation that sustained water damage. Ceilings might also be open if you are rerouting ductwork to move a wall or put an addition on the house.

This is also the time to make any necessary foundation repairs. They need to be done before you do any other work on the house, because stresses that might be released during such repairs might crack plaster or cause doors and windows to go out of plumb. You wouldn't want that to happen *after* you'd already repaired those areas.

Saving Disastrous Floor Plans

It's possible you deliberately bought a house with a bad floor plan because you were able to get such a bargain deal. Now is the time, when the walls are open, to make any planned structural changes to open up the floor plan or reapportion space for a better layout.

As we mentioned earlier, *never* remove a wall without first having a structural engineer determine if it is load bearing. If it is a load-bearing wall, you must install an appropriately sized beam to bear the weight before you remove the wall.

> **FLIP TIP**
>
> If your house has adequate bedrooms but very small closets, sometimes it is possible to take a 3-foot-wide strip between two adjoining bedrooms and apportion half of it to a closet in each room. It will only take 1 foot from each bedroom, so a 10-by-12 bedroom will end up a 10-by-11 bedroom with a spacious closet. Make two-thirds of the closet hanging room and one-third shelves, and suddenly a house with inadequate storage has plenty of room to hide things out of sight.

Make changes to open sight lines and provide a large central gathering place for the family, centered around a great room or den. The trend is to have a family room, den, and kitchen all open to each other. If your floor plan does not allow for that, at least try to open up the kitchen to the dining area or to the den.

Another popular structural change to make in an older home is to change an adjoining smaller bedroom or nursery into an en suite master bath. That can be a huge selling point.

Order of Work

Just as with demolition, there is a specific order of work to follow when you are doing a rehab. If you do jobs out of order, you'll make things harder on your crew and can even cost yourself additional money, because jobs done out of order frequently must be torn out and rebuilt, only this time in the proper order.

In this section, we'll discuss the proper order of work as it should be performed, starting with any structural issues and ending with the final cleanup. For your convenience, there's a checklist with this order of work in Appendix C.

Exterior Repairs

A leaking roof must be repaired before you start any interior work, but exterior repairs, such as new siding, doors, or windows might get done later in the schedule. If you plan to replace any windows or doors, do it after you have finished any structural changes inside the house. Once the new windows and doors are set, then you can redo the siding or resurface the stucco, replace any missing bricks, and the like.

If you need to replace the driveway or walkways, wait until the rehab is completely done to do so. You don't want someone dropping a 300-pound bathtub in the middle of a beautiful new sidewalk. If your old walks and driveway get damaged during the rehab, they can be repaired or replaced once the heavy daily traffic flow of workers and materials is over.

Plumbing

While the walls are open, your plumber will repair or replace any damaged or leaking pipes and drains. They will also install any new plumbing fixtures, such as bathtubs, shower enclosures, sinks, toilets, and drains, along with any decorative elements, such as faucets and showerheads.

If the water heater needs to be replaced, that should be done now as well.

Your plumber is also the one responsible for making repairs to or installing any natural gas appliances, such as a stove or oven. A licensed plumber must install new furnaces as well. This is to ensure that the natural gas connections are properly done and don't represent any hazard for the future homeowners.

Once your plumbing repairs are done, but *before* you close in the walls, call the plumbing inspector so he or she can review the work that has been done and approve it or give you a list of required changes.

Electrical

Plumbers and electricians often work alongside each other as they both have work to do before the walls are closed in, and they usually are working in different areas of the house. Before you schedule them for the same time, check with them to make sure they are fine with working together.

At this point, your electrician will install a new electrical panel, if required, and also replace or repair electrical wiring, switches, outlets, and junction boxes.

Electricians will also install all your light fixtures, ceiling fans, hard-wired smoke alarms, door-bells, garage door openers, and so on, but they will return and do this work later after the walls are closed.

Mechanical

If you need to replace your furnace or air conditioning unit, schedule it now while the walls are open. If attic access is restricted, HVAC technicians might need to open up ceilings to repair or replace ductwork or add new ducts, so don't be alarmed if you see a ceiling coming down.

They'll replace the outside condenser on the AC unit at this point and add a new thermostat. They should also check the attic fans and vents to make sure they are working properly.

Sheetrock/Drywall

Once everything that needs to be repaired or replaced inside the walls has been completed and passed inspection, it's time to install the sheetrock. Also known as *drywall* or *gypsum board,* sheetrock is the plasterboard nailed to studs that forms the walls of your house.

 FLIPPER BEWARE

> A sheetrock job is only as good as the framing upon which it's installed. If your contractor was careless about squaring corners, your sheetrock will bulge and be impossible to line up. Make sure your contractor is precise with his framing by testing several walls with a level to make sure they are perfectly flat.

Sheetrock requires several days to install properly, so consult with your contractor to make sure you have allowed sufficient time in your schedule.

On the first day, all the sheetrock is nailed or screwed into place. Then a paper tape is laid over the seams using a plaster called *joint compound.* Crewmembers use a special tool to smooth the wet plaster compound over the seams and cover all the nail or screw holes. This must dry for at least 24 hours, longer if the weather is humid.

When the compound is completely dry, the crew will return and sand down the seams and nail holes then apply a second coat of joint compound over the first and smooth it down again. Once again it must dry for at least 24 hours.

On the third day, the crew will return and place a *skim coat* over the entire wall. They will then check for imperfections using a halogen light. This final step will produce a smooth, even finish over the entire wall, and provide a good surface for painters.

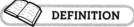 **DEFINITION**

> A **skim coat** is a thin coat of plaster applied all over a sheetrock wall as a final step to prepare the wall for painting.

Modern drywall manufacturers have now introduced a special kind of sheetrock constructed in such a way that it eliminates the need for a skim coat. It is more expensive than regular basic drywall, but looks great. You'll have to do some math to determine if the savings in labor and materials offsets the additional cost of this type of sheetrock.

Painting

There are two different schools of thought regarding interior painting. Some contractors prefer to do it as soon as all plumbing and electrical repairs and upgrades have been completed and the drywall has been installed. Then they install new cabinets, tile, countertops, backsplash, flooring, and so on.

Other contractors like to paint after the cabinets and countertops have been installed, and they just drape and tape everything they want protected from the paint, which is applied with a sprayer.

Arguments can be made for both approaches, but fortunately, it's not an argument you have to get into. Just ask your contractor when he wants to schedule the painters so you'll know when to order the paint.

On your schedule, allow enough time for one primer coat and two coats of paint to be applied and dry.

Cabinets and Countertops

Cabinets are next on your list. This includes kitchen cabinets and bathroom vanities. If the cabinets are in good shape, you'll be able to skip this step. If they're solid wood, but need refreshing, have them stripped, sanded down and stained or repainted. However, you can't do this on cabinets made of laminate or that have a thin veneer of wood on top of a composite.

Once all the cabinets are installed or refinished, you can move on to installing new countertops. No matter what material you have selected—granite, quartz, Corian, or Formica—manufacturers will not make your countertop until after your cabinets and vanities are installed and they can take precise measurements.

Light Fixtures and Switch Plates

Now it's time to install any new light fixtures, plus new switch plate covers and electrical outlet covers.

> **FLIP TIP**
>
> If you have bought attractive light fixtures, complete the good job by paying a few dollars more to replace all the switch plate and electrical outlet covers in the house as well. These covers are inexpensive; yet many an aspiring flipper will install gorgeous new light fixtures, but to save $3, leave ugly old stained switch plates with fingerprints you can see from across the room. Replace them all. They'll add a special subtle gloss to all your rooms, and it won't cost you much.

If you're not replacing all the light fixtures, be sure to have your electrician check the existing fixtures to make sure none of them have shorts or damaged wiring.

Flooring

There is some argument about whether floors should be installed before or after cabinets. We do them after for two reasons.

- If you install flooring first, you will be wasting a lot of flooring material that will be forever hidden underneath the cabinets where no one will ever see it.
- Also, there is still plenty of work to do at this point, and by installing floors this early in the schedule, you run the risk of them being damaged by the heavy traffic going in and out of the house every day.

If you are using a combination of flooring materials, such as laminate in the living areas and carpet in the bedrooms, be aware that two different crews will do the installations. The laminate, wood, or tile floors should be installed first, and the carpet last.

Tile

In this section, we are not referring to tile flooring, which should be installed at the same time as the rest of the flooring. This section refers to the decorative tile used in kitchens and baths.

Install the tile in the tub or shower surround. After the tile is in, you'll have to call the plumber back to install the faucets and showerheads. At the same time, install any tile backsplash you have planned for the kitchen and baths.

Installed Appliances

The type of appliances that are installed in rehabs vary from one part of the country to the next. In California, refrigerators are rarely included, but in Texas, they are always supplied as part of the kitchen. Check with your Realtor to determine which appliances are commonly offered to potential buyers in your area.

Installed appliances can include a full stove or cooktop, dishwasher, refrigerator, garbage disposal, ice maker, wine refrigerator, microwave, and even a washer and dryer pair.

Trim Carpentry

Trim carpenters, also known as *finish carpenters,* provide all the final finishing touches on your renovated house. They are usually the last contractors on the job.

Baseboards; quarter rounds; wooden molding around doors and windows; wainscoting; chair, plate, and picture rails; thresholds on the exterior doors; windowsills; and built-in bookshelves are all examples of the trim carpenter's art. Trim carpenters also install modular closet systems and shelving.

Scheduling Glitches and Cost Overruns

No matter how carefully you plan, you will inevitably run into at least one or two scheduling glitches and cost overruns. It could be your cabinets that hold you up. They were promised from the factory in 2 weeks and now suddenly, it's going to be 4 weeks before they arrive. Or, an inspector comes by and informs you that you have to replace your electrical panel, only you haven't budgeted for that, so you'll end up going two to three thousand over budget to get it done.

In the case of scheduling glitches, if the problem involves overlapping work crews, or crews scheduled in the wrong order, it's best to work out the problem with the crew chief or chiefs right on the spot. Be apologetic and humble and remind them you are new to this and learning the ropes. Reschedule crews so there is no conflict between them. If you have scheduled crews in the wrong order … in other words, brought in trim carpenters before the flooring crew has installed the new floors, once again consult with the crew chiefs to find out how long the flooring crew needs and then reschedule the trim carpenters as soon as they are available after the floors have been installed.

In the case of cost overruns, you should have allowed for at least 10 percent over your budget to accommodate cost overruns. You can save yourself a lot of headaches when you do this. When you need the money, it's already there. If you haven't budgeted for contingencies, then you must review your budget to find where you can cut things out to free up the needed funds. Although this will certainly work, it's not an ideal situation when you have to cut corners on your rehab at the last second.

The Final Cleanup

The final cleanup is what puts the shine on your flip. You've completed all your rehab work to a high standard and the house looks great, but the truth is, contracting work is a dirty business and your house is probably covered in a layer of dust so fine you might not even be able to see it. There might also be odd bits of trash lying around or construction debris that didn't quite make it to the dumpster.

My recommendation is that you hire a professional cleaning crew to clean every inch of your house. That means dusting (and polishing, if necessary) all the light fixtures, windowsills, and horizontal surfaces. Clean the windows, wipe down the cabinets, polish the tile and marble floors, and thoroughly vacuum all carpeted areas. Pay particular attention to the kitchens and bathrooms.

FLIP TIP

Your cleaning crew might not know this tip, but after rinsing out a sink, you should then dry it completely with a towel. If you don't, the leftover water droplets will dry and leave unsightly blotches that are particularly noticeable on stainless steel sinks. Remember to wipe the sink dry after cleaning, and it will shine and look great for potential buyers.

Don't forget the outside. Hire a crew to mow the grass, weed the beds, and sweep the driveway and sidewalks. You want your house to look pristine and ready for visitors, inside and out.

The Least You Need to Know

- Match the style of the interior to the style of the exterior of the house.
- Vintage materials can add a special touch to rehabs.
- Save on materials by following sales.
- Handle structural issues first.
- Do work in the proper order to save time and money.

CHAPTER 17

The Power of Curb Appeal

When your landscape is well designed, people assume, rightly or wrongly, that the interior of your house must be well designed, too. An eye-catching yard can truly enhance your odds of getting potential buyers to ask for a showing of your home.

Conversely, you can build out the most gorgeous flip in the history of home renovation, but if you leave the lawn patchy, the driveway cracked, and the garden full of weeds, no one may ever go inside to see your fine work. Why not? Because you've forgotten an important aspect to flipping a house … the cherry and hot fudge sauce (otherwise known as *curb appeal*) on top of your ice cream sundae of a house.

Curb appeal is what makes potential buyers pull over in front of your house and stop their cars. It makes women go digging through their purses for a cellphone to snap a photo of the selling agent's name and number. If your flip has compelling curb appeal, that potential buyer might even call the agent to make an appointment to see the inside while they're still sitting in front of your house. They don't yet know a thing about the interior of the home other than what little information is on the flyer, but your curb appeal makes them want to go in and check things out.

In This Chapter

- The importance of a great-looking yard
- Blend landscaping and hardscaping for a pleasing look
- Do you need a landscape architect?
- Buying new plants and trees: wholesale or retail?
- Pulling everything together

That's what well-planned and executed curb appeal does. It makes people want to see the inside of the house, to find out if the same style sense, eye for color, and careful attention to detail evident on the exterior, is also on display throughout the interior of the home. Curb appeal is the magnet that draws potential buyers into your home.

In this chapter, you'll learn all about creating pockets of bliss in your yard, by the pool, patio, or along a walkway. We'll show you how to tie the entire exterior of your home together thematically so that it presents a cohesive and appealing look from the street. Focusing on great curb appeal helps increase the odds that any potential buyers who happen to drive by will stop to take a look, make an appointment for a viewing, and maybe … even place an offer.

Create a Plan

Just as with the interior of your house, before you do any landscaping or cleaning up in the yard, take the time to look at what you have and what needs to be done, and make a comprehensive overall plan of action.

First, make a list of all the trees, shrubs, and *hardscape* items that already exist in the yard. Examine each one to determine its condition and aesthetics. Then decide if it fits in with your overall final plan for the exterior look of the home.

> **DEFINITION**
>
> **Hardscape** refers to any inanimate, manmade object that exists in your landscape, such as walkways, driveways, gazebos, arches, trellises, fences and gates, fountains, benches, patios, pools, and the like.

If your yard is full of mature but overgrown trees, you have some decisions to make. You don't want the trees to overshadow the house to the extent buyers can barely see it, but neither do you want to chop down every living stick in sight. Cutting trees down is a fairly expensive proposition, so that's why we suggest you evaluate each tree individually before you decide to keep it, trim it, or cut it down.

Any and all trees that directly overhang the house should either be removed entirely or, at the least, have the limbs that extend over the roof cut back. There are two reasons for this. The first is safety. Large limbs that overhang a roof can break off and land on the house in storms, causing lots of damage, and even, on occasion, injury or loss of life of the occupants inside the house.

The second reason to remove or trim back an overhanging tree is for maintenance reasons. If your house has a literal tree umbrella hanging over its roof, you will spend half your life up on a ladder scraping out gutters and raking your roof clean of leaves and twigs, or worse yet, pine needles and pinecones, which leave a nasty resin stain if they're not removed promptly. That's hard, dangerous work. It's much easier to remove the source of the problem than to spend back-breaking hours trying to keep up with the ongoing mess it creates.

It goes without saying that any diseased or rotted trees or shrubs must be removed and disposed of properly.

> **FLIP TIP**
>
> If you have a lot of green waste such as tree trimmings, branches, bags of leaves, grass clippings, and so on, investigate how best to dispose of it in your community. Most cities and towns now have a green-cycling facility where citizens can dispose of their green waste. From there, it might be made into mulch or compost, but it's important to note that by properly disposing all of green waste, you will be helping the environment.

Safety experts recommend trimming all low hanging branches from all your trees. Trees with low branches interfere with sight lines and give burglars a handy way to climb up and into your home through a second floor window that might be open. But don't go mad with the chain saw. The idea is to have trees that are attractive, neatly trimmed and symmetrical, not denuded of branches and leaves.

Follow the same procedure for existing shrubs. Any shrubs that are completely overgrown or that hide any part of the house, should be cut back to give the house more curb appeal and also for safety reasons. Law enforcement officials recommend trimming all shrubbery planted next to your home to no more than 3 feet in height to discourage intruders.

Of course, this advice is great for enhancing curb appeal as well. Creating a yard full of neatly trimmed and well-shaped shrubs accented with colorful flowers and a few well-placed trees can really improve the curb appeal of your house.

Finally, assess the hardscaping around your home. Are the driveways, walkways, and patio area in good shape? Is the concrete stable, or does it have cracks and missing chunks? Is it starting to crumble? If so, you should replace it. You might be able to patch small areas, but if the entire walk or driveway is falling to pieces, it's best to put in new concrete.

How about the fences and gates? Are they attractive, or do they require repairing or replacing? If there is a fountain, swimming pool, or fish pond in the yard, what does it look like? Does the pump system work? Is the water feature clean or covered with algae and staining? If it has tiles, are the tiles whole and undamaged, or discolored and broken?

The same goes for outdoor lighting fixtures. Do they all work? Are they dated looking? If so, consider replacing all of them. New light fixtures are a reliable and relatively inexpensive way to update the curb appeal of your home.

Once you have finished your checklist, make a budget for landscaping and add it to the main budget for the rehab of your house. Just remember, landscaping is the last job you will do. If you put in new landscaping before the rest of the rehab is done, it will likely get destroyed by painters, carpenters, and other crewmembers trampling it down as they carry heavy equipment and materials into your house and debris out.

Landscaping vs. Hardscaping

As you learned in the last section, there is more to creating curb appeal than just sticking a few flowers in the garden. The best yards make use of both landscaping and hardscaping to create an alluring vision that will attract buyers to your home.

> **FLIPPER BEWARE**
>
> If the interior of your house is ultra modern, don't flip-flop and make the outside Pennsylvania Dutch. The look and feel of your outdoor space should echo the look and feel of your home's interior. If you have a mid-century modern inside, make sure you carry that same design theme outside so that your house and yard complement each other and don't clash.

The idea is to make the yard appear almost as if it came from a cover of a gardening magazine. You want a few tranquil spots that can serve as oases for people seeking outdoor relaxation, such as a porch swing, a reading nook in a gazebo, a chaise lounge by a pool. None of these spots are created with plants alone, or with hardscaping alone. They are a harmonious blend of both elements.

It is not so much a case of landscaping versus hardscaping as it is landscaping accented by judicious use of hardscaping that helps create a unified theme for your outdoor spaces. You can tie the theme together with color or with style. Use all modern hardscaping accented with bright pops of turquoise that look great on metal loungers next to a pool, or try more traditional wooden lounge chairs made cozy with warm shades of orange.

Whatever style you choose, make the yard design, with both landscaping and hardscaping, part of your overall design for the property. That way, when people walk into your house, there will not be any jolts that make them feel as if they have suddenly been transported to another era.

Landscape Architects

If you're someone who is all thumbs when it comes to plants and shrubbery, consider hiring a *landscape architect* to create an overall plan for your outdoor space. Some charge by the hour, on average from $70 to $150 per hour, depending upon where you live. Some landscape architects charge a percentage of the total value of your job, ranging from 5 to 15 percent. So, if you plan a $5,000 job, your landscape architect might charge you anywhere from $250 to $750. Considering that the landscape is the first thing your potential buyers are going to see, it is well worth the small investment to hire a pro to do this job. Fees in larger cities tend to be higher than those in smaller towns.

> **DEFINITION**
>
> A **landscape architect** is a person who has been specially trained to develop land for recreation and enjoyment through the coordinated use of plantings, walkways, and hardscaping elements including structures, such as gazebos, pools, fountains, and fences. It is considered a multidisciplinary field, as degree candidates must master elements of botany, architecture, horticulture, the fine arts, industrial design, storm water management, and soil science, among others, in order to graduate.

A landscape architect will visit your site, ask you some questions, take notes, and ask for your budget and your timetable. They will want to know what look or feeling you are going for in the yard and also ask to tour your house to get an idea of how to match the design for the outside to what you have planned for the inside. He or she will then draw a plan of your entire lot with the house and the precise location of each tree, shrub, flower, and plant on the lot. They'll also map out the location of any new hardscaping elements, such as new walkways, a driveway, fountain, or gazebo, down to elements such as a barbecue grill or fire pit. If you're working on a high-end flip, you might even consider adding an outdoor kitchen to the yard.

Another advantage to working with landscape architects is that they know which plants thrive in your climate.

> **FLIP TIP**
>
> If you can't afford a landscape architect, some big box stores offer free yard design service if you buy all your plants at their store. Find the garden department, and let them know you need help planning the landscaping for a house you're rehabbing. Give them your budget and they'll recommend suitable plants. It's useful to bring a plot plan showing the size of the yard and the size and location of your house. That will help determine the right number of plants, shrubs and trees for your landscape.

As with the other pros on your flipping team, ask for recommendations of landscape architects, and interview several before settling on one you want to work with.

Wholesale Nurseries

While it's tempting to drive to the nearest big box store and throw a bunch of plants and shrubs in the back of your truck, that's not always the smartest option. Since you are doing a rehab, you'll want to buy wholesale as often as you can. This is especially true of wholesale nurseries. Not only will you save money and get better quality, primarily locally grown plants, but you also won't pay sales tax on wholesale purchases if your business is properly registered with your state. That 5 to 10 percent in saved sale taxes can really add up over the course of a flip.

Tell the person who assists you what you are trying to accomplish and ask for plant recommendations. Share your budget and expectations. The person assigned to help you will give you a tour of the nursery so you can look at the various options and choose what you like best.

Try to coordinate your schedule so that you only have to make one trip to the nursery. Many wholesale nurseries will deliver your order for an additional fee, usually $50 or so, plus mileage. If your nursery does not offer delivery, you'll need to either hire someone with a truck to go pick up the plants, or negotiate with your contractor to see if he can send someone. Of course, you can always go get the plants yourself, but just remember, the more physical labor you perform on your flips, the less time you have to manage your business properly or to plan your next flip.

If you hire a landscape architect, it's likely that he or she will take care of the selection and purchase of plants, so you might not have to do this job yourself.

Inviting Entrances

The entrance is a vitally important aspect of your landscaping. It is what invites people into your home and makes them feel welcomed. You want it to be a focal point that draws the eye. If you do not incorporate an attractive entrance into the overall plan of your landscaping, you are missing an opportunity to make your home stand out.

You must make sure that people can easily see how to get to your entrance. Some people focus a lot of effort in making an entrance look great, but then forget about how people are supposed to get from the curb or driveway to the entrance. You need a walkway, stepping stones, or path to guide people to your entrance without confusion about where they should go to get to your doorbell.

Nothing is more off-putting than a completely bare entrance devoid of color or design. Ideally, you want your entrance to reflect the personality of the house and to be so vivid that it almost seems to say "Hello!" to your guests. In order to accomplish this goal, you should incorporate the following elements into your entrance design:

Protection from the weather   It's not going to make your guests very happy if they have to stand out in the rain while they are waiting for you to come to the door and let them inside. If your house has a covered porch, you don't need to worry about this, but if it does not, you need to make some sort of weather protection over the front door, such as a small *cupola* or awning, part of your landscape plan.

DEFINITION

A **cupola** is a small rounded roof or part of a roof that is often used to provide protection from the weather over the entrance to a building.

Flowers or greenery　Whether you use a planter box, an urn or a hanging baskets, nothing is quite so welcoming as a lovely floral or green display, particularly if the flowers you choose have a pleasing scent, such as lavender. Set off to one or both sides of the door, flowers offer a great accent for your entrance.

Lighting　This is particularly important at night. If you don't have proper lighting along the path to your entrance, and also at your front door, how are family members and guests who arrive after dark going to find their way into the house?

The front door　The front door should draw the eye from the street. The current trend is to have either a very dark door, such as a navy or black, or a very colorful door, such as a turquoise or bright red door, beckoning from the street. Avoid painting the front door white, particularly if the house is painted a pale color. It will just get lost. Whether you choose to stain or paint your door, be sure to select a high-quality exterior-grade paint that will stand up to extremes of weather and sunlight for a long time. And go for glossy!

Leave adequate room　Don't allow yourself to become so focused on decorating your entrance that it becomes cluttered. Your goal is to make the entrance feel warm and welcoming, so that it serves as an ideal transition from the outside of your house to the inside.

FLIPPER BEWARE

House numbers should be large and clearly visible from the street. If they're not, the post office might refuse to deliver mail until the numbers are in a more visible spot.

Front and Backyard Upgrades

There are a number of ways to upgrade your front and backyards to increase your overall chance of a fast sale. Of course, only front yard upgrades will enhance curb appeal since backyard upgrades cannot be seen from the street, but backyard upgrades are equally important. Putting put all your money and effort into just the front yard is the same as icing only one side of a cake. It will look all lopsided and not very well planned.

The following sections cover some easy upgrades that will help inspire buyers to take out their checkbooks.

Pleasing Patios and Porches

Patios and porches are highly desirable features that can serve as outdoor focal points for family fun and entertaining. It's not too big a statement to say that every home should have, at the very least, either a porch or a patio, but preferably both.

It used to be that patios were strictly a backyard amenity, while porches ruled the front of the house, but no longer. Front patios are becoming more popular because they can serve as a social focus and gathering place for the entire neighborhood, whereas a porch can seem a little more closed off and private. The same can be said for back porches. Porches that run the entire length of the back of the house are a high-demand item, particularly in warmer climates where people want to spend time outdoors but don't want to bake in the sun.

When designing patio spaces, you'll have to decide if you want the patio covered, partially covered, or open to the elements. That decision will be governed by the climate where you live. If you live in area that has hard winters, you should cover the patio so that the future homeowners have a place out of the weather where they can go for a brief outside respite during the cold winter months.

> **FLIP TIP**
>
> If you're building out a flip that targets families with young children, you can make your patio a real selling feature by constructing it with rubber tiles. If a toddler falls on a soft rubber surface, they are far less likely to get seriously injured than if they take a header on concrete, which can knock out teeth and break delicate bones. Best of all, rubber tiles come in a variety of colors and attractive styles, including pavers and squares, and they are quite affordable.

If you live in a hot climate where sun beats down during the summer, a covered patio might seem too stifling, but you do need sun protection. A better solution in such hot climates might be to do an arbor or trellis covered with climbing vines, such as wisteria, that offer partial shade from the hot sun but still allow cool breeze to waft through. Also, consider a retractable awning as a way to offer some sun protection but with good air circulation.

The least expensive option is to leave the patio open to the elements. If future residents decide they want some coverage, they can invest in an awning or patio umbrella.

The most common material for patios is poured concrete, but we have also seen them built of brick pavers, asphalt, stepping stones, concrete with a pebble finish, and other decorative materials. Make the patio large enough to hold a table and chairs to seat four to six, with room for a grill or fire pit where people can gather and relax.

If the house has no existing porch, we would advise not to add one. They can be quite expensive to add on. If you do have a porch, make sure it is renewed and refreshed with all new screens (if it is a screened porch) and new paint and lighting fixtures. Put at least two pots or urns full of colorful flowers around to draw the eye and help integrate the porch in with the rest of the house.

Water Features

There is perhaps no sound more soothing in the world than the sound of running water. You can add this pleasant thrum to your landscape with a fountain or small pond.

That said, this is a feature you would likely reserve for use on a high-end flip, as installing a fountain or pond can be expensive. If you are building a modestly priced flip, you won't have room in your budget to add amenities, such as water features.

Rock Gardens

In hot desert climates, such as Arizona and New Mexico, where daytime temperatures routinely reach into the hundreds, you might not be able to find many plants that can survive those harsh conditions. Grass certainly cannot. Clever landscapers came up with the idea of rock gardens to add some beauty and eye appeal to houses located in such areas.

A rock garden consists of a gravel base of some kind, with the color of pebble chosen to complement the color of your house, and several large boulders placed as focal points throughout the yard. In addition, you might have a few desert plants, such as succulents or cactus, that don't require much water in the garden as well. That's important because many states with low rainfall impose strict water rationing in the hottest months, which means you might not be allowed to water your plants at all for extended periods. Fortunately, rock gardens don't require much water.

Consult with a local nursery for advice about which plants are suitable for use in areas where extreme temperatures are common.

Soil and Borders

Don't waste money on beautiful plants if you just plan to stick them in the awful dirt already existing in the yard. You can get high-quality garden soil for a few dollars a bag, so do it. Give your plants and shrubs the best chance of thriving by providing them with a nourishing soil.

But what's the sense of building a garden with great soil if you don't put a border around it? Borders are essential for keeping soil where you put it, in the garden, instead of on your walkways or leaching out across your driveway, or running down into the street.

Borders are available in an amazing variety of materials, ranging in cost from cheap to wildly expensive. You'll probably want to choose something somewhere in between.

A border can be as simple as a roll of black vinyl edging you place around your gardens, although this is not a permanent solution. Or it can be as elaborate as full brick or stone walls that require the skill and services of a mason to build.

As with the other design elements we've discussed so far, make sure that the borders you choose complement the style of your house.

Mulch on This

No garden looks quite complete without some sort of mulch topping. Mulch serves several purposes. Of course it's a terrific design element that gives your yard a crisp and professional finished look. But mulch also reduces the number of weeds that sprout in your gardens, and conserves moisture, which keeps your plants happy.

If you're looking for inexpensive walkways to connect different parts of your yard, mulch is a great idea. It comes in several attractive colors, and is made from a variety of materials, everything from pine bark to wood to rubber. Choose a color that complements the house.

Gazebos and Sheds

While gazebos and sheds are both outbuildings, they serve completely different purposes. Gazebos are somewhat fanciful buildings that have existed in some form or another in warm climates all over the globe for hundreds of years. However, they came into real prominence in England with the 1750 publication of a book about rural architecture in China. The author popularized the use of the word *gazebo* for such garden structures, and the classic English summerhouse version of a gazebo, the turreted tower with glass windows all around, was born.

If your yard already contains a gazebo and it is in good condition, good for you! If there is no gazebo, this is another thing you are not likely to add due to its expense.

A garden shed is another story. If you are working on an older home that has no garage or walk-out basement where things can be easily stored, the addition of a garden shed might make your house far more attractive. They're not cheap but not as expensive as gazebos. You can get a small garden shed delivered and installed for about $2,000.

Outdoor Lighting

Outdoor lighting is an essential part of any landscaping plan. At the minimum, you need a light over every entrance, and if your house has a garage, over the garage as well.

Lights are not only necessary so that residents can find their way around their house in the dark, but also as a safety feature and crime deterrent. Law enforcement officials stress that a house with sufficient outdoor lighting has a significantly lower risk of being targeted for burglary than a house with inadequate or missing exterior lights.

During the day, the role of a light fixture changes from providing illumination to becoming a design feature in your landscape. The style and placement of lighting fixtures is a significant element in the design of your hardscaping. Select lights that complement the style of your home. You'll find many different kinds of lights, such as coach lights, overhead porch lights, walkway lighting, freestanding pole lights, and so on, available within each design family, so you can create a unified lighting plan.

Upgrading Driveways and Walkways

Fortunately, most of the houses you buy will have driveways and walkways in good condition. After all, it's pretty difficult to destroy concrete. But after a while, even concrete can degrade and start to crumble. And when a tree root decides a concrete driveway is in its way, the driveway always loses. Winter weather can also do a number on concrete hardscaping.

In most cases, it is easiest to replace an ugly driveway or sidewalk. Patching usually only makes bad things looks worse. While most driveways are made from concrete or asphalt, many drive-ways are made from gravel and some are nothing more than dirt. Of course, if your house has a gravel or dirt driveway, you are going to want to upgrade that look. An attractive driveway is a critical element in curb appeal.

When you replace a driveway or walkway, you have to make drainage provisions to catch the water that flows off hard surfaces during a rain shower. You might need drain pipes or even a *French drain*. Some driveways are built over drainage culverts that empty into ditches in front of the house.

> **DEFINITION**
>
> A **French drain** is a sub-surface trench filled with gravel that uses a special perforated pipe that directs both ground and surface water away from things you want to protect from water damage, such as building foundations and concrete pavement.

It's important to install proper drains when you put in new concrete work. If you don't have them, standing water will start to collect around the driveway and walkways and eventually degrade the concrete to the point where it starts to crumble.

Fencing and Privacy Screens

The last thing you must address in your yard is your fences, gates, and privacy screens. If the fence or gate has damaged or missing boards, those must be replaced. If you have a basic structure, such as a chain link fence in your back or side yard, you might want to consider upgrading to a privacy fence if your budget will allow it. Chain link fences do nothing to enhance your home's curb appeal.

If your house is in a neighborhood that doesn't allow fences, use landscaping to form privacy screens that potential buyers will appreciate.

You can also use half-fences to define certain areas in the yard, such as a vegetable garden or play area.

Once you finish your landscaping and hardscaping repairs and upgrades, your curb appeal should make an exponential jump that will translate into more buyers.

The Least You Need to Know

- Great curb appeal translates into faster sales and higher offers.
- Use landscaping and hardscaping for the best results.
- An inviting entrance welcomes buyers in.
- Lighting plays a key role in curb appeal.

The Flip

The day your first flip is ready to market is a landmark, but the day it sells is even more special. That's when you'll realize that you can do this, that you *have* done this and launched yourself into a new career and a new way of life. There are not that many careers where you get to help people solve big problems and also get paid well to do so.

To achieve this milestone, you'll have to master staging, learn the best pricing and marketing strategies, and master the mountains of paperwork and legalese that accompany the sale of real estate property. When you split the profits of your first sale with your investor and set out to look for your next property, you'll know beyond a doubt that you have transformed your own life and become a flipper.

CHAPTER 18

To Stage or Not to Stage?

The halcyon day has arrived! You are finally ready to flip or sell the house you've put so much time, energy, money, and effort into reviving. Now that you have completed your flip, you have some decisions to make. Even though the renovation is complete, you can still do a lot to enhance the desirability of your property and increase the odds of a quick, full-price sale.

You certainly want to show all your hard work to its best advantage and give people who tour your house a compelling picture of its livability, traffic flow, and energy. You want to demonstrate in a clear way what the master bedroom or den could look like, so potential buyers can picture themselves in that setting.

We've learned through experience that staging a rehabbed house with attractive furnishings and accessories that complement the style of the home is the best way to accomplish all this and more. Think about it from a personal point of view. If you were looking for a home and had a choice between two identical homes in the same neighborhood, same price, but one was a blank, empty canvas of white walls and neutral floors, while the other was a colorful tableau of sofas, chairs, beds, table settings, lamps, plants, and colorful

In This Chapter

- The goals of staging
- Making an emotional connection with your buyers
- Choosing the right stager
- Matching staging style to the style of your home
- Managing staging costs

accessories, which one would appeal to you more? We can guarantee you, you'd pick the well-staged house. It will sell first every single time.

Home staging gives potential buyers an idea of what their own furnishings might look like in your house. It helps people imagine themselves and their families living in the house, and encourages them to consider what life might be like if this was the place they called home. When people are able to make this type of emotional connection with a house, a sales contract usually follows. Staging paves the road for this type of interaction.

Not only does good staging help houses sell quickly, data proves it also helps properties sell for higher prices. If you want to get top dollar and a fast turnover for your flip, whether or not to stage should not even be a question. Your only questions should be how many rooms to stage and how much you should spend to do it.

> **FLIP TIP**
>
> The National Association of Realtors reports that the value of a staged home increases an average of 6 to 10 percent over a comparable home that is not staged. That increased revenue on the sale means that staging often not only pays for itself, but also brings you additional profit over and above the cost of the staging. It's important to note that while staging can help improve a home's value, it is rare that staging alone would make a home sell for more than its appraised value.

So now the question is, how do you find the right stager and get the best staging job possible for an affordable price? You'll learn all you need to know to create a gorgeous, inviting staged scenario in this chapter.

What Does Staging Accomplish?

Some of you might not even be sure exactly what staging is, so a definition is in order. The term actually started out as *home staging*, but over the years, as the concept grew in popularity due to near-constant television exposure, that was shortened simply to *staging*.

> **DEFINITION**
>
> **Staging** is the art of using furniture, accessories, lighting, scent, and plants to create an inviting space that appeals to the largest possible number of buyers. Staging is completed prior to putting a house on the market.

The primary goals of staging are not just to make your house look its best and get a better sales price as a result but also to elicit an emotional reaction from potential buyers that encourages them to buy the home. Great staging should make visitors say, "Wow!" when they step through the door and then lead them to start thinking about living in the house. In their imaginations, you want buyers to feel like the home is already theirs.

Building Emotional Connections with Buyers

Why is it so important to grab your buyers by the heartstrings right away? Have you ever noticed that many TV commercials never mention the name of their brand or product at all? That's because marketers know it is more important to establish an emotional connection with potential customers than try to hard sell them right away. People who feel an emotional bond with something are far more likely to buy than those who don't. This isn't just us voicing an opinion. It's a scientific fact that's been proven in study after study, some conducted by scientists, others by advertisers and marketing researchers.

The same is true of the entire process of buying a home. It is an experience fraught with emotions for the buyer, seller, agent, and sometimes, even the lender. A buyer can go up, crash down, and soar up again literally dozens of times on a single transaction, and believe me, the selling agent is right there with them. Buyers want to be logical and think about smart things, such as potential resale value and such, but all too often their emotions get the upper hand and they make buying decisions based on that.

Emotional vs. Logical Buyers

Now, not all buyers are emotional. Some are as emotionless and logical as Mr. Spock on *Star Trek,* and naturally, the way you approach these buyers is completely different than how you interact with emotional buyers. The conundrum is that you frequently encounter couples where one is ruled by emotions and the other is coldly logical. While one is busy rhapsodizing about the granite countertops and how much Fido will love the fenced yard, the other will be inquiring about the average cost per square foot in the neighborhood, to make sure your house is a good deal, and grilling you about annual property taxes.

> **FLIP TIP**
>
> In 2005, neuroscientists at the University of Southern California conducted studies that showed emotions are a necessary component in all decisions. Emotions assign values and create preferences for various options in a process that ultimately leads to a decision being made. Without emotions, making a decision literally becomes impossible because people get stuck in an analytical loop. That's why staging is so important, because it stirs emotions in buyers and helps them reach buying decisions faster.

The point is even getting to these buying conversations, no matter whether they are logical or emotional, would take you longer if you had not invested in staging your home.

Can I Stage a House Myself?

Let's get this out of the way right now. The short answer is of course you can. But why would you? Staging homes is not your business, flipping houses is, and everything you do that takes time and energy away from that hinders your progress as a flipper.

If you happen to have a degree in interior design, we can understand why you would want to stage your houses, to put your own personal design imprint on them. But once again, this is something that can more easily be accomplished by hiring someone else to do the work for you. If you're a designer already, consider hiring a design student to make your vision for your house come to life. Give them your budget, color palette, and design sketches, and turn them loose. You will get just what you want for a smaller cost than if you hired a professional stager.

 FLIPPER BEWARE

> Many flippers start in the business by staging their own homes to save money. This can be one of those false economy situations though. Statistics prove that staging increases sales prices to the extent that it usually pays for itself, so don't feel like you absolutely must stage your homes yourself, particularly if you don't have any experience in staging. Just budget the money you need to do a proper staging, and you will soon see the wisdom of letting a pro do the job.

The only question you'll have to answer after you've sold the home you've staged yourself is what you will do with the furniture and accessories you bought. The simplest solution it to try selling them to the family that buys your home. Buyers frequently want the exact furnishings they see in a staged home. But if your buyers don't want them, either sell them or rent a storage unit to keep them for your next house, assuming the style will work in your next house. If you do store the items for future use, please be aware that you've now entered the staging business, too.

If you are determined to stage your house yourself, there are businesses that rent furniture to flippers, but be aware the styles tend to be generic and available only in a limited color palette, primarily grays or earth tones. In terms of appeal, most furniture available for rent from the major furniture rental chains is not what you would want to show off the unique charms of your house. Of course, there are exceptions to that. Some places do rent high-end furniture, but their prices are high end as well.

The other problem is that some furniture rental companies want you to sign a contract for a specific length of time. If your house sells quickly, you could end up paying for a couple of extra months of furniture rental even after your flip has already gone to the act of sale and the new owners have moved in.

After you've completed a few flips, if you come to realize you cannot or do not want to manage both a flipping and a staging business, sell whatever furniture and accessories you've acquired and put your focus back on your flipping business. It will give you more time to manage and grow your flipping business if you leave staging to the professionals who do it as their full-time business.

The Right Stager for Your Project

There are all sorts of stagers, ranging from degreed interior design professionals, to people who have turned their decorating hobby into a business, and many different levels of skill and ability in between.

As with all your other team members, the stager you choose will be determined by several factors. Start by getting names and recommendations for great stagers from your Realtor.

> **FLIP TIP**
>
> Having trouble finding a local stager? Visit the Real Estate Staging Association at realestatestagingassociation.com. The website has a search function that will help you find a stager who works in your area.

Interview each candidate, preferably in person, and tour their showrooms to get an idea of their taste levels and the design style they seem to like best. During the interview, don't forget to ask if they have any questions they would like you to answer. Encouraging a potential business associate to ask questions and speak freely often gives you a much better idea of their personality and work habits than following a rigid set of questions.

Ask to see photographs of their work to determine if they choose the staging style to suit each individual home, or simply do a variation of the same basic style in every house they work on. You definitely want to go with someone who designs unique staging for every house to highlight and enhance its unique features.

> **FLIPPER BEWARE**
>
> If you live in a smaller town or rural area, you might discover there are no stagers located anywhere close to you. If this is the case, try reaching out to stagers in nearby cities to get your rehabbed houses ready for viewing. It will cost you more since trip charges will be added to your total price for staging, but you can compensate for the additional expense with a faster sale and lower carrying costs.

After you've conducted your interviews and assessed individual design esthetics, choose the stager whose sense of style, taste level, and personality are a good fit for your own. Make sure they are flexible and willing to work on your schedule, and of course, select someone whose prices are reasonable and fit within your budget.

Assessing Style IQ

We've noticed that many stagers are heavily influenced by HGTV style. While that's not necessarily a bad thing, that sleek, modern, highly stylized staging you seem to see in almost every flipped property on TV can also be problematic.

While the style suits many houses, it doesn't work for every one, so when you're assessing flippers, make sure they can handle a variety of assignments, including period homes. You don't want to hire someone who will just keep producing the same staged look over and over again on every job with little consideration for the design of the home. And it's far better to learn something like this during the interview process than in the middle of a staging project gone wrong.

Ideally, you want a stager who has what we call a "high style IQ." They are conversant with the entire catalog of home and staging styles and seem to instinctively know which staging style will best complement your home and appeal to potential buyers. They either have or know where to get appropriate furnishings and accessories to suit every architectural style.

Now that educational programs specifically developed to train stagers are available, it is becoming easier to find professional stagers who are widely conversant with all the different decorative periods and styles. But despite good training, not all stagers are prepared to stage every style of home. Many maintain a very attractive but also somewhat generic assortment of furnishings and accessories that look good in several basic styles of home. This approach keeps their costs down. But unless you always flip the same type of house, which is unlikely, you really need to find a stager whose abilities and furniture inventory are more diverse.

> **FLIP TIP**
>
> If you rehab a very specific style of home, say a turn-of-the-century Gothic mansion, you might not be able to find a stager who has the sort of ornate, heavy, dark, and dramatic furniture a house from such a unique design period requires. Try a theatrical rental company instead, and see if they have suitable period furnishings you can rent from their prop department.

Other stagers get stuck in a sort of time warp and focus their expertise on staging only one style of home. For example, they might specialize in the mid-century modern esthetic or Victorian cottage gingerbread style. That's fantastic if you're flipping mid-century modern homes or

Victorian cottages … a perfect match of flipper and stager. But if you're flipping Craftsman bungalows one after the other, those styles of staging are not going to match the style of your homes and if your stager's mind is stuck in the 1950s or 1890s, you might end up with staging that just doesn't work with your house. Instead of helping your sales, this kind of disjointed staging will hinder them, because the picture your home presents to potential buyers will clash with the image they have in their heads of the perfect Craftsman interior.

Every house, no matter how unusual it might be, can look better and more appealing with a great staging job. It might be that you work with several stagers: one who specializes in contemporary, and another who shines when staging neo-Gothic homes, and still a third whose work is outstanding in Craftsman-style homes. While recommendations are a great place to start, you will only truly know your stager's style IQ after you've done a few projects together. Eventually, as the working relationship solidifies, you might be able to communicate your ideas effectively with just a few words because you've come to know and trust each other to such a great degree. That's the ideal we should all aim for.

Checking Inventory

Be sure to check with your stager in advance about the availability of the furniture and accessories you want for your home. Most stagers work with many flippers and must deal with several demands from their various clients at the same time, particularly during the busy summer selling season. They might not be able to supply what you need when you need it just because you snap your fingers and say you want it.

Give your stager a heads up many weeks ahead of when you expect to complete your flip. This will allow them to pencil you into their schedules so they can reserve the furnishings and accessories required to complete your job to your specification. This kind of proactive communication is vitally important to keep your flip running smoothly and on schedule.

Remember that in flipping, every day your house is not on the market is a day that is costing you money. Ideally, you don't want your flip sitting empty and not yet listed for sale for more than a few days after you complete all the rehab work and cleaning.

Scheduling a Stager

Speaking of scheduling, you should never schedule a stager until your rehab is 100 percent complete and your house has been thoroughly cleaned. No stager wants to work with power drills and generators running. Nor would they appreciate being asked to stage a house with workmen tracking mud back and forth across their just polished floors. You can't blame them for not wanting to put time and effort into properly staging a home that is dusty or still has bits of construction debris lying about, either. Getting rid of dirt and debris is *not* your stager's job. It's your job. Hire a professional cleaning crew to make sure the whole house is properly cleaned before the stager arrives.

That said, once the staging is complete, you should expect the stager to leave your house sparkling clean and ready for showing. Staging creates a lot of trash when furniture and accessories are unwrapped. Your stager should remove all the trash, dust and polish all surfaces, and polish and vacuum the floors as needed. Your house should literally sparkle when the staging is complete.

You shouldn't wait until the last minute to call a stager and expect them to show up that afternoon with a truck full of high-class furniture. Gathering all the items to create a properly staged home takes time. In a sense, the stager is moving into your home with beds, sofas, lamps, tables, chairs, just about everything a normal family would bring with them if they were actually moving into the house. An operation of that size obviously takes a fair amount of time to organize and put together.

FLIPPER BEWARE

Never ask a stager to help you cover up a flaw in the home. That's not ethical. You should have taken care of all flaws and required repairs during the rehab. However, you could ask a stager to help you make a room look larger with a clever staging, or brighter by adding more lamps, but this type of staging is ethical because it's meant only to enhance a home's features and not hide defects.

It's also important to make sure the stager understands your vision for the final look of the house. The first few times you work with your stager, you will need to exercise more oversight until you become comfortable with each other and you are confident the results of the staging will be in line with your concept for the overall look and feel of the home.

Which Rooms Should You Stage?

We often get asked by beginning flippers if they have to stage every room in their house. Of course they don't. That would cost a fortune. Work with the natural traffic flow of the house and stage the first couple of rooms a visitor will see, plus the master bedroom.

We like to stage the primary living area and the master bedroom, and do a mini staging in the kitchen and bathrooms. First impressions do count, and you only have a few minutes to wow a potential buyer and create an emotional response to your house.

Remember that emotional responses must occur before buying decisions can be reached, so go for the wow factor to grab visitors from the second they cross the threshold. If the couple of staged rooms they see don't grab them right away, they will likely leave quickly, perhaps without even touring the entire house.

You should fully stage the primary living area to show potential buyers what a family gathering spot could look like. This is especially important in homes featuring an open concept where the living area is undefined … just one large room that is intended for eating, watching TV, playing games, family time, and visiting. You can help define the space in your buyers' minds and show them how the room might be used with the clever placement of furniture and accessories.

Spaces within the large room should be designated by the choice of furniture used there. A sofa, recliner, coffee table, and TV can define the entertaining and family gathering area, while a lovely table set with cheerful dishes and linens and a fruit centerpiece can designate the dining area. A toy box and colorful rubber floor mats nicely carve out the children's play area.

Since you focused much of your rehab money on the kitchen and bathrooms, they already look great and don't require a full staging. You just need to do enough to make these rooms look warm, personable and inviting. Give these areas a *mini staging* to provide buyers with decorating and lifestyle ideas.

> **DEFINITION**
>
> A **mini staging** is crafted using colorful accessories that create a sense of a desirable lifestyle. While the feeling a mini staging evokes can range from elegant to warm and homey, it is basically a shorthand way of eliciting an emotional response from buyers and expressing moods and design ideas rather than a full-on staging complete with lots of furniture.

All you need are small touches, such as a canister set and pots of fresh herbs in the kitchen, or a bowl of fresh fruit on the counter. Hanging towels, and placing a bath rug and perhaps soap in a dish are enough to stage the bathrooms.

When you are staging, don't forget scent! You want your house to smell as good as it looks. A tried and true method is to keep a tray of freshly baked chocolate-chip cookies on warm in the oven. That delicious scent will welcome in your visitors and have them thinking about making their own cookies and other treats in your gorgeous kitchen.

In the bathroom, use a natural oil diffuser to waft a light scent through the room and keep it smelling fresh. This is not meant to mask bad odors. You should have gotten rid of the source of all unpleasant odors during your rehab. This is just to add a nice, pleasant aroma to the bathrooms.

FLIPPER BEWARE

There is nothing that can kill a sale faster than an off smell with an unknown origin. When things smell musty, moldy, or damp, people automatically assume something is wrong with the house and will make a quick exit. Make absolutely certain you have completely removed all possible sources of bad odors from your house during the rehab.

Staging is meant to tell a story about the home that potential buyers can relate to. The idea is to encourage visitors to make themselves the star of the story your house is telling. If they love your staging, chances are they'll love the house and they'll want to place an offer to buy it as quickly as they can put pen to paper.

How Much Does It Cost?

The general rule of thumb is that quality staging costs about 1 percent of the selling price of your house. Of course, this price could go up or down depending on the number of rooms you choose to stage and the amount and quality of furniture and decorative accessories used.

FLIP TIP

According to Kiplinger.com, sellers spend an average of $1,800 on staging to flip a house. Of course, costs vary depending on the size of the house, but even an expensive, high-end home selling for seven figures can generally be staged for no more than $5,000 to $10,000.

If you stick to the recommended budgets, your staging should pay for itself with a fast sale and by helping you command a higher price for your home.

How Long Will It Take?

Although you must invest some time up front discussing style and design ideas with your stager and selecting items for your house, the actual process of staging can be accomplished in a day or less. Sometimes stagers only require a few hours to complete their work, especially if the house is on the smaller side.

Many stagers use moving vans or rented trucks to bring furniture and décor items to your house, so don't be surprised when you see a huge truck rolling up to your door on staging day. Most staging crews consist of two to four people, with at least two strong crew members who can effortlessly carry and place heavy furniture without nicking door frames or scuffing your floors.

Is It Worth It?

We are frequently asked if staging is worth the investment. The answer is yes, yes, and yes. Widely available data proves that well-staged homes consistently sell for more money and spend fewer days on the market. Every time a new analysis is done, the results are the same: staged homes come out on top.

On the one hand, you make more money because your sales price can be higher, and on the other hand, you save more money because your carrying costs are lower when your house sells quickly. That all adds up to more profit for you and your investor.

If you're looking to save money on a flip, staging costs are not the place to do it. It's one of the few investments you can count on to not only pay for itself but also make you more money in the end.

The Least You Need to Know

- Good staging helps houses sell faster and for a better price than nonstaged homes of comparable value can get.
- Staging can create an instant emotional bond between your house and potential buyers, and that bond leads to sales contracts.
- Choose a stager whose style and taste level are similar to your own.
- Make sure your stager can handle many different styles of house and won't just keep putting the same furniture into every flip you do.
- Use staging to define spaces and encourage potential buyers to think of themselves living in your house.
- You don't have to stage every room to take full advantage of the power of staging.

CHAPTER 19

Price and Marketing Strategies

Pricing your renovated house strategically is a crucial step in determining how fast your completed flip will sell. You must take into account all the factors affecting housing prices at the time you go to market: overall demand, the desirability of your particular neighborhood, average recent sale prices for houses of a similar size, condition, and style, available inventory compared to buyer demand, current mortgage interest rates, and even the state of the overall economy. All these factors might not only influence how you price your flip but also how quickly you sell it.

Naturally, you want to get as much money as possible as compensation for your hard work, but no matter how attractive your house is, no matter what amenities you have added or fantastic staging you've put in, if you price your house over market it's going to take longer to sell. You already know that time is money in the flipping business, so if your finished house sits on the market and sells in 30 days instead of 5 because you have it overpriced, even if you got your full asking price you'll come out with less profit after you subtract all the additional carrying costs on your property for an extra 25 days.

In This Chapter

- The importance of strategic pricing
- Why you should avoid overpricing your flip
- Fast sales should be your goal
- Creating a marketing plan

Ideally, the sale of a house should be like a surgical strike. If you've studied the market, bought a house in a trending neighborhood with high demand, rehabbed your house according to buyer preferences and priced it correctly, buyers will be tripping over each other in their haste to claim it as their own. But if you bought the first house you saw in an okay neighborhood, did a quick superficial rehab and overpriced it, you're going to be babysitting that house for a long time.

Selling a house is not just about setting the correct sales price; it's also about doing the proper marketing to let prospective buyers know your house is available. In this chapter, we'll take you through the steps you need to price your house correctly and market it effectively, all with the goal of getting a fast and profitable sale so you can move on to the next flip.

Working with a Realtor to Set Prices

When it comes to setting the correct price for a house, no one can do it better than a Realtor. They know neighborhoods; they stay on top of housing inventory, which can change hourly; they know buyer demand. They know if the market is slow or moving quickly; they know interest rates and how that is affecting house sales. On top of that, they have inside information that ordinary everyday people couldn't hope to know, such as which major corporation will be moving into or out of a location soon, and how that will affect housing inventory and buyer demand. All of these factors and more can play a role in pricing your house strategically for your market.

 FLIPPER BEWARE

It is essential to price your house correctly so potential buyers can find it in an online search. For example, say a buyer is approved for a $250,000 home. Your home should be listed at $250,000 based on comps, but you listed at $260,000 to give yourself some "negotiating" room. The problem is your target buyers will never find your home online because they are searching for houses listed at $250,000 and under. By overpricing, you might completely cut your house out of the online market, which is where 90 percent of buyers begin their search for a home.

If you tried to gather all this information on your own, it could literally take you a week or more, that is, if you could even get access to the information you need. With their professional level access to MLS, Realtors can do a search to find available *comparables,* check which houses have sold in the neighborhood recently and for how much, how long they were on the market before they sold, and also see which houses are currently on the market that might compete with your house for buyers. They then use the comps to perform what is known as a *Comparative Market Analysis (CMA)* to help set an accurate price on new listings.

DEFINITION

Comparables, or *comps* for short, are evaluations of houses of similar age, size, design, and condition that recently sold in the same neighborhood. Comps are used to help Realtors and sellers establish a fair market value for similar properties about to come on to the market.

A **Comparative Market Analysis (CMA)** is an evaluation of comparable properties located near a home about to be listed for sale. Looking at similar recently sold properties helps you set the correct price for your house. Comps are also influenced by lot size, location, and other amenities. For example, if your house is the same as a house down the street but yours has a water view, your sales price would be higher than that of the house with no view.

Realtors who regularly work with flippers are aware of the need for fast sales. They might suggest that you come in slightly under market with your starting price to improve your chance of selling quickly, particularly if there are many similar houses already on the market in your neighborhood.

Conversely, if you were able to buy a house in a high-demand neighborhood where inventory is low and it's got something a little extra or special the comps don't have, your Realtor might recommend testing the market for a few days at a slightly higher price, to see if there is enough demand to support asking a few thousand dollars more.

If an auction situation develops, where two or more hopeful buyers are bidding against each other to acquire your house, you might even get more than your asking price for the home. An auction is a good indication that you and your Realtor have read the market well and priced the home correctly.

Assessing Market Conditions

Market conditions have a lot to do with how fast your house sells, and the price you can get for your property. You can have a spectacular flip listed $5,000 under market and still have difficulty selling it if overall market conditions are not favorable.

For example, back in the early 1980s, America went through a period of ridiculously high mortgage interest, with rates peaking at 18.5 percent for a mortgage on a single-family home in 1982. Can you imagine paying credit card interest rates for a purchase as large as a home? It effectively meant that 82 percent of your house notes went just to pay interest over the life of the mortgage, about $900,000 on a 30-year loan for a house that cost just $82,500 when purchased.

Mortgage rates were so bad they priced most Americans out of the housing market entirely. Very few families could afford the monthly payments on even a modestly priced home with interest rates so high. Basically, mortgage rates killed the real estate market, and it stayed dead until some sanity came back into the Federal Reserve, which had been spiking interest rates in a futile effort to control inflation. Instead, they destroyed the American dream of home ownership and a lot of people's careers in the process. Consequences were felt in the housing market for years, and it took a long time for things to get back to a semblance of normalcy.

Today, the Federal Reserve is doing just the opposite, keeping mortgage rates near historic lows to stimulate a sluggish economy. As a consequence, now is a good time to buy and sell real estate.

Unless you happen to be on the board of the Federal Reserve, these factors are out of your control, but there are many things you and your Realtor can do to price your house attractively and encourage a quick sale. Realtors are uniquely qualified to assess current market conditions and how your house fits into with them. They have their fingers on the pulse of the local housing market and are familiar with all the factors that shape current market conditions.

FLIP TIP

Homes that linger on the market longer than 30 days can start to develop a reputation among Realtors, deserved or not, of being a problem property. Overpricing is the leading reason an attractive rehab sits around without selling. No matter how tempted you are to grab for a few extra thousand dollars, never overprice a property. It will cost you thousands of extra dollars in the end.

Realtors also know about national trends affecting home sales and financial trends affecting interest rates and the ability to finance a home. In other words, they are equipped to help you assess the current market conditions in your area and how they might help or hinder the sale of your home.

Our best advice: Don't try to figure out market conditions on your own. Let your Realtor shine here. They have the tools, knowledge, and experience to expertly assess current market conditions and price your house so that it will have a good chance of a fast sale. This is also when you challenge your agent on their research to make sure they put in the time to really think through the evaluation. You want to make sure the Realtor is getting the best return for you, not just a quick sale for them so they can move on to the next.

Weighing Profit vs. Speed of Sale

It's natural to want to make as much money as possible on the sale of your house. However, if you ignore comparables and market conditions, and price your house over the market in an attempt to rake in a few more dollars, exactly the opposite will happen. If and when you do finally do sell your house, you'll make much less money because of the excessive carrying costs you'll have to pay while the house sits on the market unsold. And believe me, you will be forced to sell it for less than comparable price if you want to sell it at all.

But let's say that against all odds, you somehow found a family that doesn't care about the inflated price; they just want your house. Now you have a brand new problem. The pros who appraise houses know the current prevailing prices for every type of property, and it is likely they will appraise your house for its true market value and not the inflated price your buyers are willing to pay. That means your buyers will have to come up with the difference between the appraised value and what they paid for the house in cold hard cash, because no bank is going to finance the discrepancy. What happens in these situations in real life is that most of these sales end up falling through because the buyers can't come up with the extra cash and the realistic appraisal tends to serve as a wake-up call served with a side of buyer's remorse. No one likes to feel they're being taken, and a low appraisal is an easy and ethical way for a buyer who's had time to think things over to get out of a bad deal.

The market is very smart. Thanks to the internet, buyers are more informed today than at any time in history. They know neighborhoods and prices very well, and a house that is over-priced will stand out like a black eye. Chances are, buyers won't even be tempted to tour an overpriced house. As more and more time goes by with no offers, the house will begin to develop a reputation as "the house that won't sell," and it becomes a self-reinforcing downward spiral until, in desperation, you drop the price below comparables just to get rid of the thing and get your operating capital back. By this time, thanks to carrying costs, there will be little to no profit left to divide.

 FLIPPER BEWARE

Nothing kills potential sales faster than an unrealistically high starting price. Too high an asking price can permanently taint your home's reputation in the market and hurt your chance of selling the property quickly.

A fast sale is key in flipping. If all other factors such as neighborhood demand and condition of the home are correctly aligned, then homes that are correctly priced generally sell within 30 days, and usually much less, of being placed on the market.

Marketing Your Flip

Once you've set your price, it's time to think about attracting buyers. If you followed the advice in Chapter 7 about location, you bought a property in a high-demand neighborhood, which is half the battle with marketing. If you have something people want, they will come to you, that is, as long as they know your house exists. That's where marketing comes in. You must let buyers know you have a desirable property available for sale. So, let's discuss the various ways you can let potential buyers know about your house.

The Power of MLS

There are many reasons why you should list your property for sale with a professional Realtor instead of trying to market it yourself. Realtors know the market, know what is selling, and have access to many buyers who might like to place an offer on your house. They know real estate law, and can negotiate dispassionately with buyers or a buyer's agent in order to get you the best offer.

But by far, the greatest advantage Realtors have over everyone else is their full, professional level access to MLS. You cannot list your property on MLS yourself. Only a licensed Realtor can do that. And if your house is not on MLS, it's basically invisible to buyers because even popular online property search services, such as like Trulia and Zillow, pull their listings from MLS.

Once your property is listed on MLS, every licensed Realtor with anxious buyers looking for just the right house at the right price can instantly access full information about your property and start scheduling showings.

As amazing as that is, if you make no further marketing efforts on behalf of your house, it might still sit on the market longer than you'd like. Marketing needs to be a coordinated effort that reaches out to as many different potential buyers as possible, through as many different means as are practical.

Photographs That Sell

If you want your house to sell quickly, make sure an experienced real estate photographer gets a full set of photos of both the exterior and the interior. Nothing frustrates a buyer who is searching online more than not being able to see all the rooms in a home. It makes them think something is wrong with the room or rooms that are not shown.

Ideally, photos should be taken immediately after the house is staged, when it is looking its very best.

 FLIPPER BEWARE

Poor quality, badly lit, unfocused photos can ruin your chances of selling your house. We assume every Realtor has a professional real estate photographer on speed dial, but judging from the dark, fuzzy photos we see on some listings, maybe not. If you are not happy with the quality of photos on your MLS listing, speak up! Even if you have to pay for them, get the photos taken again and insist that the better quality photos be used to replace the bad photos on MLS. Most buyers skip right over listings with bad photos.

Once the photos are posted on your MLS listing, ask your Realtor to let you check them out so you can make sure they present your house in its best light, and clearly show all the rooms and notable features.

Networking with Other Realtors

Many houses sell just from Realtors networking with each other. Your Realtor might not have any clients currently in the market for a house like yours, but you can bet he or she knows another Realtor who does.

Realtors network by email, phone, and at social and business gatherings. They tend to know other Realtors in their office who have clients looking for the kind of house you're selling. They talk back and forth often, both to stay informed about what is new in the market and to learn who has active listings and buyers. This casual networking really does help sell houses more quickly.

By far, the most effective way of networking for Realtors is the weekly *agents' open house* tour held for new listings. Every real estate office has them. All the Realtors in a particular office tour all that company's newly listed houses on one particular day. Your listing agent meets and greets each Realtor, answers any questions they might have about the listing, and offers a business card and a flyer containing pertinent info about your house.

> **DEFINITION**
>
> An **agents' open house** is a special open house held for licensed Realtors when a new listing first goes on the market.

These open houses give agents an opportunity to speak directly with your Realtor and preview your house for their current active buyers. If they see a house they think is right for a client, they'll tell your agent, contact their buyers, and set up a showing right away. In some cases, your house might sell from an agents' open house before your Realtor even has a chance to place an ad.

Advertising

No real estate marketing plan is complete without advertising. In the age of internet, there are more advertising options available to sell houses than ever before.

Because of the number and diversity of advertising platforms available today, it's easy to over-spend on advertising unless you make a precise plan for your ad dollars. Let's review the most popular options.

Classifieds

Classified ads used to be the bread and butter of Realtors. It was the major way they marketed their properties. Homebuyers spent hours with real estate classified ad sections from various newspapers and magazines, a magnifying glass in hand so they could read the tiny type, and a red pen to circle the listings that interested them.

There still are classified ads, even some printed in newspapers and magazines, but their significance has shrunk since any buyer can use their smart phone, tablet, or personal computer to look up any listing, complete with 20 to 30 color photos and full information for any houses that interest them. What a tiny black-and-white classified ad offers pales by comparison.

On-Site Property Flyers

On-site property flyers only used to be offered for high-end listings because of the expense associated with printing color photos. The idea of spending a thousand dollars to print a flyer to help sell an $80,000 house never entered any Realtor's mind.

That's another thing the advent of personal computers has changed. Every house now has full-color property flyers available that passersby can grab from a weatherproof plastic box on the listing sign. Realtors love these flyers because potential buyers have already identified a house they like in the neighborhood they want. If the inside of the house and price match their expectations, oftentimes a sale can result.

Craigslist

Many real estate classifieds now run on online advertising services, such as craigslist.com, where it is possible to show a couple of color photos along with basic listing information.

Some people have mentioned that craigslist ads have become the modern equivalent of the old newspaper classifieds. We think it's true, because there are literally hundreds of real estate ads on Craiglist no matter where in the country you might live.

Broker Ads

Broker ads used to be one of the most coveted forms of advertising for a newly listed house. Brokers would take out a full-page newspaper ad, preferably on the back page of the classified section. Black-and-white photos of featured homes grabbed buyers' attention in a way that small classifieds could never hope to emulate. Homeowners fought bitterly to have their house featured in broker ads, but in reality, they were reserved for only the most significant new listings.

Thanks to the advent of internet advertising with full-color photos for every listing, today broker ads have lost much of their importance, but they do still appear in some newspapers, and are still considered to be a premium sort of ad, since only the most important listings are featured.

Broker and Agent Websites

Nowadays, broker and agent websites have pretty much taken the place of broker ads. Even if they are part of a larger franchise, each individual broker maintains a website with listings generated in that office. Buyers can search the listings to see if any of the houses match their needs.

Top-selling agents also maintain individual websites featuring their listings. These websites serve not only to promote the agent's listings but also the services of the agent.

These websites are good for informational purposes, but online buyers rarely seek out individual brokers' or Realtors' websites unless they are looking for an agent. If they are in the market for a house, they are more likely to visit a large public site, such as Trulia or Zillow, where they'll be able to find information about listings from all the different brokers at once.

Emails

Email marketing has become an important component of real estate advertising. If you've done business with an agent or signed up for their newsletter, they will market to you. This is called relationship marketing. Even if you've never met an agent in person, when you receive an informative weekly newsletter from the same agent, over time you begin to feel as if you know them, and in fact, have a relationship of sorts with them.

> **FLIP TIP**
>
> Looking to the future, you can take a page from your Realtor's book and start collecting emails so you can do some relationship marketing of your own. As you grow your business and are looking for ways to expand your reach, you can use your email list to contact people when you have a new flip available for sale. It is possible that as you build your brand and become better known as a flipper that people will actually start to look for houses you have rehabbed.

Relationship marketing works. When it comes time for one of the recipients of these emails to buy or sell a house, do you think they'll go scouring the internet for an agent? No, they prefer to do business with the agent who has been reaching out to them for years. But these emails don't only serve the agent's interests. Each email contains information about new listings and a link to see the online listing and full information about the house. So emails really do help sell houses as well as build relationships.

Social Media Ads

Some Realtors have been experimenting with placing ads on social media sites, such as Facebook, Instagram, and Twitter. The idea is that you can reach a lot of customers quickly online.

While there might well be a future in this, at the moment, social media ads are not effective enough on a local basis to fully justify the very expensive cost.

Postcards

Postcards are another form of relationship marketing. They are a bit old-fashioned; Realtors have been sending them out to select neighborhoods to advertise new listings for decades. The reason they are still around is that they work. When neighbors get a personalized post card saying a house in their neighborhood is for sale, that might be enough to sell the house. Someone might be looking for a nearby home for their mother, sister, or adult child. Friends might want to live in the same neighborhood, or they might know someone wanting to move into the neighborhood so their children can go to a particular school.

Whatever the reason for their effectiveness, the bottom line is that postcards work. Despite the expense of color printing on glossy card stock and postage, a postcard mailing generally recoups its cost in terms of new business for the Realtor. They frequently help to sell homes as well.

Word of Mouth

Never discount the power of word of mouth to sell a house, particularly if your house is located in a high-demand neighborhood. People who live in popular neighborhoods always seem to be on the lookout for homes they can recommend to family members and friends who want to live nearby. Or they might want a larger house in the same neighborhood, so they turn to their network of friends to keep their eyes open for new listings.

Open Houses

While open houses can be an important component in exposing your house to the buying public, it is not physically possible for your agent to hold open houses every weekend for your home. They have to split their time among all their listings, which means you might be fortunate to get one open house over the life of your listing. And even that could be hosted by a subagent if your Realtor is spread too thin.

The truth is anyone who wants to see your house just has to pick up the phone and schedule a showing, so don't relentlessly badger your Realtor about open houses. While motivated buyers certainly do attend open houses, sometimes, no one comes through but the tire kickers who have no intention of buying a house any time soon.

You and your Realtor should discuss all the available types of advertising for your home, and draw up a marketing game plan that outlines what forms of advertising you plan to use and your advertising budget, if any. Be flexible. If you see one form of advertising is delivering better results than the others, don't be afraid to cancel the ineffective ads so you can devote more money to the ads that are working.

Maintaining Listed Property

While your house is on the market, you cannot forget to keep it well-maintained. Even if you have already moved on to your next flip, you still must mow the lawn, run the vacuum and sweep up after showings, and keep the place dusted and generally looking clean and inviting.

> **FLIP TIP**
>
> Many cleaning services offer special deals to house flippers. They will send a crew once a week to give your house a basic once over, vacuum, dust, and polish. It's well worth the modest investment to keep your house looking its best.

It doesn't make sense to spend marketing dollars advertising a house that isn't being maintained in absolutely pristine condition. Some buyers are so picky about dirt that if they see one dust bunny, they'll turn and walk out. You don't have to be the person pushing the broom. Just make sure that someone is doing the job.

The Least You Need to Know

- Pricing your flip correctly can lead to a fast sale.
- Overpricing a house can really hurt its chances of selling.
- You can market your flip in many different ways.
- The most effective marketing plans utilize many different forms of advertising.
- It's important to maintain your property while it is on the market.

CHAPTER 20

Gathering Offers

There is perhaps no more exciting feeling in the world than answering a phone call and hearing your Realtor say there's an offer on your flip, unless of course the call is to tell you that you have two offers, or perhaps even three.

That's not as unrealistic as it might sound. If market conditions and interest rates are reasonable and you've done your job well—bought in a hot neighborhood, created a beautiful and well-staged rehab, and priced your house strategically—you should get more than one offer within a short time after placing your flip on the market.

But how do you pick the best offer? There are many factors you must consider. The highest bid isn't always the smartest choice or even the best deal. You must look at what kind of offer it is, whether or not there are any contingencies attached to it, and whether it's an all-cash offer or the buyer will need a mortgage to finance the purchase. How much of a down payment is the buyer offering? How much earnest money? When will the sale close? You need to discuss these questions and many more with your Realtor before you settle on one offer to accept.

In This Chapter

* Purchase offers explained
* How to select the best offer
* The value of an all-cash offer
* Be careful of contingencies
* What to do if an accepted offer falls through

Of course, there's always the possibility that the offer on the table is not acceptable and you'll reject it outright or try to get better terms. Negotiating an offer can be a delicate dance, but experienced Realtors know exactly how to move to that music because they've done it many times.

Homebuyers can be as skittish as baby deer. One moment they love your house and can't wait to move in, and the next they're looking for ways to withdraw their offer. If you do have an attractive offer on the table, you and your agent should move quickly to get it signed and accepted.

This chapter will guide you through how to assess offers to buy your house and choose the best one.

You Have an Offer—Now What?

Congratulations! All your hard work has paid off and you now have your first offer to buy your rehabbed property. You've taken a big step into a new world, so take a bow, because getting an offer means you did a great job on your first flip.

Once you've finished your champagne and the initial adrenalin rush of getting an offer on your house has worn off, what's next? How you respond will depend upon a number of factors, including:

- How long the house has been on the market

- How close the offer is to your asking price

- What type of financing the potential buyer needs

- How soon the offer will close

- Whether there are any *contingencies* attached to the offer

- Whether you are considering one offer or multiple offers at the same time

Offers are classified from strong to weak based on the factors mentioned above. The strongest offers are full-price, all-cash offers that close within 30 days or less with no contingencies attached to the offer. If you get one of those, you're set.

> **DEFINITION**
>
> A **contingency** is a condition a buyer attaches to an offer that must be met before the sales contract becomes valid. For example, if a buyer first must sell their current home before they can pay the down payment to buy your home, they will make their purchase offer contingent upon the sale of their home. If they cannot sell their home, the offer on your house becomes invalid because the conditions set out in the contingency were not met.

Here's an example of how these factors can influence the decision you make on a pending offer. If you receive a low offer on the first day your house is available for sale, you will likely ignore it in favor of waiting to see how the market is going to respond to your listing. (In real estate, ignoring an offer is the same as rejecting it.) But if 30 days goes by with little activity on the house and no offers and then you finally receive a low offer on Day 31, you would probably want to make a serious effort to negotiate with that buyer to find a price you both can live with.

Another example is a buyer who offers full price but with the contingency that you leave your grandmother's rare and expensive Persian rug you put in the dining room to add a touch of class. If you're fine with that, go ahead and accept the offer. If you believe you should get additional money for throwing in a valuable family heirloom, then you either must negotiate new terms or reject the offer.

Your agent will review the terms of the offer with you and make recommendations for your consideration. Generally speaking, you have 48 hours to respond to an offer. You can either accept the offer, reject it, or reply with a *counteroffer* if you are interested in the buyer but don't like the price that's been offered.

DEFINITION

A **counteroffer** is a revised offer requesting a higher price that you tender to a prospective buyer after rejecting their initial offer to buy. It keeps the contract alive while you attempt to get the buyer to offer additional money for your property. Counteroffers are a common negotiating strategy in real estate transactions.

Evaluating a Single Offer

Don't worry if you only get one offer on your rehab. You really only need one. Assuming the offer is reasonable, your house will be sold just like that.

An offer to buy a house outlines the terms of the purchase in great detail, including the following:

- It includes the price the buyer is willing to pay

- It includes the amount of down payment the buyer is offering.

- It includes how much of the purchase price, if any, will be financed.

- It also specifies what type of financing the buyer plans to seek— conventional, FHA, or VA mortgage.

- It states the date for the closing or act of sale.

- An offer will also state if the buyer will be paying all cash. When you get an all-cash offer close to your asking price, that should shoot the offer to the top of the deck, because all-cash offers are the Holy Grail in real estate. Everybody is always hoping to get one.

- The offer also describes the deed to the property and calls out any restrictions, such as water or mineral rights, the property might be subject to.

- Purchase offers describe sewer and water connections, specifying whether a property is connected to a municipal system or draws water from a well with sewage going into a septic tank.

All offers to buy are contingent upon getting a clean inspection, unless the buyer specifically acknowledges he is accepting the house in as-is condition. If the inspection turns up significant previously unknown problems with the house, the buyer is allowed to withdraw his offer without prejudice and gets his earnest money back. Or, if the buyer really likes the house, he might prefer to negotiate for a lower sales price to cover the cost of repairs. Of course, since your house is a flip, ideally you should have discovered and completely repaired any defects to the house long before you put it on the market, so this should not happen to you very often.

If the buyer is pre-approved for a specific loan amount, that's a big plus because it removes a major source of worry for sellers. Knowing that the potential buyer can actually secure financing for the purchase of the house removes a big question mark.

Property taxes and utility payments are prorated, with the seller being responsible for all monies due up to the date of the act of sale and the buyer assuming responsibility for those expenses on that date. If the seller has already paid property taxes for the entire year, he or she will receive a prorated refund for the amount that is the buyer's responsibility.

Buyers are entitled to a final inspection, often called a walk-through, right before the act of sale. This allows them to check and make sure any requested repairs have been done and that the property is in good order.

FLIP TIP

All offers to buy contain some type of addenda or contingency. The most common makes the sale contingent upon the house passing inspection. Other common addenda specify who pays closing costs, a request for a seller's disclosure in which the seller declares he has represented the property accurately and to the best of his knowledge, or a hazard disclosure in which the buyer asks the seller to declare the property free of hazardous substances, such as lead-based paint or materials containing asbestos.

Some offers also include a request by the buyer to occupy the property prior to the closing. If you and your agent are comfortable with this, negotiate a price for the rental period and include this information as an addendum when you accept the contract.

Finally, if the same Realtor represents both the seller and the buyer, he or she must disclose that on the sales contract. This is called *dual agency representation,* but it is not legal in every state, so check your local ordinances to see if it is possible in your area.

You have a specific amount of time to respond to the offer, usually 48 hours. If you do not respond, the offer is considered rejected, and the buyer can then either place a second, higher offer or walk away.

As soon as you accept an offer, it becomes a legally binding contract. Each offer is accompanied by a check for earnest money, which is usually 1 percent of the asking price. For example, if the offer is for $300,000, the earnest money deposit will be for $3,000. In some locations, earnest money is just a flat $100 check. Your Realtor can tell you how it is handled in your area.

 FLIPPER BEWARE

If a deal fails because the buyer cannot obtain financing, earnest money is generally returned to the buyer, unless your agent has added a specific addendum to the contract that states the seller will keep it in case of a failure to obtain a loan.

Earnest money is meant to show the seller that the buyer is serious about buying their property. The funds are held by the Realtor in an escrow account. When the sale closes, the earnest money is applied to the total amount due from the buyer at the act of sale. If the buyer pulls out of the deal for any reason, the seller gets to keep the earnest money. If the seller terminates the deal, the earnest money goes back to the buyer.

Other Factors Influencing Your Decision

Several other favors could influence your response to an offer, including overall housing market conditions and how long your house has been for sale. If there is high demand for housing in your neighborhood but low inventory, in other words, more buyers than available houses, you can stick to your asking price more closely than if there were five comparable houses for sale in your same neighborhood but not that many buyers in the market. All these things are interconnected and work together to create current market conditions, which can change rapidly, another good reason why you should be working with an experienced Realtor who keeps up with these things and can keep you informed.

The other factor you must evaluate when you receive an offer is how long your house has been on the market. The owner of a newly listed house that is generating lots of interest and offers from several hopeful buyers has more cards to play than the owner of a house that has been for sale for 2 months with no offers.

Realtors know all the pertinent information about every listing in the market and will advise their buying clients accordingly. An experienced Realtor would never advise a buyer to come in with a full-price offer on a house that has been on the market for a while with no offers, but if they want a serious negotiation, neither will they advise them to make an offer that's so low it's insulting to the homeowner.

> **FLIP TIP**
>
> If your agent gets a lot of offers on your house very quickly, he or she might "shop" your offer to buyers' agents who have indicated they have interested clients who also want to place offers on your house. They inform the participating agents about the offer on the table and ask them to submit their best offers for you to choose from. This gets you the cleanest offer and the best possible price. Some people don't like the practice and believe it's unethical, but it does not violate any law or regulation. It's the duty of a selling agent to get top dollar and favorable contracts for their sellers, and shopping offers is a recognized way for them to achieve that goal.

On the other hand, if a gorgeous rehab has just been listed in a hot neighborhood with low inventory, where potential buyers battle ferociously to get a home, the Realtor might advise the buyer to come in $10,000 to $20,000 (or even more) over the asking price and remove any contingencies on the offer in an effort to preempt all the offers expected from other buyers. In a seller's market where housing inventory is low, it's all about making a client's offer the most attractive so that you will select it as the winning bid for your house.

Dealing with Contingencies

Like every other part of an offer to buy, contingencies are negotiable to some extent. As we mentioned earlier, every offer has them, so the only time they would become concerning is if there are too many of them or the demands made are unreasonable.

It's perfectly normal for a buyer to need to sell an existing home before being able to buy yours. No one wants to get stuck paying two mortgages, so they put a contingency on their offer stipulating that it will only become valid upon the sale of their existing home.

However, this is where you and your agent should do some digging before you decide to accept or reject an offer contingent on the sale of another home. You have to ask two questions: where is the home they are trying to sell located, and what is the average days on market there?

If it's in hot neighborhood where houses are turning over almost as fast as they're listed, the sales contingency should pose no problem for you. But if their house is in a decaying neighborhood where homes take months to sell and residents are fleeing as fast as they can, you might be waiting a might long time for that sale to happen. At this point, you would reject the offer, not because you are against contingencies, but because you only want to accept those that have a reasonable chance of success.

You should have insulated yourself against any unwelcome inspection contingency surprises during your rehab. When you are selling a house where almost everything has been renewed, you should have no reason to fear a home inspection. However, if you tried to cut corners anywhere, this is when those short cuts will come to light. The inspector will call you out on any substandard work and require that it be brought up to code before approving the house for habitation.

All Cash or Financed?

If you are fortunate enough to receive a full-price, all-cash offer, your choice is easy … you accept the offer. The only time you wouldn't do this immediately is if you receive multiple offers, which we'll discuss in the section on handling multiple offers below.

Realtors and sellers love all-cash offers. They tend to have short *escrow* periods, typically 30 days or even less and might not have many contingencies attached either. Even if they do have the normal contingencies, such as an inspection, they are still a better deal for sellers because they close quickly, which reduces carrying costs and eliminates the stress and uncertainty you experience while waiting for your buyer's loan to get approved.

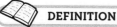 **DEFINITION**

> A house with an accepted purchase offer is considered to be in **escrow,** which means a third party is holding all monies and vital documents pertaining to the sales transaction until the sale is completed. When ownership of the house has been legally transferred from the seller to the buyer, it comes out of escrow.

Buyers sometimes don't understand the appeal of an all-cash offer. They think an offer to purchase should just be evaluated by the numbers, but that's not always the case. We frequently see all-cash offers accepted that are $10,000 or $20,000 less than the top offer just in terms of sales price. Sellers will go for a lower all-cash offer because they don't want to worry over the deal possibly falling through because a buyer couldn't secure financing. They don't have to go through the long and stressful process of waiting for the buyer's loan approval simply because cash buyers don't need a loan.

As desirable as all-cash offers are, the reality is you might not get one. Most buyers need to secure a mortgage loan in order to complete the purchase of a house. In and of itself, there is nothing wrong with an offer contingent on securing a loan. It's just that so many things can go off the rails with a mortgage application that financed offers have developed a bit of a bad rap among sellers. Everyone always grinds their teeth a little bit until they hear the loan has been approved and the sale will go through.

FLIP TIP

Agents encourage buyers to get prequalified for a loan. When you are looking for your next flip, if your offer is one of many under consideration and you are prequalified, the seller might select your offer over others even if it's $10,000 or $20,000 less, because the other buyers are not yet approved for a loan. Most sellers won't risk going after an extra $10,000 by accepting an offer that might fall through when they have an offer with preapproved financing sitting on the table.

The bottom line is, while all-cash offers are fantastic, any good clean offer that gets your house sold should make you very happy, because it means you're off to a great start in your flipping career. Once you get the proceeds from the act of sale, you can meet with your investor and get ready to go out and do it all over again.

Evaluating Multiple Offers

If you get multiple offers on your house, you're in an enviable spot. That means you truly excelled at every aspect of the flipping business, from choosing a house in the right neighborhood to doing an attractive remodel and proper staging.

As you will quickly learn, not all offers are created equal. Even two offers for the exact same amount can have enough differences to make one easily more desirable than the other.

If the offer is full price, you might be tempted to accept it immediately, but hold on. Remember to consider the history of your listing when you are reviewing offers. If your house has just been on the market a day or less and you already have an offer, chances are more offers might be forth-coming very soon. While you don't want to keep buyers waiting unnecessarily, you have do 48 to 72 hours to respond to the offer, and it won't hurt to wait for a few of those hours to see what else might happen.

On the other hand, if your house has been on the market a month with no offers and a reason-able offer suddenly shows up, you should accept it immediately, assuming all the financials are in order and there are no potentially detrimental contingencies attached to the offer.

FLIPPER BEWARE

Although contingencies can help agents put deals together that might otherwise not work, they can be very tricky and frequently detrimental to sellers. If the sale of your flip is contingent upon the sale of another house within 60 to 90 days, and if that house has not sold by the end of the 3 months, not only do you lose your sale, but you might also have lost the entire prime summer selling season. Be cautious when deal-ing with contingencies and rely on your Realtor's expertise to evaluate them.

An offer with contingencies is considered a weaker offer compared to clean offers with no condi-tions attached. They are certainly better than no offers at all, but if you can avoid dealing with a bunch of extra contingencies, you should.

The Art of Negotiation

Almost every single item on an offer can be negotiated, but only a handful ever are. That's why real estate purchase offers are preprinted, fill-in-the-blank documents. While some get accepted as is, signed and returned to the selling agent and their client, at least some alterations are made to most real estate purchase contracts.

This is where the art of negotiation plays a large role. Both the listing and the selling agent want the same thing, for the house to sell. Their job is to bring buyer and seller together on terms that make each happy. Many sales transactions would fall apart quickly if the buyer and seller had to negotiate terms directly with no help from their agents. A few punches might even fly, often over something as trivial as leaving a swing set in the yard. We should write a book about the crazy things we've seen when buyer and seller do not get along.

Believe me, negotiating is truly where Realtors earn their commissions. They have saved many a sale where the buyer and seller, despite having never met in person, took an instant dislike to each other.

From the moment a purchase offer is first presented, both agents know its intrinsic value, and whether or not it is a good offer even worth discussing. If your agent is dismissive of an offer, trust her judgment. She is going on her instincts and her instincts have been honed by years of negotiating deals. An agent can usually tell when buyers and their agents are negotiating in good faith and guide you accordingly.

There is usually about $10,000 wiggle room on either side of a listing price. A buyer who really wants the house might be willing to bid as much as $10,000 over the asking price on the first offer to get it. A seller who really wants to sell the house might be willing to accept as much as $10,000 under the asking price to sell it. The agents negotiate the often-tricky ground between the two, each bending a little or standing firm, depending on the relative strength of their positions, and report the results back to their respective clients.

Sometimes, your agent might need to negotiate with you. If your house has been on the market for a few weeks with no activity, don't be hard-nosed if your agent asks for a price drop. The lack of interest means your house is priced too high for the current market conditions. Your agent's goal is to get your house sold as quickly as possible so you can take your profits and go find another house to flip. If you stubbornly cling to a price the market has clearly demonstrated is too high, you risk burning through your profit with carrying costs, and that can end your flipping career almost before it's started.

> **FLIP TIP**
>
> If you're lucky, a new and more attractive offer will come in during a protracted nego-tiation and you can accept it instead of continuing a lengthy negotiation with the first buyer. It's perfectly ethical to break off ongoing negotiations to accept another offer. The buyer knew going in that was a risk associated with extended negotiations.

As we've discussed, when you have a hot house with lots of interest, your Realtor will likely advise you to hold your price. If your house has not received any prior offers and a month has passed, you will be advised to accept any viable offer that comes your way.

After discussing the offer with you and learning what you want to do, your Realtor will alter whatever terms you want changed and present a counteroffer to the buyers. It might be accepted or rejected, or the buyer may counter again, trying to find some acceptable price between what they originally offered and your counteroffer.

Negotiations will continue in this back-and-forth manner until you accept their offer or reject it or the buyer accepts or rejects your counter.

The value of negotiating is that it can often get you a higher price or fewer contingencies, and frequently, clever negotiation can outright save a sale.

Selecting the Right Offer

Before we get started with this section, we want to mention that perhaps 90 to 95 percent of your business with your Realtor will be conducted over the phone and via email and the internet. That's normal, so don't think your agent is neglecting you because you never see him. He is out doing business that must be done in person, such as showing houses.

In today's hyperconnected but also hyperbusy world, it's simply more efficient to take care of your real estate business over the phone. Would you really rather spend a half hour in traffic to get to your agent's office to sign a contract when you can legally sign any document online now? Yes, there's an app for that! DocuSign and similar online apps allow you to digitally sign all required legal documents pertaining to a property transaction. These digital signatures are accepted in every business venue and court of law in the land, so don't be worried they're not legitimate. They are.

Considering how busy the real estate business keeps its agents, except for occasionally touring properties together, you could go for months without seeing your Realtor, and yet still be making plenty of money working as a team. As time goes on and your working relationship solidifies, your agent might even send you to tour properties with a subagent so he or she can have more time to take care of aspects of your business that require a higher level of skill and experience, such as negotiating contracts.

That said, your Realtor will always be available to help you select the right offer. Even if you only get one bid, chances are you're not going to want to accept it exactly the way it's written. You might need to make a few changes and counteroffers before the bid becomes acceptable to you.

After you have accepted an offer, your agent might request permission to present you with *backup offers,* so that if something goes wrong with the first offer you accepted, you will already have another signed purchase offer in place and ready to go. You will not have to put the house back on the market if you have a backup offer, which is a great benefit for a seller.

> **DEFINITION**
>
> A **backup offer** is a signed and fully legal offer to purchase your house that becomes valid if the original contract falls out of escrow for any reason. Sellers solicit backup offers when they are worried the original buyer might not come through and be able to complete the sale.

When a listing agent advertises they are accepting backup offers, selling agents understand several things:

- The house is highly desirable and has already generated a lot of buyer interest.

- There is already an accepted offer on the table and the house is in escrow.

- Their clients only have a slim chance of getting the house, but they do have a chance.

You might ask why anyone would put themselves through this. When a market is hot and housing inventory is low, placing backup offers might be the only shot some buyers have of securing a house.

You don't need have backup offers on every deal. For instance, an all-cash offer is pretty solid and you would have little need of a backup offer in that situation. Backup offers are used primarily when you and your Realtor have reason to suspect your first offer might be shaky. If and when your original sales contract falls apart, your agent simply calls the selling agent associated with the first backup offer and tells them their offer has now been accepted.

Every sale will be a little different, but your objectives remain the same. You want the fastest sale possible for the best price with the most favorable terms. Your agent will work hard to bring you such a deal, but if an ideal offer doesn't come your way, you must be open to making a few concessions if you want your property to sell through.

After you carefully review all the offers on the table, and discuss the pros and cons with your agent, select the one that gives you the best combination of price, financing, few or no contingencies, and a fast sale.

No Sale? Keep on Marketing!

Even if your flip houses are amazing in every way, a day will come when one of your sales offers falls through at the last minute.

No one likes failed offers. They inevitably taint your house in some way. Instead of being a hot house with multiple offers that every buyer wants, it suddenly becomes that house with the sale that fell through.

Occasionally, if you impulsively bought a house in a less than ideal neighborhood that didn't start trending as you'd hoped it would, you might find yourself stuck with a house that will not sell at all. In that case, speak with your investor to discuss options. He won't be happy since his capital will be tied up in the house indefinitely, but he might recommend renting the house in the interim to at least cover carrying costs. The bonus to this approach is that frequently, after renters live in a house for a while, they fall in love with it and want to buy it. So you might be able to sell it to your renters eventually and get your investor at least some of his money back. Needless to say, your profit on such a venture will be close to zero.

The Least You Need to Know

- Review all purchase offers with your Realtor before selecting the one that best meets your needs.
- Remember that everything in a purchase offer is negotiable, from the price of the house to the contingencies attached to the contract.
- All-cash offers are generally the best offers.
- Rely on your Realtor's expertise to protect your interests and negotiate difficult contracts.
- If a sale falls through, don't let it get you down. It happens to all of us.

CHAPTER 21

Preparing for the Act of Sale

Once you have accepted an offer to purchase your house, you truly have reason to celebrate—but perhaps not just yet. Keep in mind there is still more work to do before you cross the finish line. You're an integral part of a professional team that will bring your property to an act of sale, and you still have an important part to play and responsibilities to fulfill.

You should immediately complete any required paperwork and turn it over to your Realtor so he or she can forward it to the bank or mortgage company financing the sale and also to the title company or attorney that will close the sale. The company handling the closing will prepare the required documents for all parties to sign at the act of sale.

If you staged the property, you must make arrangements to have the staging company pick up their furniture and accessories, and have the house cleaned and prepared for occupancy by the new owners.

You also must make the property accessible to the buyer's inspectors and provide any required paperwork requested, such as a termite inspection or proof of the date of purchase and guarantee provided for a new furnace.

In This Chapter

- Your Realtor's role
- Seller's disclosure and appraisal
- The value of a preinspection
- Dealing with the home inspection
- What to bring to the act of sale

While unlikely in a rehab, if any problems were found during the inspection that you agreed to repair, the period before the act of sale is the time to take care of that. The inspector will have to come back out and re-inspect the property to make sure the repairs were done properly.

The appraiser is one of the most important people who will be coming through your property during this period, so remember to maintain the property while you're waiting for the act of sale. Keep the grass cut, trash taken out, garden debris picked up, and the house itself dusted and vacuumed at all times.

And don't forget that now's a good time to start looking for your next flip!

Your Realtor's Time to Shine

Once a purchase offer has been accepted, your Realtor's job becomes even more critical. It's not unusual for numerous little glitches to crop up between the acceptance of the offer and the closing. Your Realtor, like the true pro he or she is, will negotiate and handle those glitches and keep the sale on track.

> **FLIP TIP**
>
> It's an especially good idea to let your agent handle all contact with the buyer's agent and the buyer. If a buyer shows up at the property when you're there and tries to talk you into or out of something, smile and politely defer to your agent, as in, "Have your agent call my agent and they can work it out."

It doesn't happen often, but buyers will sometimes try to force a meeting with a seller prior to closing in order to negotiate some perceived accommodation out of sight and hearing of the agents involved. It's never a good idea to get caught up in something like this. Let the trained professionals handle all discussions and negotiations. That's what you're paying us for. You don't want to risk losing the sale you worked so hard to get just because the buyer threw a tantrum over some innocent thing you said.

Your Realtor will stay on top of every little detail as the sale moves forward and keep you informed. She'll tell you when the inspectors and the appraiser are expected so you can have the place pristine when they arrive. Agents will let you know the results of the inspection and the amount of the appraisal the moment they come through. They'll also keep you apprised of the paperwork you need to fill out prior to the act of sale and any deadlines you must meet.

Seller's Disclosure

There's a surprising amount of work to do between signing a sales contract and going to the closing to transfer the property to the new owners. A lot of the work involves filling out various forms. The main paperwork you need to provide during this period includes:

- A valid legal description of your property including a *plot plan.*

- A *seller's disclosure* outlining precisely what is included in the sale, such as house, stove, washing machine, dishwasher, and so on. It should also disclose any known defects in the property, including potential hazards, such as asbestos and lead paint.

If, to the best of your knowledge, there are no known defects in the house, then you must state that when you sign the disclosure form.

DEFINITION

A **plot plan** is a scaled diagram showing the size and shape of your lot along with the house and any other improvements, complete with accurate measurements. It shows the exact placement of the house on the lot, plus setbacks, including utility access corridors, and the location of permanent installations, such as septic tanks, driveways, and sidewalks.

A **seller's disclosure** is a legal document provided by a homeowner to a buyer that discloses all issues with the property the seller is aware of and lists all items included in the sale. Failure to accurately disclose issues often results in lawsuits when the buyer has a problem with the house and proves through repair records or other means that the seller failed to disclose the problem.

You should have been given your plot plan at closing when you first purchased the house. If you don't have it, go to the county assessor's office, tell them what you want, and give them the address of your property and a photo ID, such as a driver's license or passport. For a small fee, the assessor's office will provide you with a certified copy of your plot plan. Ask if they can email you a digital copy so you can easily email it to your Realtor. If not, just scan your paper copy into a digital file and save it as a pdf so you can email it.

Filling Out the Forms

Your agent will send you a link to an online electronic seller's disclosure form for you to review and fill out. We really appreciate the wonders of the digital age. It saves lots of time when it comes to processing the mountains of paperwork that accompany a sale. Realtors used to have to print out seller's disclosures and hand-deliver them to their sellers. When they were finally filled out, the agent had to go back to pick up the completed forms and drop them off at the office of the attorney or title company handling the closing. Now we just send an email with a link to the online electronic seller's disclosure. It saves hours of time.

Disclosure forms vary from state to state, but all of them require absolute honesty in describing the property and any problems you know of.

FLIPPER BEWARE

Many flippers are not aware seller's disclosures are legal documents a buyer can use against you in court if it turns out you haven't disclosed all known defects in the house. You might believe the new owner will never find out, but once the problem surfaces again, (and it will) your buyers will discuss it with neighbors who will relay the conversation you had about choosing not to replace the leaking windows. You'll get nailed in court by the neighbor's testimony, so *always* tell the truth on your seller's disclosure forms.

In California, the seller's disclosure runs to a full 50 pages, but even in states with shorter forms, it is still a substantial document that requires a block of uninterrupted time to fill out. Disclosures may contain hundreds of questions, everything from the type of heating the house has to whether or not there is a garage or a carport, carpet or tile flooring, and what type of appliances are provided. You might think some of the information requested is a bit strange, such as, "Has anyone died on the property within the past three years?" or "Are you aware of any zoning violations or nonconforming uses associated with the property?" But no matter how weird you think the question is, those are things buyers want to know.

You must complete an additional form if you're disclosing a regulated hazard, such as lead paint. Consult with your Realtor for exact information about how hazard disclosure is handled in your state so that you can make sure you complete the form accurately.

The basic questions are almost the same everywhere, but every locale also has unique questions related to that particular area, such as, "Do you have a completed wetlands survey for the property?" You wouldn't find that question on a seller's disclosure in the desert areas of Arizona, but you sure will for houses located in the environmentally sensitive coastal tidelands of South Carolina.

Some questions are just boxes you tick electronically, but many require you to type out answers and explanations in the space provided.

Take Your Time

Be sure to set aside adequate time to fill out your disclosure completely. Answer everything as accurately as possible, and to the best of your ability. If there are questions that confuse you, consult with your Realtor for clarification.

> **FLIP TIP**
>
> To avoid problems with seller disclosure, you can provide yourself and your buyer with a year's worth of protection by purchasing a home warranty insurance plan for the house. Such plans repair or replace any covered mechanical system or appliance that fails in your house during the first year of occupancy by a new buyer. All the buyer must do is pay a small deductible of around $50 to $75. Ask your Realtor to recommend a reliable home warranty insurance company in your area.

If the buyer objects to any of the things revealed in the disclosure, he generally has 72 hours to withdraw his offer on the property, and the earnest money will be returned to him. Or he might choose to go forward but have his agent try to negotiate a lower price in exchange for not walking away from the contract.

Do not let the possibility of a lost sale convince you to be anything less than absolutely truthful when completing your seller's disclosure. You could find yourself in a tight legal and financial spot if you get caught in a lie on your disclosure.

Be aware that if a problem develops on the property after the closing that you were legitimately unaware of, the buyer has no legal recourse against you.

Other Paperwork

At this point you might be asking yourself, "What other paperwork could there possibly be that I haven't already done?" Well, relax, because this paperwork should be relatively easy, and there's nothing to fill out.

You should gather the instruction booklets and guarantees for all the new appliances and mechanical and plumbing equipment you installed in the house, and bring those with you to the closing in one envelope to hand to the buyer or the buyer's agent. However, if you have a tendency to misplace things, leave the envelope in a kitchen drawer where the new owners can easily find it.

Everything you installed in your flip, whether it's new windows, a roof, HVAC system, faucets, flooring, cabinets, water heater, stove, dishwasher, garbage disposal … just about all of them, came at the very least with a certificate of guarantee and a card for registering that guarantee with the manufacturer. In addition, many appliances come with detailed instruction booklets. If you have any of these available, give them to your buyer. It's a simple courtesy that can go a long way towards establishing warm feelings at an act of sale.

Inspection Issues

Passing the home inspection is a significant hurdle a purchase contract must clear before it can proceed to closing. Home inspectors go over almost every square inch of a house, not just what can be seen with the naked eye, but also what's up in the attic or down in the basement, out in the garage and sheds, under the sinks, and so on.

Be sure to leave all your utilities on. An inspector can't check to make sure all the toilets flush properly if the water has been turned off.

Since the buyer is the one hiring and paying the $300 to $500 fee for the home inspection, as the seller, you don't have much control over who gets hired. Most Realtors do have inspectors they prefer to work with simply because they have built up good professional working relationships with them over a period of time. You can look at the inspector's credentials to make sure he is licensed, and lodge a complaint with your Realtor if you think he doesn't have enough experience, but that's about it.

A savvy buyer will have read the seller disclosure and arrive at the inspection with any questions in hand, accompanied by their agent. Your agent will be there also, to serve as your eyes and ears during the inspection. However, the seller is not invited to this party, because that would create an awkward situation and make it difficult for the buyer and his agent to ask the questions they want answered.

What Happens at a Home Inspection?

The inspector takes photos of every room, with close ups of any problem areas he discovers. As he progresses through the house, he also makes notes about those problem areas for use later when writing the inspection report. It's the inspector's job to deliver an objective and truthful report about the home's condition. They do their best to uncover and report any potential problems to the buyer.

FLIPPER BEWARE

Don't fear the home inspection. It's far better for any problems to be discovered and corrected during the home inspection rather than after the buyer has moved in. A problem that pops up soon after the buyer takes possession of the home often becomes the object of a lawsuit against you, the seller, for failure to disclose the problem.

After the inspection is complete, the inspector will give a verbal report to the buyer and the two agents, pointing out any problems areas found. An extensive written report complete with photos is usually provided within 24 hours, although at busy times of the year, it can take up to 48 hours. Technologically savvy inspectors can create, print out, and deliver a written inspection report before they leave the home.

Inspections are meant to uncover major issues that could affect the habitability of a home, or that would cost quite a bit of money to repair. Along the way, dozens of other small issues might be pointed out, but don't worry too much about them. Buyers are not going to react negatively to every little flaw the inspector finds, particularly if they really want the home. They just want to feel certain the house they are about to buy is fundamentally sound. However, do expect to get pushback if serious issues are discovered.

Preempt Problems with a Pre-Inspection

An experienced Realtor will suggest that you pay for a home inspection as soon as your flip is completed. You might wonder why you should spend hundreds of dollars on something the buyer is going to have to do anyway. Here's why it's a good idea.

It is possible the inspector might find and report a problem that you wouldn't have put on your disclosure because you truly did not know it existed. Can you imagine this happening, only it is the buyer's inspector who finds such a problem and reports it to the buyer instead of to you? It could put you in a difficult situation. Having your own inspection gives you the chance to fix any problems found before your buyer's inspector can find them. It's far less stressful to find out you need a new furnace before you sell the house than after the fact. You can replace it, and then use the new furnace as a selling point.

If the buyer's inspector declares you need a new furnace, the fact that you didn't know the furnace was shot or disclose it is going to raise some suspicions with your buyer and perhaps even kill the sale. Or, the buyer could use the information to try and force you to accept a lower price rather than lose the sale.

None of these distressing events can happen when you have your own inspection performed and any necessary repairs made before you put the house on the market. With your own inspection in hand, if the buyer's inspector finds something that was not on your report, you have written proof that you were not aware of it, which can be a very good thing to have. Having your own inspection report also puts you in a stronger position when it comes to negotiating a purchase contract.

If your inspection report suggests your home needs something large replaced, such as a roof, you can even justify raising your selling price a few thousand dollars. Buyers will gladly pay for the security of having a new roof with a 25-year warranty. Something like that can be a major attraction for potential buyers, knowing they are not going to have to worry about roofing issues for a long time.

The Appraisal

The appraisal is one of the most important events that takes place after the sale of your house. Three important things are dependent upon getting a good appraisal:

- Your buyer getting the mortgage loan they need
- You getting the agreed-upon sales price
- The actual sale of your house going through

You can help matters by making sure your house looks its absolute best when you know the appraiser is scheduled. You'd be surprised at the potentially detrimental effect a poorly presented house can have on the final appraised value given to your home, so you want to do everything you can to help the appraiser see the true value in your property.

You also need to stay 100 percent out of the appraiser's way. Your Realtor can meet the appraiser and let you know how it went after the fact. Appraisers do not like homeowners hanging around pointing out all the wonderful features of the home. They can find those on their own without your help. An overly eager seller can actually hurt the appraised value of his house by irritating an appraiser, so let your agent handle this!

FLIP TIP

There's a common misconception that appraisals made for sales transactions provide the accurate market value of a house. Not necessarily. The bank hires an appraiser to find out if the house is worth what the buyer offered for it, not its fair market value. They want the appraisal to come in at the sales price to justify the amount of the mortgage they will be providing. Anything over the sales price is icing. Anything less spells trouble.

If the appraisal comes in below the sales price of the house, the buyer has to come up with a chunk of extra cash at closing to make up the difference. Most often they cannot, and unless you are willing to negotiate the price, the sale of your house will fall through.

To make this clearer, let's say your flip sells for $300,000 and the buyers are putting 20 percent or $60,000 down. That means they need to finance $240,000 plus the closing costs, which can vary from locale to locale but run anywhere from two to five percent of the purchase price of the house on average. If your house appraises for $280,000 instead of the full $300,000, suddenly the buyer has to find an extra $20,000 to make up the difference between the appraised value and the sales price.

The problem is most buyers cannot do that. So, they'll get their agent to ask your agent to lower the price of the house to match the appraised value. Suddenly, you're out $20,000 in this situation. On some flips, that could be the entire amount of your profit.

A low appraisal is basically a disaster in real estate.

Loan Approval

The day your buyer's loan approval comes through is a good day. While there's still a slim chance something could go wrong between loan approval and closing, the chances are good that you will now proceed to the act of sale. If your buyer pulls out of the purchase now, they will lose their deposit.

Now is the time we have the staging removed from the home. Some sellers prefer to do this as soon as the purchase contract is signed to save money on the rental of the staging. We don't do it then because until my buyers have loan approval, there are just too many things that could go wrong and kill the sale. Then we would need to have the house staged again (more $$$) before we could put it back on the market, or try to sell it without staging, which is not as effective.

 FLIPPER BEWARE

Many buyers don't know the difference between being prequalified for a loan, which basically means nothing, and getting preapproved for a loan. Loan officers hand out prequalification notices to buyers like candy. You can line your birdcage with these for all the value they have. It takes an actual mortgage broker or banker to issue a true preapproved loan for a certain amount to a buyer in the market for a new home. If your buyer is preapproved, it significantly increases the odds of the house actually going to closing.

After the loan is approved, the financial institution providing the funds will transfer the specified amount of money to an escrow account right before the act of sale. This is the special separate holding account the title company or attorney has been maintaining to manage all funds associated with your transaction since the first offer and earnest money check were tendered.

The company closing the sale will figure out who is owed what and pay each party accordingly.

The Act of Sale

You've finally reached the magical day. All the hurdles and barriers have been conquered and your house is going to the act of sale. You and your investor are finally about to see all your hard work pay off.

There are several items you as the seller must bring to the act of sale:

- A photo ID.

- All the keys and combinations for locks to your house, garage, tool shed, pool house, gates, mailboxes, and the like.

- The alarm code if you have an alarm system.

- The garage door opener or openers.

- Smoke detector certification if required by your state.

Depending on where you live, you might be required to bring other items to the closing. Your Realtor can let you know everything you need to bring.

> **FLIP TIP**
>
> Don't forget to call the various utility companies that service the house and tell them the house has been sold, and give them the date of the act of sale. Tell them you will be responsible for all costs until that date and ask for a final bill, plus the return of any deposit you might have been required to pay. The buyer will be responsible for all utility bills from that date forward.

It used to be that an act of sale was an event attended by all parties. There was a relaxed and convivial atmosphere, and we took time to chat for a couple of minutes after the sale closed.

Today, the buyer and seller can sign the required documents at different times and never even see each other in person. It's a less personal way to do business, but the end result is the same. The buyer leaves the closing as the proud owner of a new house, and the seller leaves the closing with a nice check in his pocket or with the funds already electronically transferred to his bank account.

If you can arrange the timing, you might even be able to go to two acts of sale in one day. First you close on your flip, which provides you the funds to pay for your next closing, the one where you purchase your next house to rehab!

To show your appreciation, take your Realtor out to lunch. You can use the time to relax and discuss strategies for your next flip.

Activating Backup Offers If the Sale Falls Through

Sometimes, no matter how well or how carefully you, your Realtor, and the selling Realtor do your jobs, a sale falls apart at the last minute. This is the time she picks up the phone and activates the first backup offer. If you have backup offers, you don't even have to go to the trouble or expense of putting your house back on the market. A simple phone call and your flip will be sold again. Of course, you'll have to go through the long loan approval process again, but it's rare to have two sales fail in a row, so keep a positive attitude and move forward.

The Least You Need to Know

- As a seller, you'll have many tasks to complete prior to your act of sale.
- Make sure you fill out your seller's disclosure completely and answer all questions accurately.
- Your appraisal is just the lender's way of finding out if the house is worth what the buyer offered for it, not an assessment of actual market value.
- Once your buyer has loan approval, you can start to relax a little.
- Have backup offers in place so that if the sale falls through, your agent will be able to pick up the phone and activate a backup offer, and your house won't even have to go back on the open market.

CHAPTER 222

After the Flip Is Over

You've closed on your first flip. You've met with your investor and received your share of the profits from the sale of your first rehabbed house. Congratulations!

If you've done a good job—and followed the guidelines in this book—you will soon discover your investor is pleased with your results and wants to you go find another house to flip. In other words, he wants you to make him some more money, which means you'll have the opportunity to make more money, too.

Those words should be music to your ears, because that means you've succeeded and have started a potentially long and mutually beneficial relationship with your investor. In short, you are now a successful flipper!

Of course, you still have more work to do. Flipping is a demanding business and you have to manage a lot of information at once in order to keep everything running smoothly. Ideally, you should be moving from flip to flip without much down time in between, but even after you reach that level of success, you still need to take time between projects to do your paperwork and balance your books, and make sure all the bills associated with your flip have been paid.

In This Chapter

- Reviewing results
- Paying the bills
- Cash flow strategies
- Don't forget income taxes
- Saving for the future

As if that weren't enough, you also have to locate and buy your next house. You must stay on top of all these things to keep yourself and your business organized and moving forward.

All we can say is to keep going. We know you probably feel like you just ran a marathon, and in a way, you did. But it does get easier as you become more experienced. If it took you 2 months to find a suitable house to rehab the first time around, you will likely find one in a month or less this time, simply because you have a better idea of what you're looking for and where you want to look.

In this chapter, we'll show you how to analyze and learn from the results of your first flip and start planning for your next one.

Analyzing Your Results

In Chapter 3, we suggested you create a spreadsheet to keep tracks of expenses as you worked on your house. As you spent money, we advised you to use the spreadsheet to compare what you spent with the corresponding line item on your project budget to make sure the expenditure fell within the amount of money you allotted for that purpose.

Now it's time to pull out your project budget and your expense spreadsheet again, and do an analysis. You should already know the sum total of your overall costs if you kept the expense spreadsheet as we advised. If you don't have that sum at hand, take the time now to add up the numbers and get your total expenditure.

Be sure to include everything from the acquisition cost of the house to all your labor and materials costs; house note; carrying costs, such as loan interest, maintenance, utilities, and property taxes; staging and marketing costs; and the cost of selling the property. If you leave out some of your expenses, your profit will appear higher than it actually is, which means you will be splitting profit that doesn't actually exist with your investor. Don't give away money and cut into your own profits by being careless with your expense tracking.

FLIP TIP

As convenient as online spreadsheets are, we suggest you print out your budget and project spreadsheets and analyze them side by side on a table or desk. Most computer screens will not display two spreadsheets at once unless you minimize them so much the numbers become difficult to read, and toggling back and forth between two spreadsheets quickly grows tiring. Not to mention, you cannot really compare things when only one set of numbers is visible at a time.

You should know what your house sold for. If you subtract your total project costs from the sales price you received for your house, that will give you your profit on the deal.

Needless to say, absolute accuracy is essential when you're figuring these numbers. The sums won't balance correctly if you have left something out of your expenses. We've read about flippers who shield their actual expenses from their investors because they have a lot of cost overruns. Investors are very savvy about numbers, especially those that relate to their money. They want you to account for every penny they gave you for the project. If you cannot, that will dampen their desire to work with you again, because they only like to work with people who take very good care of their money and make it grow. If you're either fudging the numbers or just flat out making mistakes and mismanaging the project, you are hurting your chances of being entrusted with your investor's money again.

You might be asking, "If we already know my profit, why do we now have to do more math?" By carefully analyzing each expenditure, you will find ways to be more efficient and turn even higher profits going forward. It's informative to see what sort of small nuggets of wisdom and knowledge will leap out at you as you begin to carefully review your results.

Perhaps you overspent on a luxury kitchen sink, paying $1500 for a designer farmhouse style when you could have bought an excellent-quality stainless steel double-bowl complete with cutting boards for $500. As buyers came through the house, none of them even noticed the fancy sink, and you realized you could have installed a more affordable option without negatively affecting the desirability of the property. That's $1,000 of potential extra profit you just kissed goodbye by not choosing wisely. Analyzing this sort of mistake can help to ensure you will not make it again.

This is just one example, but by comparing the budget to your actual expenditures, and factoring in what you learned during the marketing of your house and from buyer feedback you received, you'll find many more smart ways to save money on future projects, without seriously impacting either the beauty or value of your houses.

Paying the Piper, and Everyone Else, Too

Bookkeeping is one of those tasks we delegate to an expert. It is time-consuming and requires absolute accuracy and attention to detail, and we would personally rather be working on our next deal than juggling numbers a professional could juggle much faster.

 FLIPPER BEWARE

> Keep up with your expenses as you work on your rehab. Don't toss receipts and bills about because you'll lose them. Whether you use a shoebox or a leather briefcase, keep all receipts and bills related to one project in one place. Then, when it's time for your bookkeeper to start figuring out your return on investment for the project, you won't have to go on a mad hunt for a few scraps of paper or start guessing at expenditures.

If you're good with numbers, you can certainly do your books yourself, but as with all other respects of flipping that you could do yourself but probably shouldn't, you have to weigh the benefits of saving a couple of hundred dollars over the hours and hours of time hiring a book-keeper would save you. We've made it clear that you should be spending your time primarily on developing and growing your flipping business. Doing your own books accomplishes nothing in this regard and could actually distract from other jobs where your direct input is vitally important.

Why Prompt Payment Matters

People have different attitudes about paying bills. Some pay them as soon as they come in; some wait to pay them until they come due, and some pay bills on a certain day every month or every 2 weeks. Sad to say, a few people don't pay their bills on time, or at all.

It doesn't take much imagination to determine what would happen to a flipper who doesn't pay bills on time. You'd be a party of one before you could draw a breath. If you let bills slide, it won't be long before your work crews are sliding, too, right out the door. And your suppliers will refuse to sell you anything more until your current bills are paid. Finally, thanks to the reliable word of mouth network amongst contractors, work crews and suppliers, pretty soon your reputation will be shot and no one will want to work with you. And just like that, there goes your flipping career.

Contractors and suppliers are not bankers or payday lenders. They did not agree to indefinitely lend you money when they came to work for you or sold you something on credit. If you chase them all away with your poor money management and business practices, good luck. No matter how talented or capable you are, no one can rehab a flip singlehandedly, not in a reasonable period of time. However, you will soon be on your own if this is how you choose to handle your bills.

Keeping Your Investor(s) Happy

Another important reason to manage your money professionally is that it will impress your investor. There's nothing they dislike more than signing on with a new flipper, only to find they have no idea how to handle money. This scares investors and rightly so. They are money experts, and have no respect for anyone who engages in sloppy money management. How can they have any confidence that you will provide a return on their investment if you can't even remember to pay your crews on time?

We recommend you pay all bills associated with your flip as soon as you get them or just before their due date, depending on your cash flow situation. This will help you build a sterling reputation as a reliable person who is great to work with.

FLIP TIP

When you partner with an investor, he provides the money to buy a property and rehab it according to the plans you submitted. You should have sufficient funds for all expenses sitting in your project account and be able to pay all bills on time using those funds. Considering you have a big contingency cushion in your budget, if you run out of money before the rehab is done, you managed the project poorly, didn't figure costs accurately, or had really bad luck with unexpected repairs and cost over-runs.

When you develop this kind of 24-carat gold credibility, suddenly, investors will come looking for you. They have word of mouth networks, too, and a professional association and monthly meetings. If your investor starts bragging to fellow investors about what a great job you did on your flip, and how pleased he or she is with the return on their investment you delivered, you might suddenly have more offers from investors than you can handle. They are always looking for someone they can trust to help them make more money.

Managing Cash Flow

You have all the numbers figured out and you've paid the outstanding bills associated with the flip. You've met with your investor and split the proceeds, and now have a lump sum of money in your hands. That is a great feeling, and you will likely feel quite excited and happy that your payoff for months of hard work has finally arrived. You might even hoist a glass of champagne and make a toast because you did it! You flipped a house and you and your investor both made money. That's the very definition of success in the flipping business.

Believe it or not, this whirlwind period when you feel on top of the world is actually one of the most dangerous times for a flipper just starting in the business. Whether your share of the profit is $10,000 or $20,000 or even more (or less) you're going to be mighty tempted to just go do something with that money. It could be a well-intentioned something, such as paying off personal bills, or it could be a crazy something, such as jetting off to Cancun, but either way, you're blowing the money.

How Not to Blow Your Money

You should have a plan in place for your share of the profits before you ever get your hands on it. That money still has work to do, and if you spend it before you apportion it correctly, you'll be backing yourself into a corner, financially speaking. Not to mention you'll put yourself into a terribly stressful situation, and who needs that?

FLIPPER BEWARE

You might think you personally would never be subject to temptation, but after months of watching every penny, you might be. Suddenly you have lots of cash on hand, and you can't help thinking of a dozen ways to spend it. Don't do it! How will you pay taxes on your earnings if you've already spent the tax money? How will you grow your business if you're always operating on a paper-thin margin? Fantasize about that Rolex or vacation in The Bahamas all you want, but wait to buy any luxuries until you can truly afford them.

Receiving a relatively large lump sum of money is a big deal for someone who is used to getting paid a few hundred dollars every other week or a few thousand once a month. Even if your share is just $5,000 to $10,000, the check is likely one of the largest checks you have ever seen in your life. Having a big chunk of change dropped in their laps can do strange things to some people. It can make them behave irrationally and indulge in poorly thought-out decisions. That's why you read about lottery winners who are dead broke and living in a tent a few years after the big win. Their first impulse was to go out and spend their windfall and buy 10 of every single thing they had ever wanted, and so they did. They were not prepared to deal with the realities of what was going to happen to them after the money ran out.

If you do feel an urge to go out and buy a big-ticket item, don't give in to it. If you want to use every penny to pay down your personal bills, better think twice about that, too, before you do it. It doesn't matter if your intentions are noble. If you spend any of your earnings before figuring out all the government entities that are about to demand a piece of your pie, you'll be heading for trouble. When the government asks you for their pie, you better be ready to serve it and fast.

The Matter of Taxes

Before you do anything else, you should put 30 to 35 percent of outstanding your proceeds in a special savings account dedicated to paying income taxes on your earnings. Yes, you have to pay taxes on your profit, and that can add up quickly.

You'd be surprised how many new flippers forget about paying taxes and treat their profit like it was some sort of free money. Uncle Sam will definitely come calling for his share. And if you live in one of the 43 states that collect state income tax, one of his cousins will soon come calling for her share as well.

FLIPPER BEWARE

Be sure to set aside enough money to pay your taxes. Hire a bookkeeper to do a simulated tax return to find out how much you should reserve for taxes. It could be as little as 20 percent. On the other hand, if you are in one of the higher tax brackets, and live in a state with high state income taxes, such as California or New York, you might have to put aside as much as 50 percent of your earnings to satisfy the taxman.

Depending on how you set up your business, the IRS might or might not require quarterly payments of your estimated taxes. Just as you must file your annual tax return every April 15, these payments must be made precisely on time every three months. Since you're self-employed, you must also pay the employee's and the employer's share of Social Security contributions, plus your Medicare contribution, also known as the FICA or Federal Insurance Contributions Act tax. Have your accountant or bookkeeper prepare your estimated taxes every quarter and send these payments in.

Save to Build a Better Future

Correctly apportioning your profit is not just about paying taxes. It's also about working to build a better financial future for yourself and your family.

With that in mind, put 20 percent of your profit in a savings account to start building up your own investment fund, unless you're content to let your investor earn the lion's share of the profits from your work for the rest of your life. This 20 percent from each project will put you on the road to true financial independence. If you're vigilant about saving a portion of each profit check, one day you'll suddenly realize you're in a position to finance your own flips from start to finish. You might even get to the point where you're so successful that you have funds available to finance flips for other aspiring flippers. Of course, this kind of success doesn't happen overnight, but you will find the idea that you are building toward a more independent future can serve as powerful fuel for your dreams.

If you can't manage to save 20 percent from your share of the profits from your flip, shoot for 15. If you can't do 15, then do 10. No matter what, make regular deposits in your savings account or 5 years from now, you will still be in the same financial situation as you are now, and that lack of progress toward financial independence can be very frustrating.

Success doesn't happen accidentally or overnight. It's the resulting of persistence, planning, hard work, and a single-minded dedication to achieving your dreams. Plan for a better future and take positive steps now to make those dreams a reality. Flipping is great vehicle to get you there.

So How Much Is Really Yours to Spend?

Finally, we come to the part you've all been waiting for. How much of the profit from your flip can you take to live on and pay personal expenses?

The answer is about 50 percent, depending primarily on how much you must reserve to pay taxes. Of course, if you live frugally and can live on 30 to 40 percent of your share of the profits, that's great, because it will give you more money to put into savings. But you can safely take as much as 50 percent of your proceeds to live on, and up to 60 percent if you are in a lower tax bracket.

If you take more, first your savings money will disappear, and then your tax money, and finally, your finances will end up in a complete mess. It's tempting when you have bills to pay and also have $2,000 in savings that could pay those bills. You can certainly lend yourself some money from your savings to meet your immediate needs, but you must document it as a personal loan to your business in your records, and you must pay it back as soon as cash flow permits.

Accountant, Bookkeeper, or Both?

People discuss the relative merits of bookkeepers versus *certified public accountants* (*CPAs*) almost endlessly, but there really should not be a discussion. While both can accurately prepare and maintain books and other financial records for your business, they do have different training and experience. In a nutshell, *bookkeepers* compile financial information and CPAs analyze it and make recommendations to their clients based on that analysis.

A CPA is the quarterback of the financial field. They are licensed by their individual states and have to pass rigorous tests in order to be able to claim the CPA designation. To keep it, they must adhere to stringent continuing education and retesting requirements, including ongoing ethics training. This keeps them informed about changes in government tax law and changes in state law that affect accounting procedures.

CPAs help businesses by analyzing the cost of their business operations and preparing their tax returns. They prepare company financial statements and help business owners understand the consequences of various financial decisions and the impact that different approaches can have on their businesses.

DEFINITION

A **certified public accountant (CPA)** is a licensed accountant who has passed a difficult state-administered exam. The designation means an accountant has accumulated the required amount of experience in the field and also demonstrated proficiency in and adherence to generally accepted accounting principles (GAAP) when providing services such as financial audits. Their name on a set of books means that to the best of their knowledge, the information in the books is free from misstatements and adheres to GAAP.

A **bookkeeper** records financial transactions, including purchases, sales and expenditures, payroll, accounts payable and receivable, and logs and maintains receipts and payments made by an individual or a business. It is considered good business practice to have financial statements prepared by bookkeepers reviewed periodically by CPAs.

Bookkeepers are to CPAs as paralegals are to attorneys. They know almost as much as CPAs and can perform many of the same functions, but don't perform the subjective analysis that CPAs do. Bookkeepers' work is largely transactional. They maintain general ledgers for their clients' businesses where they post income and expenses.

With the advent of bookkeeping software, many bookkeepers have started to prepare financial statements for their clients, which traditionally was a job reserved for CPAs.

It is essential that every transaction conducted by your business be entered in your general ledger. This includes all sales and purchases. Depending on IRS regulations, some transactions require supporting documents, such as receipts that can be used to check the validity and accuracy of the posting.

Although many beginning flippers save money by using a bookkeeper rather than a CPA to prepare and maintain financial records, the smartest approach is to have both working for you. Use the bookkeeper to maintain your financial records and your CPA to analyze your results and make recommendations for improvement and the growth of your business.

Planning Your Next Flip

Once you finally have your money sorted out, you can devote your time to planning your next flip. Go back to the beginning of this book and follow the steps again.

Everything should feel a little more comfortable and familiar this time around. Refer to the checklists in the Appendices to help yourself get and stay organized.

You know the drill by now. Find a great neighborhood, buy a good house that meets the 70 percent rule, pick a house in a trending style, make a plan, set a budget, and present the deal to your investor.

Once you have the green light from your investor and the funds to purchase and rehab your next flip are in your bank, alert your crews and prepare your work schedule. After you close on the house, you'll be ready to go.

To Flip Number Two and Beyond

If you've read through this book and successfully flipped a house, you're already light years ahead of the thousands of would-be dreamers who just talk about their desire to flip a house but never actually do anything to make their dreams a reality. Where you go from here is up to you.

You are now equipped with the basic knowledge and tools you need to get the job done again and again. The rest of what you should know—the strategies that can rescue a flip running out of control, smart ways to save money on materials, seamless handling of crew issues and permit problems, and so on—are things you will learn over time and from on the job experience.

> **FLIP TIP**
>
> A great benefit of flipping might not become apparent to you until after you have started to establish yourself in the flipping community. Flipping houses is a great way to make new friends who share your passion for flipping. You will meet people and make many new friends from all walks of life as you expand your flipping career, and some of them will become lifelong friends.

With each flip you complete and sell, your confidence—and your bank account— will grow. It takes a lot of persistence, hard work, and dedication to get a flipping business off the ground. But if you stick with it and don't allow yourself to become distracted or discouraged by day-to-day problems, in the not-too-distant future, you will wake up one day and realize you are living the lifestyle you only just used to dream about. You are finally a professional flipper.

Now all you have to do is get your own TV show!

The Least You Need to Know

- Analyze your results to glean nuggets of wisdom you can use on your next flip.
- Pay bills promptly to maintain your reputation as an ethical, reliable business partner.
- Don't blow your profits on impulsive purchases.
- Don't forget to pay taxes on your profits.
- Start your next flip!

Glossary

70 percent rule   A formula that flippers, Realtors, and investors use to determine if a house is suitable for flipping. You should pay no more than 70 percent of a home's after repaired value (ARV) to acquire the home. The 70 percent rule helps you calculate the maximum amount you should pay for a home if you want to make money on the deal.

after repaired value (ARV)   What a property will be worth once all the necessary repairs and optional upgrades have been made. It is vitally important to know your approximate ARV on any property you are considering so you can determine if you'll make a profit from flipping that house.

agents' open house   A special open house held for licensed Realtors when a new listing first goes on the market. It gives agents an opportunity to speak directly with the listing agent and preview houses for their current active buyers.

"as-is" listing   An "as-is" listing is a property sold in its existing condition, without any warranties or guarantees. When you buy an "as-is" listing, you accept the property exactly as it is, including any damage and physical defects. You give up your right to make any claims against the seller. It must be stated within the sales contract that the house is being sold "as-is."

backup offer   A signed and fully legal offer to purchase your house that becomes valid if the original contract falls out of escrow for any reason. Sellers solicit backup offers when they are worried the original buyer might not come through and be able to complete the sale.

bookkeeper   Someone who records financial transactions, including purchases, sales and expenditures, payroll, and accounts payable and receivable, and logs and maintains receipts and payments made by an individual or a business. It is considered good business practice to have financial statements prepared by bookkeepers reviewed periodically by CPAs.

bridge loan   Also called *gap* or *interim financing*, is a short-term bank loan meant to provide financing during a period between two separate transactions. In flipping, the two transactions are the purchase of the house to be flipped, and after the rehab is completed, the sale of that same house. Bridge loans normally come due after 6 to 12 months.

carrying cost   Known as a *holding cost* in some areas, a carrying cost consists of any money you must spend to hold a house in inventory until it sells and goes to an act of sale. This includes things, such as loan interest, utility payments, hazard insurance, property taxes, yard maintenance, rental of staging furniture, and other related expenses.

certified public accountant (CPA)   A licensed accountant who has passed a difficult state-administered exam. The designation means an accountant has accumulated the required amount of experience in the field and also demonstrated proficiency in and adherence to generally accepted accounting principles (GAAP) when providing services such as financial audits. Their name on a set of books means that to the best of their knowledge, the disclosures in the books are reasonable and free from misstatements and adhere to GAAP.

change order   A legal amendment to a contract that is issued whenever jobs are added or removed from your flipping project or you make any sort of change to the work in terms of budget, schedule, scope, or materials used.

color wheel   A circular diagram in which primary and complementary colors are arranged sequentially in a circle. It is arranged so that complementary colors lie directly across from each other on the color wheel. They are invaluable in helping you select paint colors that work well together. You can buy color wheels at art supply stores and some paint stores.

comparables   **Comps** for short; these are evaluations of houses of similar age, size, design, and condition that recently sold in the same neighborhood. Comps are used to help Realtors and sellers establish a fair market value for similar properties about to come on to the market.

comparative market analysis (CMA)   An evaluation of comparable properties located near a home that's about to be listed for sale. Looking at similar properties that recently sold helps establish correct pricing for your house. In addition to the age, size, style, condition, number of bedrooms and bathrooms, comps are also influenced by lot size and location and other amenities, such as view. For example, if your house is exactly the same as a house down the street but yours has a water view, your projected sales price would be higher than that of the house with no water view. CMAs are used to establish the current market value of a property, and help you determine the correct price range for your completed flip. They are normally prepared by a real estate agent because you must have full professional level access to MLS data in order to gather information about comparable sales.

contingency A condition a buyer attaches to an offer that must be met before the contract becomes valid. For example, if a buyer has to sell their current home to get the down payment to buy your home, they will make their offer contingent upon the sale of their home. If they cannot sell their home, the offer becomes invalid because the conditions set out in the contingency were not met.

counteroffer A revised offer requesting a higher price that you tender to a prospective buyer after rejecting their initial offer to buy. It keeps the contract alive while you attempt to get the buyer to offer additional money for your property. Counteroffers are a common negotiating strategy in real estate transactions.

cupola A small rounded roof or part of a roof that is often used to provide protection from the weather over the entrance to a building.

days on market (DOM) Average DOM in your locale is an important indicator of potential for a successful flip. The lower the average DOM, the faster your flip is likely to sell.

demographics The study of human populations based upon various statistical characteristics such as age, income, and education. Demographics can be used to identify and target specific groups for marketing purposes.

distressed property Any property that has been allowed to fall into a state of disrepair due to a combination of time, weather, vandalism, and neglect. Many distressed properties have been abandoned by their owners as a result of divorce, job loss, or not being able make mortgage or tax payments or required repairs. As a result, the properties might be in foreclosure and available for a good price.

due diligence In the world of real estate, due diligence is the research and analysis of a real property in preparation for a business transaction such as an offer to buy a house.

earnest money A small deposit made to confirm that a person placing an offer on a home is serious about buying the house and acting in good faith. If they follow through and the house goes to act of sale, this money is applied to the sales price. If the buyer defaults on the sale, they lose their deposit, which goes to the seller as compensation for their property having been held off the market. Typically, earnest money deposits are 1 to 2 percent of the total purchase price of a property.

employer identification number (EIN) A nine-digit number assigned to each individual business by the IRS or Internal Revenue Service. It is the business equivalent of a Social Security number and is used to track tax filings made by each individual business.

escrow   A house with an accepted purchase offer is considered to be in escrow, which means a third party is holding all monies and vital documents pertaining to the sales transaction until the sale is completed. When ownership of the house has been legally transferred from the seller to the buyer, it comes out of escrow.

field card   Also called an *inspection card* in some locales, a field card contains all the information about your permit. It must be prominently displayed on your worksite to prove that the work underway is legal and being performed under the oversight of the local permitting authorities.

flipping   An investment method in which an investor buys a property and makes repairs and improvements to it with the goal of selling the refurbished property for a significant profit. Such sales are called flips because they can happen rather quickly after the property is marketed.

French drain   A subsurface trench filled with gravel that uses a special perforated pipe that directs both ground and surface water away from things you want to protect from water damage, such as building foundations and concrete pavement.

gentrification is the sometimes-controversial process of repairing and upgrading rundown buildings in blighted urban areas with a mix of upscale shops, office space, and residences to attract younger, better-educated, and wealthier residents to the neighborhood. It has been criticized for driving out low-income residents who frequently cannot find affordable replacement housing.

hard money loan (HML)   A loan is based on the value of the real property you are buying, and not on your credit score or perceived creditworthiness. Sometimes called "the loan of last resort" these loans provide funds in 1 to 2 weeks instead of the 30-plus days a mortgage requires. However, they're also expensive, costing as much as twice as much as a normal mortgage loan, plus they have high origination fees.

hardscape   Any inanimate, manmade object that exists in your landscape, such as walkways, driveways, gazebos, arches, trellises, fences and gates, fountains, benches, patios, pools, and the like.

historic district   A group of properties, including residential and commercial, that have been designated by the federal, state, or local government as historically or architecturally significant, or both. Property owners might have to follow strict guidelines when renovating a property located within such a district, but they might also be eligible for tax incentives to help pay for any approved renovations.

hotspot   A way to gain access to the internet through your smart phone. Located in your phone settings, when turned on, the hotspot sets up a wireless local area network you can use to temporarily get internet access on your computer when you are out in the field. Be careful though! Unless you have password protected your hotspot, anyone in the vicinity can hop on and potentially access sensitive information on your devices.

house flipping   When you purchase a house, then quickly update and sell it for a profit. Flipping can also apply to other types of real estate.

judicial foreclosure   A lawsuit filed against a borrower by the lender who holds the mortgage on their property after the borrower falls 3 or more months behind on payments. A court-appointed referee sends out a Notice of Foreclosure Sale announcing the time, date, and location of the foreclosure auction, giving the homeowner a certain period to redeem the home prior to the auction. The referee also conducts the foreclosure auction.

landscape architect   A person who has been specially trained to develop land for recreational use and enjoyment through the coordinated use of plantings, walkways, and hardscaping elements including structures like gazebos, pools, fountains, and fences. It is considered a multi-disciplinary field, as degree candidates must master elements of botany, architecture, horticulture, the fine arts, industrial design, storm water management, and soil science, among others, in order to graduate.

limited liability company (LLC)   A business that is a completely separate legal entity from its owners. It can have any number of owners and is taxed according to the underlying ownership of the business, for example, sole proprietorship, partnership, and so on. While it is governed by operating agreements like a corporation, there is no legal requirement to hold annual meetings or record minutes of meetings as corporations must do.

loan-to-value (LTV) ratio   A risk assessment lenders use to determine risk on any particular loan. Most lenders prefer loans with an LTV no higher than 80 percent. If a property has a high LTV, it can be more difficult to get financing for it. The more equity a buyer has in a property, the lower their LTV will be.

mechanic's lien   A lien placed against a property by a workman who has not been paid for work done. If the homeowner still won't pay, the lien holder can file a court action forcing the homeowner into foreclosure to get his payment. When a house with a mechanic's lien is sold at a foreclosure auction, the workman's lien is the first claim paid off.

mini staging   A staging crafted using colorful accessories that create a sense of a desirable lifestyle. While the feeling a mini staging evokes can range from elegant to warm and homey, it is basically a shorthand way of eliciting an emotional response from buyers and expressing moods and design ideas rather than a full-on staging complete with lots of furniture.

money pit   A property where unforeseen expenses keep cropping up during renovation. A money pit can quickly swallow up every penny of profit on a flip. You can avoid money pits by performing comprehensive inspections and doing everything you can to make sure you know all the problems a house has before you buy it.

Multiple Listing Service (MLS)   A database containing information on every property for sale or rent in a given locality, including address, square footage, year built, property taxes assessed, number of rooms, and other information. There is a national public database at mls.com, and more than 900 subscription-based local databases for professional Realtors in communities around the United States.

nonjudicial foreclosure   Used in states where deeds of trust are issued to convey an interest in the property to a trustee (lender) who holds the deed as security for repayment of the mortgage loan. The deed contains a power of sale clause that gives the trustee authority to record a Notice of Default (NOD) with the county clerk when a borrower fails to make mortgage payments for an extended period of time. The buyer is given a certain period of time to bring the loan up to date. If the buyer fails to remedy the debt, the trustee issues a Notice of Trustee's Sale (NTS) announcing the time, date, and place of the foreclosure auction.

plot plan   A scaled diagram showing the size and exact shape of your lot along with the house and any other improvements, complete with accurate measurements. It shows the exact placement of the house on the lot, its relationship to its neighbors, plus setbacks, including utility access corridors, and the location of permanent installations, such as septic tanks, driveways, and sidewalks.

pre-foreclosure   A period when a homeowner has missed three consecutive mortgage payments on their property. They still legally own the home, but the lender has started the foreclosure process and legally notified the homeowners that an auction is imminent. If the homeowner can come up with all the back payments plus late fees and other fees due and make a lump sum payment to the bank, the property will go out of pre-foreclosure. Otherwise, it will be auctioned off to the highest bidder.

project manager (PM)   A person who is responsible for overseeing the planning, execution, and management of every aspect of a project from beginning to end.

real estate owned (REO)   A property that is owned by a bank or another lender, such as a credit union. They become owners of the property after the original purchaser defaults on the loan and the property is foreclosed and repossessed by the lender. Lenders generally try to sell foreclosed properties at auction, but if no one bids, ownership reverts back to the lender and it becomes known as an REO property.

repipe   The total replacement of every plumbing pipe, including underground pipes, in your house. Repipes are often required on older homes in which pipes have either rusted through, or are leaching lead into the water. A typical repipe can cost anywhere from $3,000 to $20,000 or more, depending on the material used, the number of bathrooms, and the number of fixtures and appliances that are attached to the lines.

return on investment (ROI)   Investors want to know the potential ROI on any rehab property before investing.

Schedule C   An IRS tax form that sole proprietors must prepare and file with their personal income taxes annually to report how much money they made or lost in their business over the preceding tax year. Sole proprietors are considered to be self-employed, and as a result, must also pay the employer's share of any Social Security, disability and Medicare contributions in addition to the share they must pay personally on any income they have earned through the business.

seller's disclosure   A legal document provided by a homeowner to a buyer that discloses all issues with the property the seller is aware of and lists all items included in the sale. Failure to accurately disclose issues often results in lawsuits when the buyer has a problem with the house and proves through repair records or other means that the seller failed to disclose the problem.

short sale property   A property sold at a price where the net proceeds of the sale will not cover the debt remaining on the liens against the property. A short sale can only go through if all lienholders agree to accept less than is owed to them. Short sales are viewed as a more responsible alternative to foreclosure for homeowners struggling to meet mortgage payments.

skim coat   A thin coat of plaster applied all over a sheetrock wall as a final step to prepare the wall for painting.

sole proprietorship   A type of business owned by one person. Because it is not a legal business entity, the business owner pays personal income tax on any income the business generates. They are also personally responsible for any debts the business incurs. While sole proprietorships are certainly the simplest form of business to set up, they can present some major drawbacks. Chief among them is the legal exposure that is part of such a business arrangement. If you are a sole proprietor and have a client who is unhappy with their flip and sues your business, you are personally responsible to pay any resulting financial judgment against the business.

spackle   A quick-drying plasterlike compound used to fill in cracks and small holes in drywall and plaster. It can be sanded and painted to match the color of the repaired wall.

stager   a person skilled in the art of using furniture, accessories, lighting, scent, and plants to create an inviting space that appeals to the largest possible number of buyers prior to putting a house on the market.

stone remnants   Pieces of granite, quartz, or any other countertop or flooring material that are left over after a custom order has been cut from a large slab.

sweat equity   Labor, ideas, and expertise you invest in a project in lieu of cash. In exchange for your sweat equity, you receive an ownership position in the project and a share of any profits realized.

takeoff   A list of materials required to complete any building project, including a flip, along with the estimated cost of those materials.

tract home   One of many similar homes built on a large tract of land subdivided into small lots. Because developers used only 4 or so different floor plans for the entire community, even if it contained thousands of houses, tract developments became infamous for having a cookie cutter look.

uninhabitable   Any house that is considered unfit for human habitation, lacking essential comforts of living, such as working plumbing or electrical systems, hot water, and a source of heat. Conditions, such as the presence of black mold or a rodent or insect infestation, also can render a home uninhabitable. Check your local laws as the legal definition of uninhabitable varies from place to place.

urban renewal   Another word for *gentrification*. The difference is urban renewal projects are generally subsidized by government funding, whereas most gentrification projects are undertaken with private funding. The end result is the same: slums are swept away and replaced by high-rise office buildings and luxury apartments.

workers' compensation insurance   Provides wage replacement and reimbursement for medical expenses required to treat workers injured on the job. In exchange, workers covered by workers' comp are required to give up the right to sue their employer for their injury, even if they are permanently disabled as a result. Also provides a death benefit to families of workers killed on the job.

Resources

A number of organizations and websites can be of great help to aspiring flippers. Here are some of the best.

Organizations

National Real Estate Investors Association

nationalreia.org

Visit REIA's website to find meetings close to you. Networking with investors is essential to get started in the flipping business. Attending a local REIA meeting is one of the best ways to meet investors in your area who are interested in providing funds for flippers. Remember to bring your business cards when you attend a meeting.

Real Estate Investment Club

reiclub.com

Real Estate Investment Club is another organization for investors who might be looking for flippers to manage rehabs for them. Their email newsletter is free and full of information and tips about real estate investing.

Real Estate Websites

Trulia

trulia.com

Trulia is a website with real estate listings that can be a valuable source of information and comparables when you're trying to find a house or set a reasonable sales price.

Zillow

zillow.com

Zillow is Trulia's competitor and offers information about properties. You can use it for research on price and location, and also to help you come up with comparables.

MLS Multiple Listing Service

mls.com

The public version of MLS does have some valuable information, but no site can come close to the thoroughness, accuracy, and detail provided by the professional version of MLS that is only available to licensed Realtors. Access to the vast storehouse of sales and comparable data on MLS is just one of many good reasons why you should work with a professional Realtor.

Flippers Websites and Blogs

BiggerPockets

biggerpockets.com

Bigger Pockets is one of the most successful websites for flippers. It hosts hundreds of articles on a variety of topics of interest to flippers and has an active community where you can usually get questions answered pretty quickly.

Wealth-Steps

wealth-steps.com

Wealth-Steps has an extensive section devoted to house flipping and real estate investment. The blog follows an individual flipper step by step as he purchases, renovates, and sells houses.

1-2-3 Flip

123flip.com

This is another house flipping blog. This one follows a team of flippers as they go through the process of finding, buying, rehabbing, and selling houses. They have complete breakdowns of their costs but openly state they ignore some expenses to make their results look better. But there's plenty of good first-hand experience here, so worth a look. Just don't ignore any expenses on your own flips!

By reading this blog and wealth-steps.com, you will begin to get a good idea of the life of a flipper.

Sample Forms

Here are some links to the types of legal and sales forms you might come across in your flipping career. One caveat: these are just examples. Real estate laws vary so widely from state to state that no one sample contract can cover them all.

Work with a professional Realtor to get samples of the types of forms that are required to sell a property in your state. Some states require acts of sale to be performed by attorneys. Sales contracts in those states tend to be more complex and contain more legalese compared to sales documents in state where entities like title companies and notaries can conduct property closings and transfers.

Sample Property Sales Offer

cmich.edu/fas/fsr/cps/PropertyAcquisition/Documents/Sample-AgreementToPurchaseRealEstate.pdf

Here is a sample sales offer put together by the University of Michigan. It complies with the laws of Michigan. Do not use it if you live in another state. Get your Realtor to provide you with a basic form for your state if you want to review these documents before you sell your first house.

Sample Seller's Disclosure Form

forsalebyowner.com/pdf/FSBO_sellersproperty.pdf

Seller's disclosures are legal documents in which the seller of a property declares the property to be free of defects to the best of his knowledge. They are meant to protect buyers from unscrupulous sellers who try to conceal significant damage and other problems from potential buyers. As legal documents, they can be used in a court action to collect damages if the seller is found to have been less than truthful in the disclosure form. That's why it is essential to fill them out accurately. Just as with sales contracts, these documents vary widely from state to state. In California, they can be up to 50 pages long.

Sample Closing Statement Form

files.consumerfinance.gov/f/201311_cfpb_kbyo_closing-disclosure-seller-only.pdf

The closing statement is what you will receive at the act of sale transferring ownership of your property from you to a buyer. It shows exactly what your expenses are and how much money you will receive at closing after all those expenses have been deducted from the purchase price. These expenses make up what is known as your closing costs. Once again, expenses vary from state to state. For example, some states charge excise tax at closing, while others do not, so don't interpret this sample as the absolute last word in closing statements.

Helpful Checklists and Worksheets

I emphasized throughout this book the importance of doing things in proper order while working on your flip. The handy checklists and worksheets in this Appendix will assist you in scheduling work in the correct order and organizing your flip from beginning to end.

In this section, you will find a flipping timeline, order of work checklists for demolition and renovation, a staging checklist, and finally, a budget worksheet that will help you analyze your financial results after the closing.

Flipping Timeline Checklist

A timeline checklist is essential to help you manage the order of work and delivery of materials to your job site. Without it, you are more likely to forget to order cabinets, flooring, or other materials as you need them, and also forget to schedule work crews, inspections, and so on.

- ❑ Interview Realtors, contractors, and investors and start building your team—2 to 4 weeks.

- ❑ Get your office organized and set up for your flipping business—1 week.

- ❑ Research trending neighborhoods and choose one to focus on in the search for your first house to flip—1 week to 6 months, depending on your location and the amount of competition you face.

- ❑ Secure your financing with your investor—1 to 2 weeks.

- ❑ Select a house, inspect it with your contractor, place an offer, and close on the house—30 to 60 days.

❑ Reinspect the house with your contractor after you close on it, create a detailed renovation plan, budget, and work schedule—1 to 2 weeks.

❑ Review your renovation plan and budget with your investor—1 day to 1 week.

❑ Apply for any required permits—1 day to 6 months, depending on your location, the time of year, and how busy your market is.

❑ As soon as you have permits in hand and posted on your worksite, schedule your contractor and work crews to start demolition—a few hours.

❑ Rent a dumpster and have it delivered to your worksite—a few hours.

❑ Perform demolition—a few days to a week.

❑ Perform any necessary repairs—a few days to 3 weeks.

❑ Call for inspections of any repairs before you close the walls back up—a few hours.

❑ Order required materials—ongoing throughout the renovation.

❑ Perform the renovation—2 to 6 months, possibly longer.

❑ Have the yard landscaped to increase curb appeal—1 to 2 days.

❑ Have the house thoroughly cleaned—1 day.

❑ Stage the house—1 to 2 days (see separate staging checklist).

❑ List the house for sale with your Realtor—a few hours.

❑ Accept a suitable offer—a few hours.

❑ Fill out seller's disclosure and other paperwork your Realtor requests—2 to 4 hours.

❑ Renegotiate price or make repairs if inspector finds any problems—a few days to a couple of weeks depending on extent of requested repairs.

❑ Attend closing and receive funds—a few hours.

❑ Analyze your results—a few hours.

❑ Meet with your investor and split profits—a few hours.

❑ Meet with your Realtor to review available properties—1 day to several weeks.

❑ Select and purchase your next property—1 day to several weeks.

❑ Repeat steps.

Demolition Checklist

Like all jobs related to house flipping, demolitions must be performed in proper order. This checklist will keep you on track.

❑ Get a demolition permit.

❑ Order dumpster.

❑ Schedule contractor and demolition crew.

❑ Make sure contractor has workers' comp policy to cover workers injured on your worksite.

❑ Purchase insurance on your house, including liability insurance to protect you in case someone gets injured on your property.

❑ Verify that all workers (including you) have all the required safety equipment, including hard hats, safety goggles, earplugs, leather gloves, steel-toed boots, and respirators.

❑ Review the demolition plan with your contractor. If you plan to move walls, hire a structural engineer to determine if the wall is weight-bearing before you try to move it.

❑ Make sure electrical power to the house has been cut prior to starting the demolition.

❑ If you plan to repair or replace the roof, do this before you start any inside repairs so that the house will be weatherproof once you start renovations inside.

❑ Also remove any windows, exterior doors, or siding that will be redone. Make sure the interior of the house is protected from the elements before you begin any work on the inside.

❑ Remove and safely dispose of any exposed nails or screws, broken glass, or splintered wood as you find them to reduce the risk of injury.

❑ Remove cabinets and countertops if you plan to replace them.

❑ Remove light fixtures you plan to replace.

❑ Remove plumbing fixtures that will be replaced.

❑ Carry all demolition debris promptly to the dumpster to maintain a clean and safe worksite.

❑ Tear up whatever old carpeting and wood or vinyl flooring you plan to replace.

❑ Remove old tile.

❑ Remove damaged drywall and insulation.

❑ Remove damaged pipes.

❑ Remove worn or damaged wiring.

❑ Remove and properly dispose of any old mechanical equipment like a furnace, water heater, or air conditioning unit that is no longer functioning.

❑ Be aware of any weather issues that may come up, and schedule your demolition to avoid them if possible.

Renovation Checklist

Performing your renovation in the proper order is really important. If you do it out of order, you may have to go back and tear out completed work to correct it, which could blow your budget very quickly.

❑ Get a permit for your renovation work.

❑ If your renovation includes any structural changes like moving walls, complete that work first.

❑ Perform any exterior repairs or renovations such as replacing the roof, windows, doors, or siding. The house must be weatherproof before you start your interior renovations.

❑ Repair or replace any damaged plumbing pipes and drains.

❑ Repair or replace any mechanical equipment like furnaces, water heaters, wood stoves, air conditioning units, and so on.

❑ Repair or replace any worn or damaged electrical damage and conduits, electrical panels, switches, outlets, and covers. Add new wiring as necessary to accommodate new light fixtures, ceiling fans, garage door openers, hard-wired alarm services, including smoke alarms, and so on.

❑ Schedule plumbing and electrical inspections.

❑ Once your inspections have been completed, install sheetrock.

❑ Paint walls and ceilings. (Some contractors prefer to do this after the cabinets and countertops have been installed. Check with yours to see what he prefers.)

❑ Install cabinets, vanities, and countertops.

❑ Install new light fixtures, ceiling fans, doorbells, garage door openers, security systems, and so on.

❑ Install flooring, including laminate, hardwood, and vinyl tile.

❑ Install carpeting.

❑ Install tile backsplashes and tub surrounds.

❑ Install built-in appliances like cooktops, microwaves, dishwashers, garbage disposals, and icemakers.

❑ Finish up all trim carpentry like door moldings, windowsills, chair rails, and so on.

❑ Clean the house thoroughly to remove all traces of construction dust and debris.

Staging Checklist

Before the house is put on the market, stage a home to make it most appealing to buyers.

❑ Stage your house according to its traffic pattern, from front to back, from the rooms seen first upon entering to the rooms seen last.

❑ Make sure the style of the staging complements the style of the house.

❑ Meet with your stager at the house to strategize about which rooms to stage.

❑ Set your staging budget.

❑ The priority is the family room or den, dining room or breakfast nook, and master bedroom.

❑ Plan mini stagings for rooms like the kitchen and bathrooms, where the room can be brought to life with a nice set of towels, a bar of soap, and a few accessories—no furniture needed.

❑ If the house is open concept, ask your stager to create a unified look for the entire space.

❑ Make sure the house is completely clean and all workmen are gone from the site before scheduling your stagers.

Analyzing Costs and Profit Worksheet

Please note this is different from the profit analysis you work out prior to placing an offer on a property, and it is also different from the project budget you create prior to starting your flip. This worksheet is intended to help you analyze your profit or loss following the completion and sale of a flipped house.

Length of renovation: _____

Days on market: _____

Purchase price of property: _____

Square footage of property: _____

Purchase price per square foot: _____

Rehab cost per square foot: _____

Sales price per square foot: _____

Item	Cost	Notes
Property purchase price		
Property sale price		
Gross profit		
Total expenses		
Net profit		
Expense breakdown		
Survey		
Permits and inspections		
Materials		
Labor		
Design consultants		
Landscaping		
Staging		
Carrying costs		
Insurance		
Utilities		
Maintenance		
Property taxes		
Loan interest		

Item	Cost	Notes
Selling expenses		
Real estate commissions		
Closing costs		
Sales or excise taxes		
Title insurance		
Home warranty for buyer		
Total expenses		

Sweat Equity Agreement

Sweat equity agreements may seem simple and straightforward, but in reality they can be quite complex and confusing. There is a lot on the line when you are investing sweat equity, and you must have a signed agreement in place to protect your investment. All too often, aspiring flippers are too trusting when it comes to the concept of sweat equity, and they often come out on the losing end.

Our best advice is to hire an attorney to craft an agreement relevant to your particular situation. It is absolutely essential to have a sweat equity agreement signed by both parties in place before you do a minute of work. Otherwise, you can labor for months thinking you will receive 50 percent of the profits as your portion and end up disappointed when the investor decides to only give you 20 percent. Protect your investment of sweat equity with a rock solid agreement. It should contain the following clauses:

State the nature of the business agreement—are you an employee investing sweat equity in your investor's business? Are you starting a new business together where you will be equal partners, and if so, will it be an LLC or some type of corporation? It is essential to state in the agreement what the legal business arrangement is before terms are set out.

Say exactly what each partner is investing—if your investor contributes $50,000 cash and you contribute $50,000 worth of labor, you would be 50/50 partners. However if your investor contributes $100,000 cash and you contribute $25,000 of labor, you are not likely to get your investor to agree to an even split. Whatever the terms are, lay them all out in writing.

State what you are working for—in most cases, aspiring flippers investing sweat equity want cash in exchange for their labor, but there are some cases where you might be given shares in a partnership. Just be sure that whatever is offered is something you want and is precisely specified in the contract.

Define the time period the agreement covers—if it is just a one-off agreement covering one property, your attorney will craft a different document than if you are creating a partnership with an investor and working for shares of the company with the future goal of becoming a full partner.

State how the arrangement will end if you and your investor decide to end your working relationship—if a relationship goes south, you don't want to be left holding the bag. Separation criteria define the conditions under which you can be removed from the job if you are an employee or released from a partnership. Unscrupulous investors will sometimes try to fire a flipper who has invested a large chunk of sweat equity days before a payout of their profits is due. Protect yourself against this by having your attorney write clear separation criteria.

Index

Symbols

D

I-J-K